- **Watch Your Language!**

Books by Robert Gorrell

Practice in English Communication (1947)

Modern English Handbook (1953; 7th ed., 1988)

Modern English Workbook (1957; 2d ed., 1962)

A Course in Modern English (1960)

Education for College (1961)

English as Language (1961)

A Basic Course in Modern English (1963)

Rhetoric: Theories for Application, ed. (1967)

Modern English Reader (1970; 2d ed., 1977)

Writing and Language (1971)

Reading About Language (1971)

Writing Modern English (1973)

Mother
Tongue
and Her
Wayward
Children

Watch Your Language!

Robert Gorrell

University of Nevada Press
Reno   Las Vegas   London

The paper used in this book meets the requirements
of American National Standard for Information
Sciences—Permanence of Paper for Printed Library
Materials, ANSI Z39.48–1984. Binding materials
were selected for strength and durability.

Library of Congress Cataloging-in-Publication Data

Gorrell, Robert M.
    Watch your language! : Mother Tongue and her
wayward children / Robert Gorrell.
        p.   cm.
    Includes index.
    ISBN 0-87417-235-7 (cloth : acid-free paper)
    1. English language.   I. Title.
PE1072.G67   1994
420—dc20   93-33528
                                                CIP

University of Nevada Press
Reno, Nevada 89557 USA
Copyright © 1994 University of Nevada Press
Design by Erin Kirk
Printed in the United States of America
9 8 7 6 5 4 3 2 1

- For Joie

Contents

Preface   xi

1 • **Language and Society; Society and Language**   1
Turning Black to White: Public Doublespeak   3
Jew's Harp and French Horn: Language and Racism   6
Fighting Words and Flaming Flags   10
Desexing the Language   14
Mind-Softening: Lying and the Teflon Effect   19
51 Percent Truthful   21

2 • **Words and Their Ancestors: Family Trees**   24
Folk Etymology and Punch and Judy   27
Birds and Animals   31
Names into Words   36
Family Trees with Straight Branches   40
Portmanteau Words   44
Etymologists at Play   45

3 • **Growing Pains: Dealing with Linguistic Changes**   51
Semantic Change   53
New Kids on the Block   55
Workaholic and Suffixaholism   60
Autoantonyms   61
Conflicting Compounds   63

Positives and Negatives   64
Semantic Change and Reading Shakespeare   66
Draining Meaning: Making Words Empty   67
Words That Don't Change   69
Put Up, Put Out, Put In, Put Off, Put Over   70

4 • **The Ordinary Sentence: Grammar and Meaning**   74
Square Pegs and Round Holes: Meaning and Grammar   77
Two Plus Two Equals Four, Not Five   81
Equations with Modifiers   83
Varying the Pattern   84
Modifiers: Dangling   86
Modifiers: Misplaced and Squinting   89
Writing as a Balancing Act   91
Coordination and Parallel Form   92
Comparisons: Ears Like a Rabbit   93

5 • **Embalming Problems: Preserving Vestigial Remains**   95
Saving *Whom*   96
Whom-Happiness   98
Whose for Things   98
An Ending That Doesn't Know Its Place   99
Verb Forms: The Past Becoming Present   100
Verbs That Can't Make Up Their Minds   103
Take Your Choice   103
Dialect Variations   104
Keeping *Lie* Alive   106
Pitfalls and Complications   108
Sitting Bull, Setting Sun, Rising Star, Raising Cain   109
Ghosts That Walk; Making Verbs Agree   111
How Many Is or Are a Committee?   112
More Than One Subject   114
Data, Media, None   115

6 • Bishop Lowth to Miss Groby: Dealing with Rules 117

The Victory Over *Ain't* 119

Latin Grammar in the Van: Final Prepositions 121

Grandpa's Beard and Split Infinitives 123

Bad Algebra and the Double Negative 125

Rules and Possessives 127

The Ecclesiastical *Shall* and Related Rules 129

How Not to Start a Sentence 131

Leaky Rules and Useful Distinctions 132

7 • Elegant English for You and I: Overcorrection 140

U and Non-U 141

How Do You Say It? 144

Being Careful with *Me* and *Him* 147

How Does the Dog Smell? 149

Fancy and Phony 152

Fancy Fillers and Pretentious Padding:

   Cereal in the Hamburger 155

Bondoony 156

Jammies and Other *Cozzies* 158

8 • The Writing System: Conventions 161

How Do You Spell *Fish?* 162

Spelling Reform 164

Silent Letter *E* 166

The Sounds of *K* and *S* 167

Compounds 167

Homonyms 169

Demons 170

Borrowed Plurals 171

Articles: *A, An, The* 172

Punctuating for Confusion: Errant Commas,

   Including Inverted Ones 173

Restrictive and Nonrestrictive   174
Ornamental Quotation Marks   175
Save the Semicolon   177
Conventions and Politeness   178
What Do You Call a Preacher?   180

9 • Fun with Language   182
Metaphor: Happy as a Bear   184
Word Games   188
Highbrow Games   190
Playing with Sound   192
Glorified Clichés and Twisted Idioms   194
A Low Species of Wit and Shaggy Dogs   196
Language Traps for the Unwary   198
Punditry and Puntification   199
Swifties and Merriwells   200
Palindromes   202
Oxymorons, Some Moronic   203
Taking Words in Vain   204
Giggles of Geese and A Pure of Meadowlarks   206

Index   209

Preface

This is a book for language watchers. It is a book for people who are fascinated by the infinite variety of language, by the history and vagaries of words. It is for people who love language. Who delight in a graceful sentence or an insightful metaphor or an outrageous pun. Who recognize the power of language, can feel its challenge, and can feel the excitement of using it effectively. Who respect language, but are not afraid to criticize its uses, to experiment with it, or to play with it. Who enjoy finding errors in the newspaper. Who like to read dictionaries.

The English language, this book asserts, is alive and well. It is growing, spreading, producing thousands of books, tons of newspapers and other periodicals, hundreds of hours of television and radio talk. It is the mother tongue of about 350 million people and the second language of some 400 million more. An unabridged dictionary lists half a million words, without including many uncataloged scientific and technical terms.

For centuries the most ravenous linguistic borrower, English is now also a generous exporter. Since the end of World War II, it is estimated that as many as twenty thousand English words have been added to the Japanese vocabulary. Young Swedes wear *tajt jeans* (tight jeans); a Russian may drink a *viskey* or a *dzhin-in-tonik* at a *dzhazz saission;* a Frenchman may stop in *le drugstore* or go away for *le weekend*. With its global diversity, English is probably more colorful and imaginative than it has been at any time since the linguistic excitement of the Elizabethan age.

Partly because of this diversity, however, it is fashionable these days to talk about "the deterioration of our beautiful language" and "the disappearance of correct English." Many popular columnists find the language in a sorry state.

This has been going on for a long time. Warnings about the imminent collapse of English are almost as old as the language itself. Writers urge us to sustain the "purity" of the language, to protect it from contamination. But where is the "pure" language from which we are declining? Jonathan Swift, one of the most distinguished early linguistic Jeremiahs, looked back a hundred years to find the Golden Age of English. But James Beattie, lamenting the corruption of the language in the next century, thought that Swift's time was the Golden Age. Some of today's worriers see a decline from the good old days of the 1950s, although in 1950 critics were not charitable about the state of the language in their day. "Pure" English tends to focus on whatever rules of usage the purist happens to remember, or almost remember, from school; and most of the fear for the future of the language, I suspect, is really a way of dignifying our prejudices, of justifying our resistance to the unfamiliar.

I am not worried about the future of the language. I am worried about our use of the language. I don't detect that our language today is inferior to that of Chaucer or Shakespeare. I do think that Chaucer and Shakespeare used the language better than many people do today, even though Shakespeare put prepositions at the ends of sentences.

This, then, is partly a book about usage—not about what is correct or incorrect, but about ways in which we can exploit the most useful tool available to human beings. It is not easy to speak or write well. Good writing certainly involves more than avoiding mistakes. Essentially it involves choices—of ideas, attitudes, sentence patterns, words. To make these choices we try to anticipate results, the effect our language will have on a reader or listener—understanding, acceptance, antagonism.

To make these choices wisely we need to know as much as we can about alternatives, about possibilities. We have a better chance of selecting an effective structure for a sentence if we are aware of patterns that are available. We are in a better position to choose the right word if we have a large vocabulary. Even some knowledge of rhetorical devices can help. This kind of knowledge comes most readily from experience, from reading, but it can be expanded by observing how language has developed and how it works.

Most of the time, of course, we make choices automatically, guided by habits or conventions. But sometimes we make conscious decisions especially on relatively trivial matters of usage, which are usually insignificant but have a way of provoking arguments. For instance, do I answer a telephone question "This is he" or "This is him" or "This is me"? I don't know who is calling and can't guess much about the caller's likely reaction. I tend to say "This is he," but I'm not sure whether my listener will think I am literate and conservative in my language habits or will consider me snobbish and stuffy.

Sometimes we have or can get information about how at least some people react to a particular locution. We can be fairly sure, for example, that an unconventional spelling in an application letter creates an unfavorable impression, even though it is a trivial error and not a reliable indicator of the writer's qualifications. Mixing up *lie* and *lay* may get a titter from some members of an audience, may alienate others who consider it illiterate, and may be unnoticed by many.

Even fewer would notice anything unusual in this sentence: "The man changed his name over twenty times." A panel of writers and publishers put together for the *Harper Dictionary of Contemporary Usage* voted by 63 percent that *more than* should be substituted for *over* in sentences like this. The *Oxford English Dictionary* points out that *over* in the sense of *more than* has been standard in the language for centuries. But the panel indicates the attitude of a segment of society. Their decision does not mean that the use of *over* in this sense is wrong. It means only that their attitude, though it has no linguistic justification, is part of the information pertinent to making a choice. Obviously, if we go through this kind of elaborate analysis for every choice we make, we may be doomed to silence.

Therefore, although this book discusses communication as a series of choices, it is more concerned about ways in which we can understand and enjoy language. It begins by looking at some of the ways in which a language reflects its society and also influences it. Chapter 2 looks at the origins of the English vocabulary, where some words came from, and then chapter 3 discusses language changes and how we deal with them. Chapter 4 considers the grammar of English as it becomes dependent on word order rather than inflection. Problems resulting from that change, difficulties in using the inflections that survive, are considered in chapter 5. The attitudes of prescriptive and proscriptive grammars lead to the discussions of rules in chapter 6 and to the kinds of overcorrection and false elegance discussed in chapter 7. Chapter 8 describes the writing system of English, including spelling and punctuation. Chapter 9 is about ways in which we can play with language. In its attitude it is a summary of the purpose of the book, to make readers friendlier with language—the tool that has allowed human beings to emerge from the Stone Age toward civilization.

I am grateful to Nicholas Cady and the staff of the University of Nevada Press for help and thoughtful editing. Over the past ten years, readers of my weekly newspaper column have contributed useful questions and comments. I am indebted especially to my wife, Joie, for genuine interest, imaginative suggestions, and sensible advice.

1

Language and Society; Society and Language

Man could not have gone to the moon merely with an opposable thumb . . . but with a thumb and a brain and language he can go, and so far as we can now foresee, his evolution may be unlimited.

- Charlton Laird, *Language in America*

There are 869 different forms of lying.

- Mark Twain, *Pudd'nhead Wilson's Calendar*

You can tell the ideals of a nation by its advertisements.

- Norman Douglas, *South Wind*

Advertising is a racket . . . its constructive contribution to humanity is exactly minus zero.

- F. Scott Fitzgerald, *The Crack-up*

Obviously a language reflects the society that creates it. Societies choose words and frame grammars to meet particular needs, to name something, describe actions, express feelings. Not all societies have the same needs, as a comparison of different languages reveals. The linguist Benjamin Lee Whorf in 1940 pointed out, for example, that the Hopi language often differs from English in its need for words. It has one word to designate the kind of water in a lake or waterfall and another for the kind we drink; English uses *water* for both. On the other hand, Hopi has one word for flying things that covers what we designate with *insect, airplane,* and *aviator.* Trobriand Islanders have many words for yams. Some South Pacific island languages have no general word meaning "tree," but have separate words for varieties of palms. Our modern technology has added hundreds of words to the English lexicon.

Other variations reveal different emphases behind the metaphors that create words. English *train* developed from the idea of one thing following another; the Chinese word for train is *hwoche,* which literally means "fire cart." A vacuum cleaner in Finnish is *polynimuri,* a mouth that sucks up dust. In French, the head of a cane is the apple of a cane and the head of a hammer the iron of a hammer. It is also true that some lexicons lack words that may exist in other languages. English, for instance, uses the word *aunt* for four different relationships, although it can differentiate with phrases like *father's sister* or *mother's brother's wife*. English has no words paralleling *deaf* and *blind* to designate failures in taste and smell.

This kind of evidence suggests that different societies have different ways of looking at the world, different ways of thinking. Certainly language depends on thought. Even nonsense syllables must have some kind of cognition behind them. Grammarians and philosophers in the eighteenth century postulated a universal grammar, suggesting that the structure of language results from the way the human mind works. Modern grammarians like Noam Chomsky have revived interest in this idea. "Language is the dress of thought," said Samuel Johnson; language holds a mirror up to nature. But the conclusion that differences in languages reflect differences in ways of thinking may be deceptive. The case of Eskimo snow indicates how evidence can get out of hand. Whorf pointed out that the Eskimo language has separate words for three kinds of snow but no word corresponding to our general term for snow. His observation became perhaps the most popular example of language differences, turning up in dozens of studies. As enthusiasm for the example has increased, so has the estimate of the number of Eskimo words. Bill Bryson's *The Mother Tongue* (1990) asserts confidently that the Eskimos, "as is well known, have fifty words for types of snow." But whether there are three or fifty, it seems to me that we can't be sure that the Eskimos see differences that we are incapable of seeing. Indeed, skiers have words in English to distinguish *powder, corn, hardpack, slush.*

Whorf's other contention is no easier to prove. "Language is not simply a reporting device for experience but a framework for it." That is, language causes certain ways of thinking, determines at least some aspects of a society's view of the world. To take a very simple example, one language has a single word for the colors we call blue and green; does that language cause its speakers to perceive colors differently? Or to take a more complex example, Western society has developed from Aristotle the language patterns of the syllogism, which we call logical;

does what we traditionally call logic reflect the way the mind works, or does it merely show the mind working under the influence of language? Not all societies have the same view of logic. I do not presume to speculate about these basic psychological relationships, still mysterious in spite of recent experiments by psycholinguists. I do want in what follows to consider some more mundane questions about language and society. Do officialese and double-talk petrify minds? Do Polish jokes and slurs based on nationalities encourage racism? How much are we confusing words and things in our concern about demeaning or insulting language? How sexist is the language, and will reforming it promote equality? Are misleading advertising and propaganda eroding people's ability to think independently?

• Turning Black to White: Public Doublespeak

"When *I* use a word," Humpty Dumpty said, in rather a scornful tone, "it means just what I choose it to mean—neither more nor less."

"The question is," said Alice, "whether you *can* make words mean so many different things."

"The question is," said Humpty Dumpty, "which is to be master— that's all."

The Humpty Dumpty approach, of course, is not new. Deceptive use of language is as old as language, and so is concern about the effects of linguistic deception. But the development of new media has multiplied opportunities for using language to manipulate and has also stimulated serious efforts to condemn irresponsibility.

In 1941, for example, the Institute for Propaganda Analysis was formed. It popularized terms like *bandwagon* and *plain folks* and *testimonials* to classify tricks used to influence the public. At about the same time, books on general semantics were making the best-seller lists. Both propaganda analysis and semantics proposed that exposing deceptive language would cure many problems. Stuart Chase, in his popular *The Power of Words,* saw semantics as the solution to world conflict. He did not consider that studying semantics might have given Hitler new ideas.

Today the most active opposition to linguistic deception comes from the Committee on Public Doublespeak of the National Council of Teachers of English. The committee condemns false advertising and also "semantic distortion by public officials, candidates for office, political commentators and all those who transmit through the mass media." Their efforts may not be doing much to decrease the exploitation of language to deceive rather than inform, but they may be doing something to help people recognize the distortion.

The kinds of linguistic antics that are being exposed range from relatively innocent euphemisms, such as *pass away* for *die,* used only to avoid an unpleasant reality, to inaccurate labeling designed clearly to twist the thinking of the public in a particular direction, such as *peacekeeper* as a name for a guided missile.

The euphemisms are often more amusing than dangerous. Labels to make a profession seem more important or dignified seem to me not threatening, but maybe silly—*cosmetologist* for *beautician,* which was a euphemism for *hairdresser,* and *mortician* for *undertaker.* A *nail technician* is not a carpenter but a manicurist. A *vertical transportation corps* is made up of elevator operators. A mausoleum is advertised as *an eternal condominium,* and a handbag is praised because it is made of *beautiful unleather* or *virgin vinyl* or *vegetarian leather.* The secondhand car business has produced *preenjoyed cars,* which are sold by *product consultants.*

Euphemism and other kinds of mislabeling can, however, seriously mislead a reader, and the government seems increasingly adept at distortions designed to avoid criticism. A State Department announcement that it will no longer use the word *killing* but will refer to *unlawful or arbitrary deprivation of life* seems to me more than just some incompetent trying to sound important. Its intent is surely to deceive.

Some of the contortions of business to conceal various unpleasant procedures seem more serious than just good fun. It is perhaps only a sign of the times that one business appoints a new executive, a chief information officer, to "monitor the life cycle of documents"—that is, to take charge of the shredder. Another business avoids firing anybody but indulges in "negative employee retention," and McClellan Air Force Base handles the same problem by putting some mechanics on "non-duty, non-pay status." Another company avoids firing employees by "eliminating redundancies in the human resources area." An unemployed person is "actively cultivating an employment situation." Early retirement is "special incentive separation." An airline's financial report shows a profit of a million dollars from "the one-time involuntary conversion of an aircraft." The plane crashed.

Education has also been an offender, sometimes not gaining much in spite of good intentions. The attempts, for example, to find palatable labels for children who aren't very bright or are loafing in school have had only short-lived success. We have tried *disadvantaged, nonachiever, underachiever, retarded, slow learner, late bloomer, remedial, special,* and others I've forgotten. One problem is that the game never ends. Children catch on to a term quickly, and you hear things like "I'm a retard, are you?" And then we have to think of a new term. Some different sorts of classifications have turned up recently. *Visual learners* are students who like to read; *tactile-oriented students* don't like to read but like baseball; *kinesthetically inclined students* can't keep still.

Other education doublespeak seems to me mainly pretentious. At a teachers' convention handwriting becomes *grapho-motor representation.* In one school a child causing trouble in class is diagnosed as having "an attention deficit disorder." Another child "engages in audible verbal self-reinforcement." That is, he talks to himself.

Much of what emanates from the government is hard to classify and may sometimes just reflect incompetence. For example, the National Transportation Safety Board cites the cause of a helicopter crash as "flying into bad weather and failure to maintain clearance from the ground." That is like dying from failure to maintain life. Or the Federal Aviation Administration identifies a broken propeller as just a case of "uncontained blade liberation." In one agency a windshield wiper is "an adverse weather visibility device." In another nobody ever exceeds the budget; they say, "These reports indicate if a program is excessively consumptive of funds."

The military contributes. A parachute is an *aerodynamic personnel decelerator.* A pencil is a *portable, hand-held communication inscriber.* A bullet hole is a *ballistically induced aperture in the subcutaneous environment.* A toothpick is a *wood interdental stimulator.* These sound more absurd than serious.

But other military creations are dangerously deceptive. A neutron bomb is a *radiation enhancement device*. To kill is "to terminate with extreme prejudice" or "to service the target." A bombing is a *limited duration protective reactive strike* or *coercive diplomacy* or *airborne sanitation*. *Friendly fire* can produce *friendly casualties*, caused by "accidental delivery of ordnance equipment."

The public is being protected from truth better than it needs to be.

• **Jew's Harp and French Horn: Language and Racism**

A recent NBC news broadcast included an interview with the head of a Cleveland company that professes to be the only manufacturer of what he calls a jaw's harp, a musical instrument still produced at the rate of about fifty thousand a year.

As a child I considered myself pretty good on the jew's harp, a small lyre-shaped frame with a metal tongue attached. You hold the frame against your teeth and get a vibrating twang by flipping the metal tongue with your finger. You vary pitch by changing the shape of your mouth cavity. You can get a similar effect by holding a rubber band in your teeth and strumming it, although with this instrument you change pitch partly by stretching the band to change its length.

I also played the kazoo and the comb, a piece of tissue paper stretched over a comb and held like a harmonica so that I could hum into it. I am somewhat confused to discover that Eric Partridge's dictionary of British slang defines a jew's harp as a comb with tissue paper with which "one can produce queer music."

I have not seen a jew's harp for many years, and I think my teeth are not strong enough these days to accommodate an attempt to recall my earlier prowess. More seriously, I have mixed feelings about the proposed renaming. I have some affection for the old name, which we used in total innocence of any prejudice. In fact, the instrument was sometimes known as a juice harp.

Undoubtedly, however, the name arose as a slur on Jews. It was used as early as the sixteenth century, and in northern England and Scotland it followed an earlier name for the instrument, *jew's trump,* from the

French *trompe,* horn. It apparently referred vaguely to ancient Jewish use of the harp—David's harp, for instance—combined with a suggestion of contempt for the insignificance of this harp.

There have been attempts at other etymologies, some perhaps intended to remove the suggestion of a racial slur. James Barclay's nineteenth-century dictionary positively explains the derivation as "from joue, French, a cheek, and harp, from its being held against the cheek." Obviously, Barclay never tried to play a jew's harp.

And interestingly the *Century Dictionary,* of about the same period, reports that "another proposed derivation, 'a corruption of jaw's harp' is absurd." The Cleveland manufacturer, apparently less worried about a racial slur than his name change suggests, says, probably not seriously, that *jew's harp* came from the instrument's sound, which is "oy, oy, oy."

In spite of his efforts to market the instrument as a jaw's harp, the old name seems to persist. I haven't found *jaw's harp* in any dictionary; my most recent one includes *jew's harp* with a picture.

I'm glad the change doesn't seem to be catching on, and I'm glad the word *Jew* retains its dignity in spite of some derogatory uses. I don't think the image of the Jewish people will suffer if we continue to play jew's harps.

The attempt to change, however, is characteristic of a general trend to modify our usage to conform to changing social attitudes and avoid locutions that may be considered racist. Other uses of *jew,* for example, are disappearing. To *jew down,* to bargain or try to reduce a price, is no longer acceptable, nor are *sheeny* and *kike* as derogatory terms. *Kike* apparently derives from the frequent *-ki* or *-ky* endings on names of some Eastern European Jews.

The most obvious example of the influence on the language of new attitudes on race is the near disappearance, at least in the United States, of the word *nigger.* The word has been derogatory for many years, although not quite as offensive as the Southern *nigra,* but only in recent years has it become universal bad taste. Various slang phrases have also disappeared: *nigger heaven* for a theater balcony, *nigger night* for Saturday night, *niggertoe* for a Brazil nut.

The whole question of names for members of nonwhite races remains confused, as attitudes and prejudices shift. During early years of this century, for example, Negro educators and leaders conducted a successful campaign to get members of the race referred to as Negroes, using a capital *N* rather than the lowercase *n* that had been common, along with *black* and *colored*. *Colored*, which had once been common in expressions like *colored maid* or *a person of color*, became both old-fashioned and offensive. In the 1960s and 1970s, however, preferences shifted; *Negro* was looked on as another word for *nigger*, and style books recommended *black* as the acceptable term. In the 1980s black leaders in America began urging the use of *Afro-American*, which has begun to supplant *black*, especially as a term of self-reference.

There have been attempts also to get rid of the term *Indian*, partly because of confusion with citizens of India and partly because it was an inaccurate designation in the first place, but also because *Indian* has become part of various phrases with derogatory connotations. The most common substitute, however, *Native American*, also presents difficulties, since anyone born on an American continent is technically a native American. *American Indian* is still the most widely used term.

Many of the phrases using *Indian* are dropping from acceptable use. *Indian summer*, however, although it probably started as a derogatory term, enjoys even a kind of romantic status with no racial overtones. It developed in the later years of the eighteenth century, and there are many theories about its origin. Perhaps the most plausible is that it reflects a general tendency of American settlers to associate the term *Indian* with anything false or bogus. An Indian summer was not really summer, but only felt like it. *Indian corn* probably reflects the same association with deception; it is not wheat.

Honest Injun also is probably derogatory in its origin but has become relatively harmless, like *honest to gosh* or *honest to goodness*, using euphemisms for God. *Honest Injun* goes back to the eighteenth century, when it began as sarcasm based on the notion that an honest Indian was a rarity.

To put the *Indian sign* on someone, to take advantage or perhaps to place a curse, appeared only in this century and supposedly reflects white men's fascination with Indian signals and tokens. It doesn't seem especially demeaning, nor do *Indian club* and *Indian wrestling*. *Indian giver*, however, for a person who gives a gift and then demands it back, is currently in bad odor on the assumption that it perpetuates the myth that you can't trust an Indian.

Many terms that developed from prejudices against nationalities survive, perhaps because their origins are obscure or unknown, and others have just gone out of use. *French disease* or *French pox* for syphilis grew from English prejudices in the sixteenth century, but it is now obsolete, perhaps more from increased knowledge of venereal disease than from any greater tolerance for the French. *French leave*, based on an eighteenth-century reputation of Frenchmen for leaving a gathering without saying goodbye, is still used to designate an unauthorized departure. *French kiss* and some associated sexual terms originated in attitudes—and wishful thinking—of American and British soldiers in France during World War I. *Pardon my French*, to apologize for an oath, has a similar origin.

Mexican disease or *Montezuma's revenge* for diarrhea is perhaps more geographical than national, not seriously disparaging. A *Mexican promotion*, an advance in rank with no increase in salary, is like a *Mexican breakfast*, a cigarette and a glass of water. Neither is much used today.

Francis Grose's eighteenth-century *A Classical Dictionary of the Vulgar Tongue* reflects British scorn for the Irish at the time: *Irish beauty* for "a woman with two black eyes" or *Irish legs*—"it is said of Irish women that they have a dispensation from the Pope to wear the thick end of their legs downwards." No longer current are an *Irishman's feast*, a fast, and an *Irish promotion*, like a Mexican promotion. *Irish confetti*, for bricks, refers to the alleged tendency of an Irishman to fight when he "has his Irish up."

British antagonism to the Dutch also flourished in the eighteenth century, based on rivalry in commerce and also on the battlefield, and some of the derogatory terms are still in use: *Dutch courage*, the kind that comes in a bottle; *Dutch defense*, retreat or surrender; or *Dutch treat*, originally suggesting Dutch stinginess but now hardly associated with the nationality. To *do the Dutch* is to commit suicide. To talk *like a Dutch uncle* reflects the reputation of the Dutch for strict discipline. A *Dutch rub* is administered with knuckles to the top of a head, usually by a Dutch uncle with quaint notions of child psychology.

In Australia the equivalent of a Dutch treat is a *Yankee shout* or a *Chinaman's shout,* a party where individuals pay for their drinks. In America, *Chinaman's chance* comes from the Gold Rush, in which Chinese in a segregated society were relegated to working claims that had been abandoned by other prospectors.

•   Fighting Words and Flaming Flags

It is probably inevitable that languages should develop words with which people can insult one another. Human beings have deficiencies, and pointing out somebody else's seems good for the ego. The development of fighting words may even have some practical value when words become substitutes for action. Falstaff and Prince Hal in *King Henry the Fourth,* Part I, engage in fine, creative name-calling but never come to blows:

> *Prince.* Thou clay-brained guts, thou knotty-pated fool, thou whore-son, obscene, greasy tallow-catch.
> *Falstaff.* You starveling, you elf-skin, you dried neat's tongue, you bull's pizzle, you stock-fish.

On the other hand, duels have been fought over a word, and in our less gallant world insults can lead to knifing or gunshots.

Social pressures, therefore, work to banish some clearly prejudiced or demeaning expressions at least from polite usage. Arbitrary regulation of speech, however, has never been very successful in democratic societies. I doubt that current efforts to ease racial tensions by banning allegedly inflammatory words are likely to work.

The enthusiasm for regulating language is perhaps understandable as conflicts increase not only in the inner city but also on college campuses. People probably get along better when they talk politely, but disciplinary codes for language seem to me impractical. One proposal, for example, would prohibit the use of "fighting words," and "such words include, but are not limited to, those terms widely recognized to be derogatory references to race, ethnicity, religion, sexual orientation, disability, and other personal characteristics." That's a lot of words, and I wouldn't want to try enforcing such a regulation.

More important, such proposals are not only impractical, but they are also wrong-headed. They are dramatic examples of the most ancient and common of semantic distortions, the confusion of word and thing.

The study of meaning, semantics, has long been a concern of both philosophers and linguists, and it has assumed special importance with the development in recent years of widespread mass communication. The basic concept of semantics is that a symbol represents a thought or an interpretation of something. *Pig*, a word, is a symbol for a thought about a certain type of four-legged animal. The other side of the concept, which is perhaps the most important practically, is that a symbol is not the thing it stands for. A swastika is not Nazism; a label is not a pair of designer jeans; the word *pig* is not an animal.

Failure to recognize this basic distinction has been causing different sorts of confusion for centuries. Word magic is one early manifestation, the notion that words have some kind of power in themselves. Spells, words like *abracadabra* or *open sesame* or *hocus pocus* were once considered powerful enough to work miracles. Even today enterprises like faith healing or exorcism often depend on the notion that words have some kind of power in themselves. In another manifestation of belief in word magic some societies avoid the use of words for earthquake or lightning, thinking that naming the phenomena may encourage them to occur. Some avoid words for gods or death; some never utter the name of a relative who has died. At one time in China, the names of all victims of beheading were collected once a year, written on pieces of paper, and burned in a public ceremony; only then was the execution completed.

Contemporary manifestations of word magic are not less obvious. A state senator in New York, John McNaboe, some years ago opposed a bill for the control of syphilis because "the innocence of children might be corrupted by widespread use of the term," which "creates a shudder in every decent woman and decent man." The same kind of superstition is behind our use of TB for tuberculosis and VD for venereal disease, as well as our more recent use of the *C-word* for cancer and the *R-word* for rape. Politician have taken to substituting the *T-word* for taxes, and the old fear of mentioning death is behind a dozen euphemisms, such as *pass away* or *go to one's reward*. A fraternity magazine labels its list of defunct brothers *Chapter Celestial,* which has both becoming delicacy and a suitable touch of fraternal optimism.

A child's comment that "pigs are called pigs because they're such dirty animals" or that "rabbits are called rabbits because they have long ears" reflects the mixing of word and thing. So does a comment like *"Mother* is a beautiful word." The confusion of a word with what it stands for is behind the commandment, "Thou shalt not take the name of the Lord in vain." But we don't worry much about this if the name is disguised: *gosh* or *golly* or *jeeze.*

Our attitude that some words are "dirty" is another manifestation. We really mean that we consider what the words symbolize to be dirty. Avoiding some words in polite usage depends on our failure to recognize the separation of symbol from thing. Different words, of course, are regarded as bad words at different times in history and in different locations. Words that Queen Elizabeth I used are now regarded as improper. Words that I'd have been punished for using when I was a child are now common in teen-age speech.

The same kinds of difficulties confound any serious attempt to impose taboos on "fighting words." Which words are inflammatory in which situations? Owen Wister's Virginian says, "When you call me that, *smile!"* which becomes a kind of guideline for the use of *son of a bitch*—which is now included in collegiate dictionaries. *Bloody* and *bugger* are likely to be fighting words in England but are not likely to raise much heat in the United States; someone may even be a "cute little bugger." *Motherfucker* can be a serious insult in America, like *son of a bitch,* but it is not much known in England. Shortened to *mother,* it may refer relatively innocently to a thing or person that is large or impressive. *Bastard* is often used affectionately.

All sorts of other terms are hard to evaluate. Take terms "derogatory to religion," for example. *Catholic* or *Baptist* may be used with an intent to be derogatory. Are they less so than *mackerel snatcher* or *Jesus freak?* How about *fatso* or *high pockets* or *peabrain* or *egghead?*

Are *sissy* and *macho* and *pantywaist* "derogatory references to sexual orientation?" Regulation would also have to cope with the ingenuity of language users in creating slang terms in which the derogatory origin is disguised or forgotten. An example is the word *spaz,* which had a fortunately short-lived currency in the late 1950s, to describe what was also a creep or a nerd or a drip or a jerk. The word originated as an abbreviation of *spastic.*

One of the most controversial semantic problems in recent years is the desecration of the flag as a social protest and the resultant public outrage and demand for legislation to ban the practice—even for an amendment to the Constitution. Pertinent to the furor over flag burning is a tradition in Japan in the days of emperor worship. Every schoolhouse had on the wall a picture of the emperor. If the schoolhouse burned, the first duty of any pupil was to rescue the picture, even at the risk of life.

The flag or the cross or a picture of the president or the Pope has symbolic significance like that of the emperor, evoking emotions and representing a country or an ideal. But the symbol is not what it symbolizes. Burning the flag is not attacking the country, and slashing a picture of the Pope is not hurting a person. The person burning a flag as a political protest is confusing the symbol with what is symbolized, but so is the person or government that considers the gesture a serious threat. Theoretically, legislation to protect a symbol or a word is very much like the edict of a third-century Chinese emperor who decreed that a standard first-person pronoun should no longer be used generally but should be reserved for references to him.

Practically, legislation to regulate language has never worked very well. One can think of all sorts of difficulties, some of them absurd. Is intent pertinent? Would an accidental burning of the flag be a crime? How about singing "The Star Spangled Banner" off-key or setting it to rock tempo? Would a logical next step be a law against smashing a political button of the party in power?

The real problem is that the linguistic confusion, acting as if the symbol really is what it only stands for, cheapens what is symbolized. Revering or protecting—or burning—the flag is too easy a substitute for really respecting the ideals the flag symbolizes.

• Desexing the Language

Usually the influence of society on language is slow and imperceptible, seldom the result of direct efforts to make changes; witness the fate of attempts at spelling reform. It is therefore remarkable that in two or three decades social pressures have caused stylebooks of publishers to adopt policies proscribing alleged sexist usages, have caused government agencies to revise documents and legislatures to rewrite statutes, and have sent writers scurrying for ways to avoid sexist language, especially to compensate for our language's lack of a neutral personal pronoun.

The movement is based on an assumption that language does somehow influence our attitudes and that language based on a male-dominated society encourages inequality between the sexes.

There is not much doubt that the English vocabulary generally reflects a society dominated by males—at least in activities like government or religion or business. The Christian God is male, even though the common noun *god* has a feminine *goddess* to accompany it. *Governor, ambassador, athlete, priest, bishop, senator, professor, captain, executive, poet,* and dozens of others are usually thought of as masculine. As evidence, notice that we tend to distinguish a *woman governor* but not a *man governor,* a *woman* or *female* or even *lady* athlete, a *female poet* or a *poetess.*

Clearly there is a problem. The running of our society is no longer exclusively the business of men. Women are poets and athletes and governors and actors and senators. We need to change our language habits. *Female professor* or *female executive* certainly seems condescending.

Furthermore, even without using any sexist vocabulary, we can, usually without thinking, perpetuate sexual stereotypes. The following sentences illustrate:

> The pioneers crossed the desert with their women, children, and possessions.
> The slaves were allowed to marry and to have their wives and children with them.
> Current tax regulations allow a head of household to deduct for the support of a wife and children.

The most obvious and most resented of the sexist terms in the language are *man* used to refer to all humanity and *he, him,* and *his* used as a common-sex pronoun to refer to a noun that may be of either gender. Although for centuries *man* and *he* have been used to refer to both sexes—"all men are created equal"—reformers argue that the words can no longer be thought of as sexless. *Mankind,* at least some of the time, seems to exclude women. Referring to a student or an artist as *he* suggests that all students and artists are male. I suppose it works the other way if we refer to a nurse or a teacher as *she.* I don't know how to deal with the fact that ships are referred to as *she.*

In Old English, *man* was the generic term. *Wer* and *wif* were terms for adult male and female. But sometime before about A.D. 1000, *man* became the word for any adult or nearly adult male as well as for all humankind. *Wer* disappeared, surviving only in *werewolf.* This use of *man* has become so common that it is often hard to tell whether the older generic sense is intended. In "man creates out of necessity," the generic sense is probably intended, but the masculine sense would fit. The rule today, in stylebooks and government manuals, is to avoid the generic use of *man.*

There are problems, quite apart from the mass of literature with the earlier use and the obvious jokes about *personhole* or *personikin* or *huperson.* It's hard to get agreement on substitutes. For instance, should it be *chair* or *chairperson? Chair,* the *Oxford English Dictionary* points out, has been used since the seventeenth century; in *The Pickwick Papers* Dickens has the people shouting "Chair! Chair!" when they want the person in the chair to recognize them. Or should we use *chairman* and *chairwoman* in order to have more accurate information about the presiding officer? Should we always use *salesperson,* or should we distinguish between *salesman* and *saleswoman?* I don't know what to do about *fisherman.* One publisher's guidelines specify *fisher,* which seems to me not likely to catch on. Russell Baker quipped about "Benny Goodperson playing 'Personhattan' or 'Can't Help Lovin' that Person of Mine.'" Somebody has suggested that if we are to keep things really equal we need feminine equivalents for male terms like *womanizer* and *wencher* and perhaps *wolf.* I can't produce any. *Manizer* doesn't work and *philandress* seems pretentious. Maybe *guyser* is a possibility.

There are, of course, more palatable substitutes that avoid the *person* business: *fire fighter* for *fireman, executive* or *manager* for *businessman, police officer* for *policeman, mail carrier* for *mailman*. But I have trouble with many of the revisions of titles required in guidelines established by the Equal Employment Opportunity Commission or the U.S. Department of Labor. Guidelines require *actor* for *actress, waiter's assistant* for *busboy, lodging quarters cleaner* for *chambermaid, rail vehicle operator* for *motorman*.

The use of *he* as a genderless pronoun seems to cause the most trouble, and the most fuss, in the effort to desex the language. English, unlike some modern languages, has no separate genderless pronoun, and historically, *he, his,* and *him* have served to refer to *anyone* or *each* or *one* or to a student or a writer or a person when the sex is not specified:

> Everyone cast his vote in the morning.
> A student should take his work seriously.

It is hard to divorce the pronouns from their masculine meaning in sentences like these.

It is also hard to get along without using them. Proposals for the creation of a new genderless pronoun—*himmer,* for example, or *hit* or *(s)he* or the Old English *wit*—don't get much support. *He or she* or *he/she* is cumbersome. Using *he* and *she* alternately seems to me not to solve anything. There are methods that are advocated in the style books and that work most of the time. Essentially they are just ways of writing without using a singular genderless pronoun. Here are the most workable:

1. Shifting the sentence to the plural: "Students should take their work seriously." This doesn't seem to weaken the sentence. But I have trouble trying to revise "Every dog must have his day." "All dogs must have their days" doesn't seem quite the same.

2. Shifting to the pronoun *you*. "If a person tries, he can succeed" becomes "If you try, you can succeed," which says pretty much the same thing.

3. Shifting the sentence to the passive: "The economist should revise

his estimates" becomes "The estimates should be revised by the economist." This seems to me to weaken the sentence and perhaps change meaning slightly.

4. Just drop the pronoun: "A student should take work seriously." This device often works without much sacrifice in clarity. Or notice: "If a person wants work, he can find it" shifted to "A person who wants work can find it."

5. Use *they* and *their* to refer to singular nouns. This has the advantage of simplicity, and a considerable number of people already indulge in this device, although it is a schoolroom sin, faulty agreement. I am uncomfortable with this construction, although it is becoming more common. I don't mind too much something like "Every dog must have their day," which is probably better than other ways of avoiding *his*. I don't like sentences in which the plural pronoun follows both a singular subject and a singular verb form: "Any person who puts their gum under the chair . . ."

Using these devices is not always easy, and I think that some of the contortions required to avoid the sexist use of *he* tend to tie a writer in knots. But I think that the genderless *he* is gone, at least from anything being published.

Campaigns to abolish other allegedly sexist terms are less uniformly successful. One word that seems to resist attempts to obliterate it is *girl*. A male executive refers to "the girls in the office" at his peril. But I think the word—and in a different way *boy*—illustrate the difficulties of dealing with sexism in language. *Girl* occurred in Middle English as a noun for a young child of either sex. It, and also *boy,* probably came from Low German. One theory is clearly sexist—that *girl* comes from Latin *garrulus,* meaning talkative or chattering.

By the sixteenth century, *girl* had specialized to refer to female children but had also generalized to refer to any unmarried female. It had also come into use as a term of endearment for any woman. After another century, *girl* had developed another meaning, to refer to a servant. Echoes of that meaning are probably behind current uses that seem demeaning: "I'll get one of my girls to type it" or "My girl Friday takes care of the coffee." But banning it is complicated because there is no quite suitable substitute and because *girl* remains in use as a term of endearment. Popular songs could not get along without a "girl of my dreams."

A male child was a *knave child* in Middle English or sometimes just a *knave*. *Boy* was derogatory, probably because it also could refer to a servant. Like *girl* it became a term of affection. More recently it has reverted partly to its unfavorable sense. There is something humorously contemptuous in mentioning "the good ol' boys." Or calling someone "boy" can be seriously insulting, especially to a black.

I am not totally in sympathy with all the concern over *girl* and *boy*, and I also don't understand some of the feminist objections to *lady*. I understand that *lady lawyer* or *lady barber* implies discrimination, but I see no reason for abandoning the old polite address of "ladies and gentlemen." *Women and men* isn't quite the same thing. *Lady of the house* sounds old-fashioned, but I'm not sure what to substitute. *Lady's Day* at the ballpark may not always reflect the behavior of the women attending, but *Women's Day* doesn't quite work. There is often some reason for indicating the sex of a *salesperson*, and *saleswoman* seems to me no better than *saleslady*.

I don't object to *ladies' rest room*, and I'm not ready to abandon all feminine counterparts of male terms. It is often useful to distinguish between an actor and an actress, a lion and a lioness, a waiter and a waitress, a widow and a widower. *Actress* doesn't seem to me disparaging. But I don't like *authoress* and *poetess*, which do seem demeaning. *Student* as a substitute for *coed*, as guidelines suggest, doesn't say the same thing, although the implications of *coed*, echoing the condescending acceptance of women as educable, are clearly sexist. I don't find *freshman* to refer to a first-year student especially sexist. Using *homemaker* or *consumer* to avoid *housewife* is pretentious and doesn't solve the problem of *house husband*, which is a little cute.

It is worth noting that a majorette is not a female major, nor is a governess a female governor.

• **Mind-Softening: Lying and the Teflon Effect**

It is a commonplace that we live in an age of communication. Language is everywhere: radio, television, tapes, newspapers, magazines, computers, even books. I'm not sure what this deluge of words is doing to us. Obviously, I suppose, there is some increase in our ability to use language, in spite of the frightening figures about illiteracy in the United States. But it also seems to me that something is happening to our understanding, to our reactions to language. We are, I think, developing a kind of immunity to language, an ability to hear sounds without interpreting them, a cynical assumption that much of the language we see or hear can be dismissed automatically as trivial or untrue. Paradoxically, we are at the same time becoming more gullible, as attested by the successes of advertising campaigns, the triumphs of the public relations offices, and the surrender of politics to the authority of the sound bite.

Advertising, especially the television commercial, provides the most obvious illustrations. The advertiser's distortions have become blatant, not quite lies but seldom the whole truth. For example, the skillful use of qualifiers is apparent in almost all ads. *Virtually* is a good example. The word means, in one dictionary definition, "in effect although not in fact; for all practical purposes." That is, two things that are "virtually identical" are not really identical, although they may be almost so. The word has become a favorite with advertisers, possibly because it is easily associated with *virtue*. So a birth control pill offers "virtually 100% protection," a washing machine is "virtually trouble free," or a dishwasher soap leaves dishes "virtually spotless." What the qualified statements really say is that the product is not really trouble free or does not leave the dishes spotless.

Another useful word is *help*, especially convenient for health remedies that have to claim some kind of superiority. The snake oil advertisers of some generations ago could promise directly to cure everything from hives to hemorrhoids, but government regulation on truth in advertising has forced a new technique. Making a strong claim and qualifying it works on the assumption that if you make the claim attractive enough, people will believe the claim and overlook the qualifier.

This pill will "help relieve tension," this ointment will "help reduce hair loss," this cream "helps keep you young looking," this toothpaste "helps prevent cavities." Slightly different in their effect are *new* and *improved*, which sound important but may mean almost nothing. One laundry detergent is "ultra new." Regulations require some change in a product before it can be advertised as new or improved, but the changes do not have to make it any better. A cereal may be "new" or "improved" because the box is different or because it has more—or fewer—raisins in it. A detergent may be "improved" because its color is changed.

It is assumed that anything new or improved or "state-of-the-art" is also "better," and comparative forms of modifiers are among the most useful terms in advertising copy. The advantage is that the other side of the comparison never has to be specified. The advertiser can say that a battery lasts longer, and nobody asks, "Longer than what?" We assume that the statement means longer than other batteries last, but the advertiser is not committed to that. So we have ointments that heal faster, razors that shave smoother—or occasionally more smoothly— detergents that make clothes cleaner, fruit that is fresher, champagne that is drier, or deodorants that make your armpits drier. More doctors prescribe aspirin, and more dentists use Crest. And so on.

The ad agent is also a master of euphemisms, especially those that can deceive an unwary prospective customer. "Genuine simulated diamonds" at a low price are more attractive than paste or fakes, especially to somebody not sure of the meaning of *simulated*. This ad in a Sunday paper is even more skillful: "The $3,000 diamond anniversary ring—re-created with 3 full carats of cubic zirconia diamonds set into a genuine 18 karat gold vermeil band." *Vermeil* is an old poetic term for vermilion that can also refer to gilded copper and has been resurrected by the ad writer to make the phony sound real. *Genuine imitation leather* and *virgin vinyl* suggest that artificiality is an advantage. Long ago advertisers popularized *halitosis* for bad breath; more recently sweat has become *nervous wetness* as constipation has become *occasional irregularity.*

It's hard to assess the effects of all this business on people generally. Certainly some people have become so skeptical that much Madison Avenue talk has lost its effectiveness. Words like *fabulous* and *tremen-*

dous and *colossal* have lost their meaning for anyone paying attention. People assume that calling olive oil "extra virgin" doesn't mean anything. On the other hand, some people must be impressed by the statement that "Certs have a little drop of Retsyn," whatever Retsyn is, or that "Liquid Drano is the liquid strong enough to be called Drano."

• **51 Percent Truthful**

Of all the techniques of public relations language these days, the use or misuse of statistics seems to me the most intrusive. We live in an age of numbers, dominated by computers and pocket calculators. We identify ourselves with social security numbers, make purchases or telephone calls with credit card numbers. Addresses include increasingly complicated zip code numbers. We observe the Dow Jones index in the morning paper. The compiling of sports statistics is a thriving business; the record number of home runs—or of strikeouts—is available for zealous fans.

An early example of the use of statistics is the Ivory soap ad that hailed its product as 99.44 percent pure. Nobody asked, "99.44 percent pure what?" Nobody wondered what was in the .56 percent presumably impure. And nobody suggested that the purity might be air, which might account for the product's other slogan, "It floats." The use of the figure gave the soap a scientific respectability that was apparently not seriously questioned.

Advertisers have continued to see the benefits of percentage figures. We find that one medicine has 30 percent or 40 percent or 50 percent more pain-relieving ingredients than a rival or than it used to have. Or we see a drawing of a human stomach and watch as a concoction graphically "absorbs 32 percent more stomach acids" than some other all-purpose remedy. I am totally puzzled by an ad for cups and plates that claims, "Our dishes are 20% more appetizing." The figures give credence to the logical fallacy that more is necessarily better.

But sometimes less is better, and ads claim that their cigarettes have various lower percentages of coal tar or nicotine. We don't know what the percentage is lower than—lower than it was in the same cigarette a year ago or lower than it is in other cigarettes. Dairy products do the same thing to emphasize dietary suitability. Milk may have 1 or 2 or 0 percent fat, and ice milk may be 96 percent fat-free, which may mean that it has 4 percent fat, but I'm not sure.

Some supermarkets have moved to a more inclusive approach, simply claiming that they have 10 percent or 15 percent lower prices than their competitors, even though the rival store may make the same claim, perhaps with equal validity.

A variation is to quote a statistic on some authoritative group that endorses a product—especially doctors. "In a survey 60 percent of dentists recommended our toothpaste which has 40 percent more tartar-resisting ingredients."

Advertisers of breakfast cereals, facing increasing competition, have worked out ingenious ways of comparing their products. Not satisfied merely with pointing out that their product contains 30 percent or 40 percent more of some ingredient—oat bran or fiber or vitamins—than another, they pile up boxes of different brands to demonstrate relative nutritional value.

Statistics can be even more confusing in other settings. I'm never sure whether a 41 percent chance of rain means that I should carry an umbrella. More important, I don't find great comfort in a medical decision based on statistics. This drug was successful for 38 percent of its users and that one for only 33 percent; better try this one.

Or consider, "Crime climbed 5.5 percent in 1990, a 30 percent increase since 1978." This sounds ominous, but we don't know what kinds of crimes are involved, whether reporting requirements have changed, or how the figures relate to population growth. Or a statistic that classifies 33.33 percent of a school class as unwed mothers becomes less worrisome when it is clear that the school is small and the class has three members.

The most disturbing manifestation of this age of statistics seems to me our reliance on polls. Market surveys regulate policies in all sorts of businesses. Public officials make decisions on the basis of answers to questionnaires—or by weighing stacks of pro and con telegrams. Some polls are not very accurate; they are based on samples that are too small or badly chosen, ask confusing questions, often are conducted on telephones by inexperienced questioners, are influenced by temporary conditions, and so on. But the record of political polls in predicting election results has recently been impressive, perhaps because the polls influence voters. Political polls seem to me clearly to violate the principle of the secret ballot—presumably basic in a democratic system—but they provide attractive material for press releases and lucrative jobs for various statisticians and seem to be here to stay.

I'm not sure whether the numbers games are being successful or are mainly driving us to cynicism about advertising and government. But I can't forget that there is apparently enough gullible acceptance of the deluge of figures, enough faith that anything "scientific" must be good, to tempt anyone with a reason and no scruples to create statistics. I sometimes wish we'd go back to "It might rain this afternoon" or "You're likely to survive for another year."

People are reacting to this sort of deception in two ways. Some assume that lying is the standard way of life for advertisers, business people, and politicians. They find it not surprising that NASA should dismiss mistakes, like that with the Hubble telescope, by referring to "a string of bad luck." Other people, however, believe the lies, accept what they read or hear at face value, and are numerous enough to keep advertising agencies and public relations firms in business. I'm not sure which reaction is more frightening.

2

For the most part our words came deviously, making their way by winding paths through the minds of generations of men, even burrowing like moles through the dark subconsciousness.
- John Moore, *You English Words*

Words and Their Ancestors: Family Trees

Trace back almost any of the common English words and you will get a rich and rewarding glimpse of the history, the customs, and even the beliefs of earlier ages.
- Margaret Bryant,
  Modern English and Its Heritage

There must have been a time when there was no language. Then there was a time when there was language. We don't know when or how or why this happened. But today more than three thousand different languages are in use, and we can observe a good deal about how at least some of them have developed. In particular, we can trace the history of English and notice the several ways in which words have come into the language.

A great portion of the words in an unabridged dictionary can be traced ultimately to a reconstructed language spoken as early as 3500 B.C., probably by nomadic people who moved from Siberia to various parts of what is now Europe. We have no direct knowledge of these people or their language, Proto-Indo-European, with *proto* meaning earliest or original. We can, however, fairly accurately guess about details of the language as the result of ingenious comparisons begun by nineteenth-century linguists. Working with languages as diverse as Latin and Celtic and Old Norse and Sanskrit, linguists discovered similarities indicating that most of the languages of Europe and America and parts of Asia have a common ancestor. Then by analyzing similarities and differences, discovering patterns of change from ancient to modern languages, linguists were able to reconstruct an Indo-European language, made up of words that can account for related words in a variety of languages. Modern dictionaries are able with some confidence to include lists of Indo-European roots. Nobody knows why the

Indo-Europeans should have picked the sound *ped to name a foot or the sound *kaput to mean head. (The asterisk before a word indicates that it is hypothetical.) But the evidence shows that they did, and the sounds developed into related words in many languages, including in English *pedestal, pedestrian, foot, fetlock,* even *pioneer,* and *capital, chapter, chief,* and *cap.*

One group of Indo-European languages was spoken by a number of Germanic people, mainly Angles and Saxons, who came to the British Isles during the period from about A.D. 450 to 650. The Lord's Prayer in the language of the Anglo-Saxons begins like this:

> Faeder ure þu ðe eart on heofnum si þin nama gehalgod. Tobecume þin rice.

Modern English retains much of the structure of this Old English as well as a vocabulary of basic words for the everyday activities of people.

But fairly early in their history, the British people began borrowing from other cultures and other languages—the Danes during three or four centuries of conflict and then, after 1066, the Normans. Norman French became the official language and added a new commercial, educational, and ecclesiastical vocabulary, all new words, to the language. Often the new words duplicated existing words, and both new and old survived, sometimes revealing a difference in the status of their users. Early lexicographer Nathaniel Bailey recorded a pat example. Farm work was done by English farmers, and farm animals were called by native names: *cow, bull, calf, swine,* and *sheep.* But when the meat of these beasts had been dressed (a French word) for the Norman seignior's table, it had borrowed the names *beef, veal, pork,* and *mutton.*

The borrowing continued, accelerating with the Renaissance, although it was not always approved. Here is Alexander Gill in 1619 in *Logonomia Anglica:*

> O harsh lips! I now hear all around me such words as *common, vices, envy, malice;* even *virtue, study, justice, pity, mercy, compassion, profit, commodity, colour, grace, favor, acceptance.* But whither, I pray in all the world, have you banished those words which our forefathers used for

these new-fangled ones! Are our words to be exiled like our citizens? Is the new barbaric invasion to extirpate the English tongue?

Nevertheless we went on, borrowing religious terms from Latin through French, *bishop, monk, mass, priest;* music terms from Italy, *piano, piccolo, andante, concerto;* and hundreds of others. Eventually almost every language in the world contributed to English: *guru* from India, *alcohol* from Arabia, *sauna* from Finland, *rodeo* from Mexico, *spoor* from Holland by way of Africa, *teriyaki* from Japan, and so on.

The result is that a large percentage of the words in any English dictionary are borrowed, more than half from Latin and Greek and the Romance languages. Borrowing usually accounts for more than half the words in any piece of prose. The commonest words, however—the most useful ones—are mainly native.

Direct descent from Old English and borrowing account for most of the extensive vocabulary of English, but words originate in other ways, especially in modern times. For example, a few words are simply coined. *Kodak* was created as a trade name and became a common noun, as did *victrola* and *frigidaire.* Many more words are created by combining existing words, compounding: *roughneck, bulldog, bedroom.*

Especially in America we have produced hundreds of new words with affixes, nouns from verbs by adding suffixes such as *-ment* or *-tion* (*establishment, demonstration*) or verbs from nouns with suffixes like *-ize* or *-ate* (*finalize, capitalize*). Many new words have been created in recent times with faddish affixes like *-orium, -wise, -orama,* and *-burger.* Words are also formed from proper names: *sandwich* from the Earl of Sandwich, or *watt* from James Watt. In recent years the government has produced dozens of acronyms, which function as words, *WAC, NASA, UNICEF.* Back-formation is an interesting phenomenon, the creation of a word by the opposite of the usual processes. For example, the word *editor* looks like *edit* plus an *-or* ending. Actually, *editor* is the older word, and *edit* is a back-formation from it. *Enthuse,* a back-formation from *enthusiasm,* is still regarded with suspicion.

Perhaps the most interesting extensions of the vocabulary come about as metaphorical applications or shifts in function give a word new meanings. We turn the names of animals into verbs: we *dog* someone's footsteps or *bull* our way through a crowd. The adjective *green* becomes a name for part of a golf course or a village meadow. A recent example of a functional shift is the word *collectable* or *collectible,* which has long been in the language as an adjective to describe anything which can be collected. I don't find it listed as a noun in any dictionary before the 1980s, but recent enthusiasms for collecting baseball cards or decorated plates or old tobacco tins have created the noun *collectable.* The word suddenly has great use because it has great usefulness, especially for promoters of Marilyn Monroe dolls or plastic models of antique cars.

Because of the great flexibility of the language and the imaginative ways in which the vocabulary has been created, etymology, the study of a word's ancestry, is especially fascinating for English. Sometimes the history of a word can be traced with confidence from roots as far back as reconstructed Indo-European or origins in Latin or Greek or a modern language. Often, however, origins are elusive and histories become speculative or fanciful.

• Folk Etymology and Punch and Judy

I read recently an explanation of the derivation of the names of Punch and Judy, principal characters in a puppet show popular since the Renaissance. According to this account, the two names have their origin in early moral teaching and represent the two most dangerous threats to male virtue, wine and women. Punch, of course, is a drink, and a *judy* in contemporary slang is a girl, particularly one of questionable morals.

Attractive as the story may be, it is only a rather elaborate example of false or folk etymology, expressing people's enthusiasm for making up stories to account for the origins of words, jumping to conclusions that depend on apparent similarities more than the actual workings of language. In this case, a kind of anachronism is also operating, since the explanation depends on meanings attributed to the words long after their origin.

Etymology is certainly not an exact science, but it does require some knowledge of language history or at least a look at some of the many reliable sources of information. The *Oxford English Dictionary—A New English Dictionary on Historical Principles*—is an obvious starting place. It suggests that *Punch* is a shortening of *punchinello,* an Italian clown or buffoon or puppet and specifically the chief character in the Punch and Judy shows, which became popular street entertainments about 1600. *Punchinello* is a diminutive of *pulcino,* a young chicken or child, and the character may have acquired his name from feathers in his hat.

Punch is a short, humpbacked, hooknosed puppet who beats his wife to death, strangles his child, and fights a policeman but still remains more a comic figure than a serious villain. *Judy* is a familiar form of *Judith.* There is no obvious reason for selecting the name for the heroine of the puppet show.

Another example of folk etymology is the erroneous assumption that the word *gaudy* comes from the name of the Spanish architect Gaudi i Cornet, who died in 1926 and was known for unusual designs. Actually, the word has been around a long time, deriving from Latin *gaudere,* to rejoice. A popular Latin students' song in the early nineteenth century used the word in *gaudeamus igitur,* "let us therefore rejoice." The meaning of *gaudy* developed in two directions, one suggesting exaggerated decoration or showiness and the other retaining the root meaning. Shakespeare used the word in this latter sense when Antony proposes to Cleopatra, "Come let's have one other gaudy night." Dorothy Sayers used *Gaudy Night* as the title for a novel.

Another example of a mistaken etymology is this account that appeared in a newspaper column by L. M. Boyd: "Mythology had it that souls were ferried to Hades across the river Styx. And fancy fiction writers let that river symbolize any faraway place next door to nowhere. Plain talkers wouldn't put up with it. So it wound up in the vernacular as 'out in the sticks.'" I have no notion where Boyd got this, but it is pure folk etymology. The origin of *sticks* as a term for back country is neither very complicated nor very glamorous and can be documented in standard dictionaries. *Stick* was used as early as the eighteenth century in England to refer to timber. In Australian lumbering talk it was used to refer to a tree fit for logging or to a log. It was used occasionally to refer to a grove of timber in the United States in the nineteenth century, and a Canadian book, *Black Canyon* (1857), includes the following bit of dialogue: "Before sun up you whitemen go. Go back to the stick [forests] far, far, far." The Stick Indians were those who lived in the timber country. By the beginning of the twentieth century the plural form *sticks* was used to refer to the backwoods, the country. A 1905 book, *Northerner*, comments, "Billy is a cane-brake nigger; he'll take to the sticks like a duck to water when he's scared." In theatrical slang the sticks is likely to be any place outside New York.

Boyd's explanation of *the sticks* is a little like the theory that *Hoosier* comes from the cries of settlers along the Ohio river yelling at passing boatmen "who're ya." Or there is the story that *gringo* developed because a sailor in a Latin-American port sang "Green Grow the Lilacs," and a native thought he was being addressed in the first two words of the song. The most likely precursor of *Hoosier* is a dialect word *hoozer*, used of anything large, but there is no clear evidence for the guess. *Gringo* may be Spanish gibberish based on *Griego*, the word for Greek.

Mistaken notions about a word's ancestry sometimes work to create new words or change the character of an existing word. One example that we can see occurring at present is the Americanization of French *chaise longue*, literally a long chair. Americans, uncomfortable with the French, assume that *longue* is an error for *lounge*, a familiar word in English that fits the context. Current dictionaries list *chaise lounge*. Similar is the popularity in the Middle West of *hi-bred* corn, the result of an adman's ignorant or possibly calculated misunderstanding of *hybrid*.

An older example is the word *shamefaced*. It developed from an earlier English word, *shamefast*, which had nothing to do with the face. It combined *shame*, a synonym for *modesty*, with *fast*, which meant fixed or confirmed, and was a complimentary term. Popular association of the sound of the second part of the word with *face* changed over the years both the spelling and the meaning. Similarly mishearing has altered the spelling of *duct tape*, the name of a strong adhesive tape designed especially to cover the seams in heating ducts. The tape has become useful for all sorts of quick repairs, but it has also become *duck tape*, although none of its uses involve ducks.

Eating *humble pie* implies contriteness or humbleness, but it developed this association through folk etymology. Originally the pie was made from *umbles*, the inferior parts of a deer, or offal. *Belfry* has nothing to do with bells. It came from Middle English *berfrey*, a name for a tower. No matter how much wood a woodchuck can chuck, *woodchuck* has nothing to do with either wood or chucking except through folk etymology. Its origin is the Algonquian word *otchek*, the Indian name for the animal.

Sirloin is a compound of French *sur*, above, and *loin;* it specifies an anatomical location for the cut of meat. Naming a restaurant *Sir Loin's* gives the beef knighthood through folk etymology. *Penthouse* has added the idea of *house*, presumably to make it more accurately descriptive. Its Middle English form, *pentis*, from Latin *appendere*, to hang, has nothing to do with *house*. *Cold slaw* appears on menus, a folk etymology revision of *cole slaw*, from Dutch *kool* for cabbage plus *sla* for salad. With the change to *cold slaw* we can have *hot slaw*.

Sound often produces the erroneous assumption behind folk etymology. I was taken fishing years ago in Australia on Coal and Candle Creek. I discovered later that the creek had been named originally for Colonel Campbell. Similarly, attempts to pronounce French turned *route de roi*, the king's road, to *Rotten Row* in England.

Sometimes folk etymology is reflected in blunders. Student comments on the Mid-evil Age in history perhaps reflect popular misconceptions about the period. "You can take it for granite" is increasingly common, and perhaps as expressive as the usual cliché. I like the ring of *sourcastic* comments. I'm not sure whether the following misspelling is a conscious pun or unconscious folk etymology: "I've been frightened so much lately that I'm getting parannoyed." I won't speculate about what was going on in the mind of the student who misspelled the name of a wild fungus as a *toad's tool*.

• **Birds and Animals**

Metaphoric expansion is one of the most interesting ways in which the vocabulary of a language grows. I started thinking about the names of birds and animals as sources for metaphorically created words when I heard, for the first time, the cry of a loon and began to understand why "crazy as a loon" should have developed. The cry seems to be the basis of the phrase, in spite of the similarity in spelling of *loony* and *loony bin*, which have nothing to do with the bird. *Loony* comes from *lunatic* and ultimately from *luna*, the moon.

I'm not familiar enough with coots to be comfortable with "crazy as a coot," although the coot is apparently considered an unusually stupid bird, and *coot*, especially in British slang, names a simpleton. In America coots are usually old coots.

All this led me to some of the obvious epithets involving birds: *bird-brained, owl-eyed, eagle-eyed, raven-haired, henpecked, chicken-hearted, pigeon-toed*, Hamlet's *pigeon-livered*. More interesting, however, are bird names that have become dead or moribund metaphors, sometimes with clear relations to the bird in the background but sometimes only dimly connected.

I'm not sure, for instance, why a pigeon should give its name to a dupe or person swindled or cheated; in Elizabethan times rabbits, or conies, had that honor. The transfer may go back to the fact that at one time pigeons were tied to a stool as decoys for other pigeons, hence *stool-pigeon*, meaning a decoy. From that apparently came both the notion that a pigeon is easily deceived and the current slang meaning in which a stool-pigeon is an informer.

Turkey is still sometimes used not only for a failing dramatic performance but also for a person—for whom it can convey mild reproach or humorous endearment or complete exasperation. The dictionary's explanation that turkeys are considered "comparatively easy to catch" does not fully warrant our verbal exploitation of the fowl.

The greed and voracity of ravens produced *ravening* and *ravenous*. But quails have no responsibility for *quail* as a verb meaning to cower or draw back in fear. The verb probably comes from an old French word meaning to coagulate. And the seagull is not the source of the Elizabethan slang word *to gull,* meaning to cheat or swindle, and of the word *gullible.* The verb *gull* comes from an old word meaning to swallow. *Gullet* is unrelated, going back to Latin *gula,* meaning throat. The guinea hen is not responsible for *guinea,* the name of an obsolete British coin worth twenty-one shillings, but both the coin and the fowl were named because they were imported from Guinea on the west coast of Africa. The hawk is not related to the verb *hawk,* to advertise or peddle, which is a back-formation from *hawker,* derived from a German word meaning huckster. *Grouse,* to gripe or grumble, and *lark,* a prank or good time, also developed with no help from the birds. *Grouse,* related to *grouch,* comes from an old French word meaning to complain. *Lark* goes back to an Old Norse word meaning to leap or play.

A crane, the lifting machine with an extended arm, looks like the bird, and the verb *crane,* to lean out with a stretched neck, imitates the bird. *Jay,* for a stupid or talkative person, apparently reflects the tendency of jaybirds to chatter. A popinjay was originally a parrot and in slang is a person like a jay. A jaywalker is a stupid pedestrian. To *crow* is to boast or gloat, but to *eat crow* is to admit a mistake, to accept humiliation.

The snipe, a long-beaked marsh bird, is responsible for a number of common words, although the connection is not always obvious. The verb *snipe,* to shoot from cover and pick off an enemy, probably referring to methods of hunting snipe, has generalized to refer to any kind of verbal attack. In British slang the common snipe was sometimes called a guttersnipe, apparently from its habit of picking up refuse from a gutter; by extension a street urchin became a guttersnipe. This association with the gutter probably accounts for another use of *snipe,* as a slang term for a discarded cigar butt.

Canary, by an interesting twist, goes back to Latin *canis,* dog; the Canary Islands were named for large dogs that inhabited them. Then the birds, native to the island, were named for the islands. As a fairly obvious metaphor, a canary can be a singer or a stool-pigeon singing.

The characters of common barnyard fowl seem established in metaphors—the duck as cute, the chicken as cowardly, the rooster as arrogant, and the goose as stupid. The verb *to duck* reflects the duck's dive.

To *be chicken* or *to chicken out* is to quit because of fear. The car game called *chicken* tests which of the participants will chicken out first. *Spring chicken,* for a young or inexperienced woman, is almost always used in the negative, "She's no spring chicken." The rooster or cock obviously produces many adjectives like *cocky* and *cockeyed* and less obviously the verb *cock,* to tilt or raise, as a dog cocks his ears, referring apparently to the way a rooster moves his head. One interesting application is the British slang *cock a snook,* for what in American slang is thumbing one's nose. *Queen Anne's fan* is another British term for the gesture. The cock also is behind *cockney,* which referred to a spoiled child or simpleton in Chaucer's time and then was applied to a native of London's East End. Presumably the word originally referred to a cock's egg, which was assumed to be either impossible or not very impressive. The size of the goose's egg probably gave it preference as a metaphor for zero. I'm not sure how accurately a goose's behavior is portrayed by the verb *goose,* to prod suddenly in the backside. But the extension to refer to pumping gas into a car engine seems logical.

All this leads to things like robin banks and oriole cookies, which you can't swallow without going stork raven mad.

Animals have been equally useful in expanding the language. The bat, for example, has produced a variety of set phrases, most of them referring to its erratic habits in flight: *blind as a bat, crazy as a bat, like a bat out of hell, bats in the belfry,* and just *batty.* The connection of *old bat* with the winged mammal is less clear. In the early seventeenth century, *bat* referred to a prostitute, probably because, like the bat, she was a creature of the night. The word then became a more general term for a gossipy or mean old woman. Some of those meanings were probably influenced by another word *bat,* which comes from Old French *battre,* to beat, and means to blink or flutter. "Not to bat an eye" comes from this word. But "to bat one's gums" comes from still another *bat,* for a stick or cudgel, like a baseball bat.

The word *dog* turned up in late Old English, and its early history is unknown. It ultimately replaced an earlier word for all varieties of canines, *hund.* *Dog* became the general term, and *hund* became *hound,* specialized to refer to only a particular kind of dog. Although the adjective *dogged* refers to an admirable characteristic of man's best friend, its persistence or steadfastness, most of the extensions of *dog* emphasize the animal as inferior or miserable, the liver of a dog's life.

To dog it is to loaf or avoid responsibility. A derogatory term for a World War II private was *dogface*. When times are bad, we're "going to the dogs." A dog may be merchandise that won't sell, a racehorse that runs last, a book or actor or play that fails. "A dog in the manger" is uncomplimentary in a different way, emphasizing the dog's alleged self-ishness as displayed in the Aesop fable. Various guesses about the origin of *hot dog*, for a wiener, suggest that it came from the resemblance of a dachshund to a sausage or that it reflects a humorous allegation that the sausage is made from dog meat. To refer to a show-off athlete as a hot dog is fairly recent, as is the verb *to hotdog*.

Although *dirty dog* is in the pattern of canine disrespect, some refer-ences to human males are different. A *gay dog* or a *lucky dog* may not be totally respectable, but he's usually admired or even envied. Even an *old dog* is looked on with tolerance. But a woman called a dog is insulted; at worst she is an "ugly, unrefined, or sexually disreputable girl or woman," to quote one dictionary. *Bitch* has become disreputable enough that many speakers hesitate to use it even in its traditional sense to name a female dog.

A male who is a *tomcat* or given to *tomcatting* is accused only of excessive "maleness." In macho company, at least, the terms are even complimentary. But to call a woman a *cat* may suggest that she is *catty*, given to gossip, or even that she is a resident of a *cathouse*.

The animal metaphors tend pretty consistently to follow a pattern like this, illustrating the male orientation of the language. The animals used to designate males emphasize strength, virility, and sexual prowess, usually with favorable connotations. Those applied to women tend to suggest wantonness, with unfavorable connotations. Sometimes, how-ever, they are combined with cuteness and possibly helplessness.

Thus a man may be a *buck, stag, tiger, wolf,* or *stud*. He may be a *moose* or a *bear*, but even these are not completely derogatory. He may eventually become an *old goat*, annoying to women but admired by others for his durability. A woman, however, is not flattered by being called a *cow* or a *sow* or a *pig*. She may be a *filly* in some places, or a *bunny* or a *lamb*. In the 1920s a "fast" woman was a *vampire*, usually shortened to *vamp*. But the vampire may become an *old bat*. *Crone*, another word for an old bat, derives from the Danish noun for an old ewe.

Fox, applied to a female, a near parallel to the male *wolf*, indicates something of the new status of women. *Vixen*, like *shrew*, is uncomplimentary. But *fox*, the male counterpart of *vixen*, distinguishes a sexy female, usually without criticism.

The horse is not treated as contemptuously as the dog in the expressions it inspires, although parts of its anatomy, notably its rear and its neck, are the basis for uncomplimentary epithets. "To horse around" often has sexual implications. The advice against beating a dead horse echoes experiences of riding, as does the use of *horse*, or more often *pony* or *trot*, to refer to a translation or a set of answers used to carry a student through an examination. I'm not sure why a horse's mouth should be especially authoritative, or why *horsefeathers* should have been picked to express incredulity rather than, say, *bullfeathers*.

The bull has, however, inspired a considerable number of metaphoric uses, focusing not on feathers but on his excrement. *Bull*, both noun and verb, as well as *shoot the bull* and *bull session*, all refer to talk, often empty, nonsensical, exaggerated, or lengthy. These slang meanings may all be euphemisms for *bullshit*, but they may also be related to Old French *boule*, a lie, which goes back to Latin *bulla*, a bubble. A bullpen is not only a place to keep bulls but a small room in a penitentiary and in baseball an area beside the diamond where relief pitchers warm up. I'm not sure why the eye of a bull should have been chosen to name the central mark of a target, but some non-English languages have made a similar selection: French *oeil de boeuf*, Danish *kooie*, cow's eye.

The uses of *rat* as a verb refer often to the notion that rats desert a sinking ship. *To rat* is to desert companions, to squeal or inform. *Rat race* refers to the image of rats on a treadmill or in a maze. *To squirrel* emphasizes the animal's industry in providing for the future. But the use of *squirrel* to mean a psychologist apparently suggests a person who examines nuts. *Squirrely*, to mean eccentric, may refer to the animal's behavior in a cage.

Some dictionaries make the chipmunk responsible for the development of *chippy* as a term for a prostitute; others relate *chippy* to *chip*, suggesting a parallel with *piece*. I'm not sure how either explanation works. The skunk has never been a popular animal, which accounts for the use of *skunk*, often accompanied by *low-down*, as an insulting term for a person. But I don't know how the verb developed, *to skunk*, to overwhelm an opponent in a game. *Weasel words* and *to weasel* result from the animal's reputation for sneakiness.

- **Names into Words**

Some of the most interesting word histories are those in which a word has a source in a proper name. *Bloomer* provides a place in history for Mrs. Amelia Jenks Bloomer, a nineteenth-century reformer and advocate of modesty who promoted the garment. Chaucer's character Pandarus, who sponsored the love affair of Troilus and Cressida, is remembered in the verb *pander*. Mary Magdalene was often depicted with eyes red and swollen from weeping. *Magdalene* became the modern word *maudlin*.

A more complicated example is *Nosey Parker*. *Nosey* or *nosy* has for a long time referred to either a bad smell or an oversized nasal organ. In Australia the phrase "on the nose" indicates something that stinks; in the United States the phrase means accurately or exactly or distinguishes a bet on a horse to place first. Both Oliver Cromwell and the Duke of Wellington had *Nosey* as a nickname, celebrating their looks and not their curiosity.

Nobody is sure when the name Parker was first associated with *nosey* to signify an inquisitive, prying person, but the *Oxford English Dictionary* notes a 1907 picture postcard describing the adventures of Nosey Parker. It comments that "the original 'nosy parker' was one who played Peeping Tom to love-making couples in Hyde Park."

Peeping Tom does have an established identity. According to the legend, when Lady Godiva rode naked through Coventry to relieve the citizens of a new tax burden, Tom bored a hole in a wall. Although his eyes were blinded before he had a look, his name and title were established.

Nosey Parker may have existed long before it turns up in print, and there is one plausible candidate for the original prying person. Matthew Parker (1504–75) was one of England's most distinguished and influential divines, ultimately Archbishop of Canterbury. He was constantly in the center of controversy, looked on as an instigator of investigations of unacceptable religious behavior. Etymologies making him the original *Nosey Parker* have some plausibility, but no supporting evidence.

An alliterative companion for Nosey Parker, Paul Pry, is less well known, but he has a known origin. Paul Pry was the main character in a popular farce by John Poole produced in 1825. Pry, a meddlesome and inquisitive fellow, was supposedly modeled on a journalist of the time, one Thomas Hill.

A news story quotes a professor of law asserting that "the state cannot present a police officer with the Hobson's choice of incriminating himself or facing a penalty." The phrase is sometimes used this way, but in its origin and standard meaning it refers to a different kind of choice, a choice which is not a choice.

Supposedly the expression refers to a Cambridge livery stable keeper named Thomas Johnson or Hobson, who died in 1631. He let out his horses in strict rotation. Each customer was obliged to take the horse nearest the stable door or to take none. Hobson's choice is not a choice between alternatives but between what is offered and nothing. *The Century Dictionary* quotes T. Ward:

Where to elect there is but one.
'Tis Hobson's choice, take that or none.

This etymology is the kind of interesting story that thrives on frequent repetition, and Ernest Weekley spots a 1617 comment by one Richard Cock: "We are put to Hodgson's choice to take such privileges as they will geve us, or else goe without." This early quote suggests that the expression may antedate the Cambridge carrier.

The pedigree of *guy* does not command much respect. The word is a common noun developed from a proper name, that of the notorious Guy Fawkes, villain of the Gunpowder Plot, an unsuccessful attempt to blow up the houses of Parliament and James I of England in 1605. Fawkes was executed, and Guy Fawkes Day is still celebrated in England, a little like American Independence Day.

For a long time, the major character in the celebration was an effigy of Guy Fawkes, made of old clothes and stuffed with straw or rags. For a day or two before the November 5 event, it was customary for children to drag the effigy about, asking for "a penny for the guy." In England *guy* still designates someone grotesque enough in dress or appearance that he recalls the effigy, the guy.

In America the word has developed differently, with almost no derogatory connotations. *A regular guy* and *a good guy* are complimentary. And relatively recently the word has become a common way of simply referring to a male: "guys and dolls" or "that's my guy." It is widely used colloquially, a synonym for words like *fellow* and *chap*. The verb *to guy* has the same meaning on both sides of the Atlantic: to make fun of, to tease, to badger.

Sometimes common names get adapted to use as common nouns for no discernible reason. I don't know why we have a good joe rather than a good charley—but a good-time charley—or why we have a jack of all trades. I don't know why we have a jim-dandy and a weary willie and a joe college and tomfoolery.

I got involved with *billy* by wondering about the origin of the billy that the jolly swagman boils in the Australian song, "Waltzing Matilda." *Billy* has a lot of uses, and there are a lot of guesses about their origin. The word is a variation on *Willy* as a shortening of *William*. One of its uses is to designate a male, as in *billy goat*. But the *billy* of *billy club* has a different source and is a shortening of *billet*, which seems to have descended from Indo-European *bilia*, a tree, and is a dialect word for a stick of wood. The swagman's billy, a kettle or can for carrying water or boiling tea, has a still different ancestry, the aboriginal word *billa*, meaning water. *Billa* appears also in another word in the song, *billabong*, a pond or channel holding water in the rainy season.

A billiful is an imprecise quantity, which has not taken the same route as *bellyful*, which is in its original meaning just a reference to enough food to fill the belly, a sufficiency. *Belly* is a native word developed from an Old English word meaning bag or skin or referring to the hull of beans or peas. In Middle English it came to refer generally to the body and was restricted to the middle part of the body in Modern English. It is also related to *bellows* through an old Teutonic ancestor meaning to be inflated. A bellyful, however, has come to be more than a sufficiency, more than one wants, as in "a bellyful of sermons" or "a bellyful of your complaining." A belly plea, in the eighteenth century, was a plea of pregnancy used by convicted female felons to avoid execution. Francis Grose observes that the females prepared before their trials, "every jail having, as the Beggar's Opera informs us, one or more child getters, who qualify the ladies for that expedient."

Billycock produces another complication. It's the name of a low-crowned, wide-brimmed hat, especially the one worn by Australian soldiers with the brim turned up on one side. One explanation of the name's origin is that it honors Billy Coke, a nineteenth-century sportsman for whom the first hat in this style was made. It seems more likely that the word is a variation on *billycocked*, used in England in the eighteenth century to describe this sort of hat without the turned-up brim. *Bullycock* probably refers to the person who was likely to wear the hat, but it's hard to be sure just what kind of bully that was. Captain Grose again defines an eighteenth-century bullycock as "one who foments quarrels in order to rob the persons quarreling." The word *bully* is not related to the old English word *bull* but comes from Dutch *boele*, meaning a lover of either sex. It retained something of this meaning in its early uses, as in Shakespeare's *Bully Bottom* in *A Midsummer Night's Dream*. Something of that early sense is retained in the use of the word as an informal approval, "bully for you." But the word's meaning degenerated, and the lover became a blustering gallant, a swashbuckler. Then a bully became especially anyone who attempts to exploit the weak or helpless. *Bully beef*, however, is innocent of any of these characteristics and comes from French *bouilli*, a shortening of *boeuf bouilli*, boiled beef.

Adaptations of female names, like the applications of animal names I mentioned above, tend to emphasize the masculine orientation of the language, frequently at least generalized as uncomplimentary terms. A *judy*, for example, has been slang for a girl, especially one of dubious morals, since early in the nineteenth century. It is a familiar form of *Judith*, well known to the English language mainly through the popular English Punch and Judy puppet shows. Judy may have had her name attached to the role of the nagging wife in the playlet partly as an echo of the exploits of Judith in the *Apocrypha*. In the biblical story Judith is treated as a heroine for weakening Holofernes, chief captain of King Nebuchadnezzar, an enemy of Israel, "with the beauty of her countenance" and then whacking off his head.

Other proper names that have become common nouns include *jug*, a pet name from Joan or Joanna, which became a common noun for a woman, usually a homely one, or for a servant or mistress. Then by extension *jug* acquired its most common meaning for a receptacle for liquids, as in *milk jug* or *little brown jug*. *Moll*, a diminutive of *Mary*, has been a name for a prostitute in England since the seventeenth century. In America it most commonly designates a gangster's companion, at least in B movies. In England *molly* is slang for an effeminate man and is part of the verb *mollycoddle*, although *nancy* is a more common term.

Fanny is now a common noun in America, almost respectable as a cute name for the human rump, but in English slang it refers to female sex organs, presumably an adaptation from the eighteenth-century pornographic novel, *The Memoirs of Fanny Hill*. *Fanny* developed another meaning in British naval talk of the nineteenth century when *Fanny Adams* became the term for canned mutton, honoring a Fanny Adams who was murdered about 1812 and whose body was cut into pieces and thrown in the river.

In Queensland, Australia, an aboriginal woman is a *mary*. A wicket-keeper among British cricketers is an *aunt sally*. *Sally,* what the army does forth, has nothing to do with the name. A *bertha* is a kind of wide collar; *big bertha,* the large cannon introduced in World War I, comes from a proper name, *Bertha Krupp,* of the Krupp munitions works in Essen. *Prissy* is not related to *Priscilla* but is a blend of *precise* or *prim* and *sissy. Patsy,* for a dupe or sucker, is unrelated to Patricia.

• Family Trees with Straight Branches

For many words a specific source can be found—an event, a coinage, a literary character, a place. What happens to the word as it is used, however, may be complicated, and often family trees that can be documented are more interesting than etymologies that keep linguists guessing. *Serendipity* is an example. It has acquired recent popularity as a pseudo-learned word meaning something like a general state of well-being. It is unusual because it is one of the few words in the language that someone created out of whole cloth. (*Out of whole cloth*, by the way, referred originally to something cut from cloth of the full size as manufactured. It developed in the nineteenth century to refer to something completely fictitious or made up.)

In a 1754 letter, author Horace Walpole told a friend that he had invented the word from the title of a fairy tale, "The Three Princes of Serendip." *Serendip* is an old name for Ceylon, which is now Sri Lanka. Walpole coined the word to designate the faculty for accidentally making happy discoveries, a faculty the three princes possessed. I have never noticed any great demand for a name for this faculty, and I suppose that is why the word in its current minor popularity has become vague in its meaning.

Backlog is an old word in America, appearing as early as 1684 to identify a large log placed at the back of a fireplace. The smaller log in front was the forestick. Sometime in the nineteenth century the meaning of the word began to generalize to refer to any kind of supporting material. A backlog was a reserve of supplies or an excess of work or orders for goods.

As huge log fires in fireplaces disappeared, the need for the original meaning of the word disappeared. But the figurative senses have become more useful, and a secretary may work at night because of a backlog of dictation or a factory may double production because of a backlog of unfilled orders. The word has also become a verb, and to backlog supplies is to build a reserve, to stockpile. To backlog an order is to put it on hold, or, to use a similar metaphor, to put it on the back burner.

Tules has become generalized, especially in the American West, to refer to any remote area, the sticks. Its origin is direct; it comes through Spanish from an Aztec word *tullin*, for a rush or bulrush. It was adopted in the United States in the middle of the nineteenth century, and it keeps the original meaning, referring to various kinds of reeds or rushes or to an area overgrown by tules. The word *tulare* has also developed through Spanish as a name for a rush-covered area, a tule. And "He's out in the tules" is like "He's out in the boondocks" or "boonies." *Boondocks* apparently comes from the Tagalog word *bundok*, meaning mountain, and was given its current use by World War II soldiers in the Philippines.

Teetotal seems to have an authenticated story to explain its origin. Richard Turner, an early English temperance advocate who stammered, made a famous speech in 1833 in which he kept repeating that nothing but t-t-t-total abstinence would do. The temperance society adopted *teetotal*, now sometimes spelled *teatotal*, revealing further speculation about its origin.

I remember from my childhood hearing the word *shitepoke*, and I remember it as something uncomplimentary and something to do with a large bird. It is not, I think, one of the most important words in the English vocabulary, but its origin is interesting and elusive. I don't find the word listed at all in a number of modern dictionaries, but it does appear in some older ones, and the old *Century Dictionary*, produced a hundred years ago, has a detailed description and a picture of the blue heron, known as a shitepoke and also as a poke and a fly-up-the-creek. The *Century* tactfully avoids any mention of the word's origin.

The word appeared in Canada or the United States as early as the eighteenth century, combining the common vulgar word for excrement with *poke*, a word for bag. The same combination with the word *sack*, *shitesack*, is recorded in the eighteenth century as a name for "a dastardly fellow," also a nonconformist. The bird probably got its name from the way it behaves on taking flight. A popular myth explains that the bird has an anatomical peculiarity responsible for its habits and the name. The notion is that the bird has only a single straight alimentary canal, unimpeded from gullet to exit.

Other variations on the word are *shagpoke* and *shidepoke*, both probably partly the result of efforts to avoid echoes of the word's vulgar origins. But *shagpoke* makes sense in another way, since *shag* is an old name for a cormorant.

Dubrovnik, on the east coast of the Adriatic, was an early center of commerce and culture, with many historical buildings still standing, at least until the disasters of the 1990s in Yugoslavia. The Italian name for Dubrovnik in the sixteenth century was Ragusa, and a ship sailing from the port was called a ragusa. In England the spelling for the port and the ship name was modified to *Aragouse*. The term generalized to refer to any large merchant vessel, especially one with a valuable cargo, and then to a fleet of such ships. With a shift in spelling it became the modern word *argosy*.

This seems very neat, but there are complications. For example, there is also a port called Ragusa in Sicily, and the *Oxford Dictionary of English Etymology* thinks that this port, rather than early Dubrovnik, gave its name to the merchant ships. And then there is Jason's ship, the *Argo*, in which he set out in search of the golden fleece. It may have influenced the English shift to the spelling *aragusa*. The *Argo*, however, was probably named for its builder.

The story of the word *shibboleth*, a password or any sign or symbol to distinguish a group, is interesting because it can be traced so clearly. It comes from a Hebrew word for a stream or flood, but its modern meaning has a special background.

In one bit of biblical fighting, the Gileadites successfully smote the Ephraimites. After the battle, many of the Ephraimites tried to escape, and the Gileadites had trouble identifying them. They hit on a device not unlike that of GIs in World War II, who tried to identify spies by asking about the Brooklyn Dodgers. They would ask, according to Judges 12:5–6, "Art thou an Ephraimite? If he said Nay: Then said they unto him, say now Shibboleth, and he said Sibboleth: for he could not frame to pronounce it right. Then they took him and slew him at the passage of Jordan."

Macassar is a district in the island of Celebes in Indonesia east of Borneo. The Strait of Macassar was the site of a 1942 battle between the Allies and Japanese. In the early nineteenth century some enterprising merchant imported into England an oil, perhaps made from berries from the sandalwood tree, which was alleged to be especially good for grooming hair. At least some of it came from Macassar, and it became known as Macassar oil. The name stuck long after the original formula had been replaced by concoctions of coconut or safflower oil. An advertisement in an 1895 journal offers "Rowland's Macassar Oil, known for 100 years as the best and safest preserver of the hair, and is far preferable to ordinary hair restorers."

Careful housekeepers obviously needed something to protect furniture from the oil, something to be anti the Macassar oil. The doilies placed on the backs and arms of chairs were called *antimacassars*.

Historians of locomotives and of army vehicles both claim the first uses of the word *jeep*, now associated primarily with the versatile army car. Probably both are right, since the word was applied in a number of ways during the 1940s, when it apparently came into use. In 1936, E. C. Segar's comic strip, "Popeye the Sailor," introduced a new character, Eugene the Jeep, a small animal with supernatural powers. The word *jeep*, like many other comic strip creations, caught on and was applied in various ways: to an army recruit, to ill-fitting coats and hats, to an autogiro as a jumping jeep. At some time it was applied to a new all-purpose military vehicle, and there the name stuck.

• Portmanteau Words

I once confidently explained *flustrated* as a folk blend of *frustrated* and *flustered*, only to discover that I was wrong and that *flustrated* or *flusterated* has been in the language since the early eighteenth century, an adjective from *fluster*, especially to mean confused with drink. The *Oxford English Dictionary* labels it "vulgar."

I was partly right, however, in the sense that the word is now often a confusion between the two words it sounds like. That is, it acts like a blend or like what Lewis Carroll's Humpty Dumpty called a portmanteau word, a word that packs more than a single meaning into one portmanteau or suitcase.

Humpty explains that *slithy* in the poem called "Jabberwocky" means slimy and lithe. *Mimsy* is flimsy and miserable. Neither of these caught on outside the looking glass, but *chortle*, combining *chuckle* and *snort*, and even *galumphing*, from *gallop* and *triumphant*, are now in dictionaries as Carroll coinages.

Portmanteau words are frequently more whimsical than useful and don't survive, but many exist—*brunch* from *breakfast* and *lunch* and *smog* from *smoke* and *fog*, to mention obvious examples. *Dumbfound*, from *dumb* and *confound*, was put together in the seventeenth century.

Flabbergasted, one of the more contrived, is apparently an eighteenth-century blend of *flabby* and *aghast. Gerrymander* combines the name of Governor Elbridge Gerry and *salamander,* referring to the shape of a redistricted Massachusetts county. *Anecdotage,* adding the implications of *dotage* to *anecdote,* and Clifton Fadiman's *hullabalunacy,* from *hullabaloo* and *lunacy,* are clever enough to deserve survival.

* **Etymologists at Play**

Many words lend themselves to speculation about their origin, producing comments ranging from obvious folk etymology to scholarly research articles. Sometimes the words seem to offer a challenge because they look as if they should have a clear history. The results are usually interesting but inconclusive. The best example is what is probably the most widely used of all English words, *OK* or *okay.* In spite of hundreds of pages of guessing about its origin, nobody is very sure where it came from.

The most frequently accepted explanation relies on a use of the term in 1840, when it was published as the name of the Democratic O.K. Club, an organization supporting Martin Van Buren for a second term in the White House. O.K. was supposedly an abbreviation for *Old Kinderhook,* the name of the village where Van Buren was born. The name was attractive to radicals in the party known as Locofocos. (*Locofoco* combines *loco,* as in *locomotive,* and Italian *fuoco,* fire. The prefix *-loco,* from Latin *locus,* place, was mistakenly assumed to mean "self"; *locofoco* originally meant "self-lighting" and was applied to both a cigar and a match.)

A gang of Locofocos invaded a political meeting of the rival Whig party shouting *OK* as a war cry. The initials became a campaign slogan and spread throughout the country. Van Buren was not reelected, but various kinds of attention focused on the word. The Whigs, observing that the Locofocos had been overcome and chased from the meeting, said that *OK* derived from an Arabic word and, when read backward, meant "kicked out." Other Whig proposals were "out of kash, out of kredit, out of klothes," and "out of karacter." The word gained further popularity in 1840 with the publication of two musical compositions, "The O.K. Quick Step" and "O.K. Gallopade."

Although this explanation seems plausible, it is not certain enough to forestall dozens of other proposals. The guesses include:

1. That the expression comes from *aux quais,* used by French sailors in the Revolutionary War to make appointments with American girls, or from French *O qu-oui,* an emphatic form of *yes* found in Sterne's *Sentimental Journey.*

2. That it may be derived from Finnish *oikes,* meaning correct.

3. That it comes from the first letters of Greek *ola kala,* used by teachers of Greek to approve student themes.

4. That it stands for *oll* (that is, *all*) *korrect.*

5. That it comes from a Choctaw word, *okeh,* meaning "it is so." The 1934 edition of *Webster's New International Dictionary* accepted this explanation. There are others.

A headline reads: "Does government give a tinker's damn about consumer?" The question is not whether the government does or doesn't but whether it should be *damn* or *dam.*

Francis Grose's 1785 *Dictionary of the Vulgar Tongue* points out that a dam was a small Indian coin and suggests that the phrase "I don't care a dam," like "I don't care half a farthing," reflects the worthlessness of the coin. But the phrase "don't care a curse" or "not worth a curse" was also current in the language by the fifteenth century. It was logical that *damn,* as a specific curse, should get into such phrases.

Tinkers got into the act very early. They were menders of pots and pans, often tramps, who moved from town to town looking for household odd jobs. Christopher Sly in Shakespeare's *The Taming of the Shrew* was a drunken tinker. An Elizabethan statute provided for sentencing "all jugglers, tinkers and petty chapmen" and other vagrants who were "rogues, vagabonds, and sturdy beggars."

Tinkers also had a dam different from Grose's small coin. Even into this century tinkers mending pots and pans built what they called a dam, a mold of wet sand or mud or bread, around the hole to be repaired. When the job was finished, the dam was worthless. Something absolutely worthless is "not worth a tinker's dam."

This explanation of *tinker's dam* is plausible; however, lexicographers record no use of *dam* in this sense before the nineteenth century, and both "not worth a dam" and "don't give a dam" were around in the eighteenth. Both the useless coin and later the tinker's mold may have influenced the development of *tinker's dam*. But *tinker's curse* or *damn* also had early currency, reflecting the tinker's alleged tendency to drunkenness and profanity, which made his oath worthless.

So you can take your choice, depending on whether you prefer a tinker's unreliable oath or his worthless mold or a small coin. Nobody, incidentally, ever says something *is* worth a tinker's dam or damn.

Damn sight is not related to tinkers and has nothing to do with *dam site*. It depends on a secondary meaning of *sight*. *Sight* can refer to some kind of unpleasant appearance: "The house was a sight after the party." Or it can refer to a spectacle, an unusual appearance, "a sight to behold." Or it can mean a lot or a large quantity: "The old house will take a sight of fixing." "Not by a damn sight" apparently developed in America in the nineteenth century, meaning "not by a good deal" and exploiting the use of *damn* as a general intensive. Mark Twain uses "not by a considerable sight." Joel Chandler Harris has a character say, "That ain't all by a long sight."

A guest on a recent television program answered a question confidently and explained that the word *cocktail* had its origin in the practice of an early bartender who stirred drinks with a feather. This bit of folk etymology is fanciful, but so are other suggested etymologies for the word. The truth is that nobody knows where *cocktail* came from.

One suggestion, with some support, is that the word comes from French *coquetier,* an egg cup, and was attached to a drink invented in New Orleans about 1800. The inventor, according to the story, used brandy made by Sazerac du Forge et Fils, and his cocktails were called *sazeracs*. A similar suggestion is that the word came from French *coquetel,* a mixed drink known for centuries in the vicinity of Bordeaux. It was supposedly introduced to America by French officers during the Revolution.

Other stories involve cockfighting. *Cock-ale* was a mixture of spirits and bitters and probably other ingredients fed to fighting cocks to prepare them for a match. *Cock-ale* became associated with all mixed drinks. In a variation, spectators at cockfights used to toast the cock with the most feathers left in his tail after the contest; the number of ingredients in their drink corresponded to the number of feathers remaining in the tail. There have been other proposals equally speculative.

There's a fairly widespread notion that *hooker* as a term for a prostitute came about as an expression of the aggressiveness or resourcefulness of certain women, referring especially to a woman who "hooks" a man by pretending to be pregnant.

The word *hook* comes from Old English *hoc*, meaning hook. *Hooker* has developed a host of metaphoric and slang meanings. It can refer to a fisherman, the person who tries to hook the ball out of a scrum in a rugby match, or a substantial drink of liquor. In the sixteenth century it referred to a thief or shoplifter, especially to a pickpocket, who sometimes used a hook to snatch a purse. These uses all seem compatible with the use of *hooker* to designate a person who recruits others for illicit purposes and then keeps them hooked by threatening exposure.

And these variations all seem to explain the origin of *hooker* to mean prostitute. But according to etymologists the facts are different. *Hooker* to mean prostitute comes from a region in New York City called the Hook, a center for prostitution in the nineteenth century. A hooker was a resident of the Hook, therefore a strumpet or a sailor's trull.

Cop appeared in the early eighteenth century as a verb meaning to capture and, a little later, to steal. It apparently comes from French *caper*, to catch or seize. Probably from this use *cop* became a name for a policeman in the middle of the nineteenth century, although there are other theories about the origin of the term. One of them is that *cop* is a shortening of *copper* and refers to the copper buttons once used on police uniforms. Another is that it comes from Yiddish *cop*, to grab.

But *cop out* had appeared as a phrase even earlier, with various meanings. It was a variant of *cop it hot*, which meant to be scolded or to get into trouble. In the Boer War it was slang for dying. In American slang of the late nineteenth century it could refer to winning a girl, as in "Why don't you cop the lady out?"

Current slang uses, primarily related to police business, are further variations: to be arrested or caught in a crime or to plead guilty to a crime. The latter use, of course, is almost the same as *cop a plea*, to plead guilty as a trade for a lighter sentence. But the term has also generalized beyond criminal proceedings to refer to any kind of confession or to any inglorious withdrawal from a project.

Jerry-built or *jury-built* has been around a long time, but nobody is sure where it came from. *Jury-mast* was a nautical term as early as 1616, a temporary mast contrived at sea to replace a broken one. There are half a dozen theories about the origin of the term. One of the more plausible is that *jury* in this sense goes back to a Latin word for aid or support. Another is that the word here is the same as the one for a court jury, and that a jury-mast is simply one hastily put together with the captain and carpenter consulted as a jury. I don't have a choice and don't find any of the theories conclusive.

But the term *jury* was quickly extended to new applications. *Jury-rig* or *jury-rigged* developed to describe any makeshift device. A *jury-leg* was a wooden leg in the seventeenth century. *Jury-built* is no longer confined to nautical construction.

Jerry-builder appeared in the late nineteenth century as a name for a person who tossed together unsubstantial houses built of inferior material. Something that was *jerry* was unsubstantial, and a speculator who built flimsy houses was a *jerry*. The word is presumably a nickname for Jeremy or Jeremiah or Gerald, but how it got associated with shoddy building nobody knows.

Other uses of *jerry* seem not related. Jeroboam in the Old Testament was "a mighty Man of valor." His name was adopted to name an oversize wine bottle and then any large bowl or bottle, partly perhaps because "he made Israel to sin." The name was shortened to *jerry* and in British slang became a name for a chamber pot. American soldiers in World War I memorialized the resemblance of German helmets to chamber pots by calling German soldiers *Jerries,* a term generally replaced in World War II by *kraut.* Both *jury-built* and *jerry-built* now have extended meanings to apply to any kind of makeshift construction.

The phrase *it's not cricket* is one of the hundreds of metaphorical uses of athletic terms, but this from England is less obvious than some. *Cricket* comes from old French *criquet,* a stick used as a mark in the game of bowls, and was adopted by the sixteenth century in England as a name for their supposedly most British sport. Bergen and Cornelia

Evans, usually quite objective in their usage manual, have an opinion on this one: "Only Americans seeking to ape or to ridicule the English ever say *it's not cricket,* and they are likely to be bores." We probably do have enough sports clichés of our own that we need not import any. And since cricket is primarily an upper-class game in England, and since the phrase refers only to something not sporting—not something dishonest or criminal—it has a touch of snobbery about it.

Cricket may have contributed to another colloquial expression that grew up mainly in America, *to stump,* meaning to confuse or baffle. In cricket, stumps are sticks that are parts of wickets. One way to put a batter out is to stump him, by knocking over a stump at the right moment. One etymologist suggests that the batter's frustration is generalized into the broader sense of *stump.*

I suspect that this explanation is more ingenious than accurate and that *stump,* meaning to baffle, is another of many colloquial terms that refer to what's left after a tree is cut down. "To make a stump speech" or "take to the stump" reflects that in early political campaigns the candidate often found a tree stump the best available platform. "To be up a stump" is like being up the creek, stuck in some difficult spot. "To stir one's stumps" depends on the parallel between the base of a tree and the base of a human being. I have no guess about the origin of "to whip the devil around the stump," which grew up in America in the late nineteenth century, meaning to overcome or avoid difficulty by roundabout means.

Cab Calloway's "Minnie the Moocher," and Hoagy Carmichael's "Hong Kong Blues" popularized the phrase "kickin' the gong around" more than fifty years ago. Its general meaning is obvious and depends on the fact that an opium pipe is a *gong*—as well as a *gonger, dreamstick, joy-stick, bamboo, saxophone,* or *stem.* Most of these are obviously related to the pipe through shape or the presumed effect of the smoke. The only guess I can make about the connection of *gong* to the pipe is that we tend to associate both gongs and opium with the Orient or that the user may consider the smoke as exciting as the sound of a gong.

As a summary, I cite Mark Twain on etymology. He derives *Middletown* from *Moses;* you drop *-oses* and add *-iddletown.*

3

Growing Pains:
Dealing with
Linguistic
Changes

There is nothing permanent except change.
- **Heraclitus, Fragment**

Change is not made without inconvenience, even
from worse to better.
- **Richard Hooker,**
  Of the Laws of Ecclesiastical Polity

A verb has a hard enough time of it in this world
when it's all together. It's downright inhuman to split
it up.
- **Mark Twain, "The Disappearance of Literature"**

Languages change; they grow. English differs from Anglo-Saxon—in grammar, in vocabulary, in pronunciation. English today differs from Chaucer's English or Shakespeare's English or the English of ten years ago. It is not better or worse, but it is different.

Although this growth has been going on for centuries and is likely to continue, it causes confusion for users of the language, particularly those who are serious about using the language effectively. At an extreme are several popular critics of the kinds of changes occurring today. Most of them are journalists, writers who use language skillfully but have limited knowledge of the history of language or how language works. In general, they lament changes they observe, warning society that the language is being ruined, mainly because so many people are using it. Jim Quin, a knowledgeable writer on language, calls journalist Edwin Newman the "leading, but not only, linguistic Chicken Little." Newman asks, "Will America be the death of English?" He answers yes.

John Simon feels about language that "things have at last been sufficiently established—classified and codified—that there is neither need nor excuse for changes based on mere ignorance." He suggests, for example, that we defer to Anglo-Saxon to condemn *between* referring to more than two. "Now I realize that in our sadly permissive dictionaries, 'between' is becoming acceptable as a synonym for 'among.' But do not buy this, good people; the 'tween' comes from the Anglo-Saxon 'twa' meaning two, and if we start meddling with such palpable etymological sense (who cannot hear the 'two' in 'tween'?) we become barbarous or trendy, even if we happen to be in the dictionary business." Sterling Leonard made fun of arguments like this as early as 1929, suggesting in his parody that only "an ignorant barbarian" would use *let* "in any sense but that of *prevent*." And *prevent*, according to the etymological argument, can mean only *go before*, from its Latin origin; its use to mean *hinder* is a baseless innovation.

The writings of pop grammarians have been popular, their books best-sellers. People seem to accept the notion that changes they are able to observe must be somehow dangerous. And all of us are prone to defend what we learned in school, or what we have always done, against encroaching dialects or against what seem to us sloppy or silly innovations. It is comfortable to feel superior to speakers who fail to observe grammatical distinctions still considered part of standard English. There are good reasons to condemn the vacuity of public utterances consisting mainly of "you know" and "yeah, man," or at another extreme of stale or pretentious set phrases. But the problem is not that changes are ruining the language; the language is in good health, changing as it always has, but remaining a very useful instrument for communication.

Writers and speakers, as they always have, sometimes use this instrument skillfully, sometimes badly. Their success depends partly on decisions about usage. These decisions often require dealing with linguistic change, anticipating how a listener or reader will react to various locutions. For example, 86 percent of the Harper usage panel would not use the word *finalize* in writing, and 74 percent would not use it even in casual speech. This does not make the word "wrong" in any sense or "bad English." But the panel's attitude reveals a fact that needs to be considered in any decision on usage. The fact is that even though *finalize* has been widely used and accepted in the language since the 1920s, there is a significant amount of mainly frivolous prejudice against it from educated users of the language. This is a fact to be considered in deciding whether to use the word. Mainly, I suppose, just because it has produced so much controversy, I find myself avoiding it.

The following comments consider aspects of language change: the status of various newcomers and some linguistic eccentricities.

- ## Semantic Change

Semantic change is a standard phenomenon in the history of language; the effect a word has changes through use, through the company the word keeps. And linguists observe patterns in the kinds of changes that occur. One pattern of change is pejoration and amelioration, to use technical terms, or, less pretentiously, degradation and elevation. Another is generalization and specialization.

An obvious illustration is the case of *knight* and *knave*. In Old English there were two words to designate a boy or lad, *cniht* and *cnafa*. The words were both taken over into Middle English, where they acquired a more specific use to refer to a boy employed as a servant. In the Middle Ages, however, specialization and generalization began occurring. The meaning of *cniht* specialized to designate particularly a military servant or attendant; *cnafa*, on the other hand, generalized to refer to any servant or menial.

Cniht became *knight* and gradually changed to become a clear example of elevation, referring to a fair damsel's champion in a medieval romance and later to a modern British rank. *Cnafu*, on the other hand, became *knave* and an example of degradation, now referring to a base, crafty, or unprincipled person.

There are many similar examples of degradation. *Boor* and *villain* started as names for a peasant and farm worker, with no uncomplimentary implications. *Churl* meant simply a man, a male person. *Lewd* meant nonclerical; a lewd person was a lay person. *Uncouth* was uneducated. *Silly* meant happy or blest and then later innocent or simple. Chaucer speaks fondly of "sely sheepe." *Demagogue* comes from Greek words meaning people and leader and originally was a complimentary term for a popular leader. It has come to suggest dishonest or deceptive leadership.

Examples of specialization and generalization are also common. In the sixteenth century *deer* could refer to any animal; by specialization it has come to apply to a particular group of animals. *Nice* once meant foolish, but shifted to mean something like precise, in "a nice distinction," or to mean particular or scrupulous, then generalized to indicate anything agreeable or satisfactory. *Shambles* comes from Old English *scamel*, a bench or stool. It referred to the bench or stall where a butcher sold meat and by extension to a slaughterhouse. But the word has generalized to refer to any scene of confusion, bloody or not.

Sometimes it is not easy to label a change. *Harlot,* referring to a young male servant, shifted in the Middle Ages to refer to a woman and became uncomplimentary. *Buxom* meant obedient, and the conjecture here is that it changed partly because of its sound, which associated it with words like *bosom* and *bust*.

Another complicated example is *boy.* In Shakespeare's time it was insulting to call a person a boy. Then the meaning of the word was elevated, and the word became an unprejudiced name for a young man. But it has slipped again and is often regarded as derogatory, partly because it was used in the South as a contemptuous term for blacks.

We can observe changes like these going on at present, as words get associated with a particular context that makes them ineffective in other uses. *Collaborator* was used so frequently during World War II to refer to a person working with an enemy, a Quisling or traitor, that its more general earlier meaning was tainted. As occasions for collaborating with an enemy occur less frequently, the word has tended to shift back to its earlier meanings.

Gay is interesting because the shift is partly degradation and partly elevation. It has developed unfavorable connotations in its relatively recent shift to mean homosexual. We can't say "It was a gay party" if we just mean that everybody had a good time. On the other hand, the word comes closer to being an unprejudiced term for homosexual than others—*queer,* for example—and has been pretty much adopted officially.

I regret the loss of *gay* in its earlier sense. I think of Mehitabel, the corybantic cat of Don Marquis's "The Lives and Times of Archie and Mehitabel." Among the productions of Archie, the cockroach, is the song of Mehitabel, the cat:

there's a dance in the old dame yet
toujours gai toujours gai

I've gone through half a column in a thesaurus looking at synonyms: *cheerful, merry, vivacious, happy, mirthful, cheery, gleeful, joyous, joyful, genial, convivial, jolly, blithe, zestful, bonny, fun-loving,* and so on. None of these seems quite to fit Mehitabel.

(*Corybantic,* by the way, is Mehitabel's favorite word for describing herself. It comes from the Corybants of Greek mythology, attendants of the Phrygian goddess Cybele, who accompanied her nightly wanderings with dancing and revelry.)

• **New Kids on the Block**

When does the new kid on the block become one of the gang? New meanings and new applications of words get spread rapidly in this age of mass communication, but they are confronted always by resistance from some users of the language—often for good reasons. Coinages, changes, new metaphoric applications of words enrich the language, make it more versatile. But there are differences among the candidates for admission into the language. Those that depend on only a kind of mild mass hysteria, our curious assumption that imitation produces distinction—pet rocks and Cabbage Patch dolls—are boring and don't last long. They are so obviously attempts at originality and so clearly not original that they sound phony. Sports announcers take advantage of the flexibility of the language to create verbs like *to audibilize* (when the quarterback uses audible signals at the line of scrimmage), *to ball control, to possession,* or *to nonchalant* (used when a fielder seemed preoccupied and didn't throw promptly). *Mob,* after nearly three centuries of rejection, is finally accepted as standard English. Usage questions on words like *finalize* or *hopefully* or *workaholic* or *lubratorium* are not easily resolved. But the reaction of people to the words is information pertinent to any decision about using them.

A number of words are old favorites of so-called purists, who object to them on various grounds—logic or etymology or just that they are new. Some of them have been waiting for approval for more than a century. For example, *transpire,* which means breathe in its root sense, was extended by the early nineteenth century to mean happen or occur. The new meaning has been condemned from the beginning. Richard Grant White in an 1870 usage book commented on *transpire* that "of all misused words, this verb is probably most perverted." More than a century later, Leo Rosten, of the Harper usage panel, says, "*Transpires* for *happens* is tantamount to lifting your pinkie while drinking tea." Rosten's objection may make some sense.

Another word condemned by White is *aggravate,* which is suffering from an effort to keep a word true to its ancestry, almost always futile. The word comes from Latin *ad* plus *gravis,* meaning heavy. In 1870, White asserted that "it means merely to add weight to." In his day he found that the word was being "misused by many persons ignorantly" to mean provoke, irritate, or anger. This latter use now seems firmly established, and the sense that preserves the Latin has nearly disappeared. Nevertheless, more than half the members of the Harper usage panel condemn the current usage.

On *enthuse,* White's 1870 comment was: "This ridiculous word is an Americanism in vogue in the southern part of the United States. I never heard or saw it used, or heard of its use, by any person born and bred north of the Potomac." *Enthuse* is a back-formation; that is, it was created from the noun *enthusiasm,* which existed before the verb. And this seems to be the main basis of White's objection. He has the same concern for the verb *donate,* which he calls "utterly abominable." He goes on, "It has been formed by some presuming and ignorant person from *donation,* and is much such a word as *vocate* would be from *vocation* or *orate* from *oration.*"

I think *vocate* hasn't developed, but both *donate* and *orate* appear without restrictions in current dictionaries, although some English purists still have reservations. Another back-formation, *resurrect,* has been generally accepted, and even *burgle* is common colloquially. Curiously, however, *enthuse* is still suspect; only 14 percent of the Harper usage panel would use it in writing. The objection may be partly to its overuse, or a feeling that it often is an exaggeration.

In its most frequent current meaning, *unique* has had even more trouble than *enthuse* in getting acceptance into the prestige dialect. The usage panel for the *American Heritage Dictionary* disapproves by 89 percent expressions like "rather unique" or "very unique." The argument is that the word is an absolute adjective that cannot be qualified in any way. Because it goes back to Latin *unus,* meaning one, the argument goes, and means *only,* as in "his unique son," no degrees of uniqueness are possible.

The word was adopted in English from French in the seventeenth century with two meanings, "being the only one" or "having no equal." It was seldom used, treated as a foreign word, until the middle of the nineteenth century, when it became popular to mean remarkable or unusual or maybe just desirable. This is certainly the most common use of the word today. Many users of the language, however, are still reluctant to accept the current meaning, perhaps partly because the word has become so popular with advertising copywriters.

Actually, many adjectives in the language are absolute or incomparable, too narrow or technical to be compared. We wouldn't call something very ancillary or most residual. Furthermore, in a literal sense we think of adjectives like *square, perpendicular, circular, eternal, absolute, complete, perfect,* and *full* as absolutes. "A more perfect union" logically should be "a more nearly perfect union."

Many of these words, however, are commonly used with qualifications and a shift in meaning. We mention the fullest glass or the most complete plan. In George Orwell's *Animal Farm,* the ruling pigs assert that all animals are equal, but some are more equal than others. One account may be more correct than another. In these contexts, the meaning of the adjective has broadened; we understand that *more perfect* means *more nearly perfect.*

Still, many users of the language feel logical pressure to avoid such comparisons. Curiously the same logic is not applied to the word *singular,* which, like *unique,* has oneness in its background, but is accepted without question to mean unusual.

Both *loan* and *lend* are verbs derived from the noun *loan. Lend* is earlier, but both verbs can be found in modern English at least as early as the sixteenth century. The *Oxford English Dictionary* calls *loan* as a verb an Americanism, from that British authority a condemnation. The verb is less common in England than in America, but it is used in both places. The attempt to restrict *loan* to use as a noun and use only *lend* as a verb has never been successful. I tend to make the distinction out of habit, I suppose, but it seems to me not a very important distinction.

Hopefully, used to mean *I hope*, is probably suffering mostly because of its surge to popularity in recent decades. The word was used in this sense as early as the eighteenth century but was not much used. Today it is one of the favorite targets of the guardians of the language. Some years ago the *New Yorker* lamented that "this frightful, earbending virus has wormed its way deep into the national vocabulary." Jacques Barzun calls the usage "an example of misdirection in logic." He's right, of course, if one doesn't recognize changes in meaning. That is, *hopefully* until fairly recently was an adverb from *hopeful*, meaning full of hope. In this sense it can refer only to the one having hope: "He looked hopefully into the future."

Logic, however, does not always govern meaning change, and the word has shifted to a new meaning, shorthand for *I hope* or *it is to be hoped*. It has become a kind of sentence modifier, not attached to any individual word in the sentence. It is similar to other words that have been adapted to such a use, usually at the beginning of a sentence: *supposedly, regrettably, thankfully,* and *evidently,* for example. Compare:

> Hopefully, there's plenty of gin.
> Luckily, there's plenty of gin.

The new usage seems to be here to stay and is useful, but the fact is that some people react unfavorably when they hear it. If you want to avoid their disapproval, wait some years before using it.

There is still a good deal of resistance to using *contact* as a verb, partly because it has become business jargon. The argument that it is illogical to contact someone on the telephone makes little sense, especially if one prefers *get in touch with*. I should guess that the great majority of users of the language would say "Let's contact him at once" without hesitation, but 65 percent of the Harper panel would not write it. I still don't use the word as a verb, perhaps only because my father objected to it—which may be as good as most of the reasons for our prejudices.

I have equally untenable reasons for a number of other personal prejudices. For example, I can't be comfortable with the verb *to debut*. *Debut*, a noun adopted from a French word meaning to lead off in a game like bowls, has recently become popular as a verb: "New actress debuts this week." Coining verbs from nouns is a standard procedure in English, but I don't like this one. Maybe it's partly that I don't know how to pronounce it. *Debews* or *debewing* sounds a little silly, and *debutts* loses all the toniness of the French. A similar adaptation is easy enough to pronounce, the verb *to premiere*, but I tend to avoid it also, just because it produces unfavorable reactions in a number of users of the language.

A sector has a clear definition in geometry: any part of a circle bounded by two radii and an arc of the circle. Therefore sectors are the pieces of the familiar pie figures used to tell us where our tax dollars go. It is currently applied more broadly in *public sector* or *private sector* or *nonprofit sector*, which to me are not very precise terms and perhaps are a little euphemistic. *Sector* seems to me to be a vogue word often used to avoid saying anything too clearly.

H. W. Fowler describes vogue words as "words owing their *vogue* to the joy of showing one has acquired them." I find myself resisting using them. *Viable* and *relevant* and *paradigm* had their day in the sun but now seem settled into the regular vocabulary. Often vogue words are, like *parameter,* words with a scientific background that become fancy substitutes for more common words—*dichotomy* for *division,* for instance. *Parameter,* which has some precise mathematical uses, generalized in technical writing as early as the 1950s to refer to any determining characteristic or factor and then to a limit. The most usual uses today occur in the plural in expressions like "the useful parameters for judging long-term success" or "keeping within the parameters of the discussion." These definitions appear in current dictionaries, but some writers find the word in these senses an unacceptable newcomer.

I resist also the current use of *exit* as a verb that can take an object. Traditionally you exit *from* an airplane. Amplified instructions about "exiting the plane," however, have become so common that I suspect this shift in function is here to stay. Other words with similar meanings—for instance, *depart*—are following the same pattern: "They departed Minneapolis at seven." *Escape* has long been used with an object, as in "He escaped punishment," but its recent use in contexts like "He escaped prison" seems to me unidiomatic; I would still say "escaped from prison."

The current use of *plus* as a conjunction is a shift in function that seems to me fairly silly, but it is very popular, especially in television advertising: "You can get all six genuine simulated rubies for only $11, plus you don't have to pay till January." The *plus,* of course, is uttered with exaggerated stress. *Plus* is a versatile word—noun, adjective, or adverb—but there seems to be little reason for this attempt to make it a kind of conjunction.

• *Workaholic* **and Suffixaholism**

Creating new words with affixes accounts for much of the growth of the English vocabulary. It also has been producing a plethora of coinages, usually intended to be clever but often neither very clever nor very useful.

Playing with language is a legitimate sport, and cleverness is usually a virtue, but some of the current tries for novelty seem to me unsuccessful. For example, *K* may be orthographically more logical than *C* for the first sound in *cake,* but I don't find a Kandy Kitchen or a Kiddy Korner more attractive because of the cute spelling. *Barbecue* has a legitimate ancestry, going back to a Haitian name for a framework of sticks used for smoking or broiling meat. I can't see much reason for spelling it *Bar-B-Q.* I have similar feelings about a Valentine card protesting "I'm All 4-U" or about any bumper stickers using a drawing of a heart as a verb. I don't think that changing *fish and chips* to *fish 'n' chips* makes the food more palatable.

Most of the creations with popular suffixes have the same effect. Happily, the enthusiasm for *-wise* as a suffix seems to have abated; I haven't heard for some time that it is likely to be cold weatherwise. The popularity of *-gate* in the wake of the Watergate scandal has declined. But *-ology* and *-ologist* still flourish. A sign proclaims that a company's *cleanologist* will take care of your clothes. *Cosmetology* seems well established. Some of those that H. L. Mencken noticed a generation ago have disappeared: *truckologist, hoofologist, chalkologist.*

Creations developed from *hamburger* are the same sort of thing. Sometime early in this century a name for chopped beef was imported from Germany, and we began eating Hamburg steak. It became hamburger steak, without a capital letter, and then just hamburger. During World War I, as part of our effort to get rid of everything German, the steak became Salisbury steak, and *hamburger* was used mainly when the meat was put into a sandwich. In no sense was *-burger* a suffix, but it was turned into one to mean something like sandwich. Quickly a series of new words developed, attaching *-burger* to any kind of sandwich ingredient: *fishburger, chickenburger, clamburger, nutburger,* and even *Spamburger. Whinnieburger* was a euphemism for a sandwich with ground horsemeat.

By analogy with *auditorium* and *cafeteria,* a whole series of allegedly clever coinages had some commercial success: *lubratorium, tiratorium, washateria. Panorama* spawned *bowlorama* and *seafoodorama.* The suffix *-ville,* usually used in place names, flourished in *dullsville* and *splitsville.* The suffix *-ery* appeared in only a few words in the nineteenth century—*printery, grocery, bindery, groggery, bakery*—but more recently it turns up in all sorts of coinages: *boozery, learnery* (for a girl's school), *cleanery* (a home for cleanologists), and even *skunkery* (a place where skunks are bred for their fur).

Alcoholic is a fairly precise term, referring to a specific disease. The only suffix in the word is *-ic. Alcohol* is a word derived from Arabic *al kohl,* and the creation of *chocaholic* or *workaholic* is based on an erroneous assumption, that *-aholic,* misspelled, is a suffix. The enthusiasm for *-aholic* creations seems to be spreading, but I have hope that it will pass, perhaps along with *lubratorium, camelcade, scenographer,* and *lawnmowerdom.*

• **Autoantonyms**

Words readily change their meanings in different contexts, as demonstrated in business slogans capitalizing on the double meanings. "When it rains it pours" for salt is an old one, not entirely accurate. "The paint that covers the earth" depends on different senses of *cover*. A furniture refinishing company promises, "We take it all off," and a drain cleaning company in a gambling community announces, "In our business a flush beats a full house every time." A radiator repair shop boasts that it's "The best place in town to take a leak," and a riverside hotel assures us that "The only thing we overlook is the river."

Overlook in the last slogan illustrates the phenomenon of semantic change that produces words sometimes called autoantonyms, words that can be used with opposite or nearly opposite meanings. *Overlook* can mean to review carefully or not to see at all. *Rent,* in "I'm renting my house this year," can mean either that I am a tenant or a landlord. A *sanction* can be a penalty or permission. *Sanction* derives from a Latin word, *sanctio,* which referred to the act of making something sacred. *Saint* and *sanctify* have the same root. The two opposite meanings developed by specializing different meanings. In one use the word came to refer to enforcement of the law; in another, using the authority of the law. The president can "impose economic sanctions," or he can "sanction removal of the sanctions."

If you *seed* a mine you add something; if you *seed* cherries you remove something. If you *dust* a crop you add; if you *dust* furniture you subtract. *Buckle* can mean either to fasten together or to fall apart. You can buckle your belt or buckle under stress. *Critical* can mean opposed or supportive. A speech can be critical of an opponent's position or critical to the success of the project. *Downhill* may mean either getting easier or getting worse. "From now on it's all downhill" may mean that the worst is over or is only beginning. An *engagement* can be a prelude to matrimony based on affection or a military battle with an opposite basis. A horned cow may have horns or may have had horns removed.

To fight with can mean either to fight against or to fight alongside as an ally. *Fix* may mean to repair or to destroy. "I'll fix his clock" spoken by a watchmaker means one thing; spoken by a hoodlum it is different. "He lost no time reading the book" can mean that he wasted no time on it or that he read it at once. A *handicap* can be an advantage, as in the strokes allowed in establishing a golf score. It is not an advantage if it refers to a golfer's broken arm. A *knockout* may be a collapse, the count of ten, or a dressmaker's triumph: "She's a knock-out." *Oversight* may refer to supervision or the lack of it. A *fast* horse runs; a *fast* color doesn't. But this is a horse of a different color, since the two *fasts* are quite different words that just happen to be spelled and pronounced alike.

In some instances the Atlantic Ocean makes a difference. *Homely* in the United States means plain or ugly, but in England to call a woman homely is a compliment. In the United States a telephone operator asking, "Are you through?" wants to know whether you're ready to stop talking; in England the operator would wonder whether you were ready to start, whether your call had gone through. A play that bombs in the United States is a failure; in England it is a success if it bombs.

• **Conflicting Compounds**

Similar to autoantonyms are compounds in which we join two words but produce different meanings by putting the words in different order.

For example, we put *out* and *lay* together to create two nouns, but *outlay* and *layout* are quite different things. *Outturn* is a total amount produced during a given period, but a *turnout* can be the number of people at a gathering or a wide place in a road.

Output is a synonym for *outturn*, but a *put-out* is what may happen to a batter in a baseball game. *Outlook* and *lookout* can both name an observation post, but *outlook* can refer to prospects for the future and *lookout* can refer to a matter of concern or worry: "His future is his own lookout."

To *outsell* is to beat the competition, but a *sellout* may be an event with all the tickets gone or a betrayal of a trust. To *back out* is to withdraw; the *outback* is remote rural country, especially in Australia.

An *overpass* is a road or bridge that crosses above another; *Passover* commemorates the escape of the Jews from Egypt. An *overlay* is something that covers something else, like a transparency over printed material; a *layover* is a stop during a journey. To *overtake* something is to catch up with or pass it; a *takeover* is a seizing of power, in a business or a nation.

To *uphold* is to support; a *holdup* is a delay or a robbery. *Upbeat* is an unaccented beat in a measure of music or an adjective meaning happy or optimistic. A *beatup* can be a fistfight or a wild party.

An *upset* can be a disturbance, a reversal, an unanticipated defeat in a contest. A *setup* may be a plan, especially one designed to trap someone, or it may be mixers provided for a drink.

An *upstart* is a person whose arrogance exceeds his merit, who is presumptuous or self-important; a *startup* is a beginning. A *downturn* may start a *downtrend,* especially in the stock market; a *turndown* is a rejection.

• Positives and Negatives

A sentence in the *New Yorker* using the word *eptitude* suggests another curiosity in the way language develops, the formation of positive and negative versions of a word. I don't find *eptitude* in any dictionaries; but its meaning is clear enough, and there may be a use for it. *Ineptitude* has been in the language since the early seventeenth century, but like a number of negative words it has no corresponding positive. It comes from Latin *ineptus,* which is a combination of *in-,* not, with *aptus,* meaning suitable. It has roughly the same roots as *inaptitude,* which has also been in the language since the early seventeenth century. The positive *aptitude* apparently preceded both negatives and has served as a positive for both. But *ineptitude* has developed a shade of meaning different from that of *inaptitude.* It suggests awkwardness, even foolishness, whereas *inaptitude* suggests mainly lack of skill or suitability. Being inept, or not ept, is different from not being apt. *Eptitude* may not have much future, but it makes some sense.

Introducing it suggests all sorts of possibilities, since many other negative words in the language have no corresponding positive, tempting writers like the *New Yorker* staff to create one. For instance, if you have not developed *immunity,* why shouldn't you be *mune?* If you can do something without fear of punishment, with *impunity,* why can't you do it with *punity?* At one time in teenage slang it was cool or groovy, or whatever the word was, to praise somebody as *couth.* It is tempting to call people who are neither calm nor indifferent *souciant* or to call someone who is not *disgruntled gruntled*. *Impudent* combines *in-* with Latin *pudere*, ashamed; a well-behaved child might be called *pudent*.

Sometimes there is a positive version that functions as a different part of speech. *Incessant*, from Latin *cessare*, has no parallel adjective, but the noun *cessation* exists. *Incognito* is from Latin *cognoscere*, to know, which is also the source of positive *cognition* and *cognitive*, but a person traveling with the right identity is not *cognito*, a word that doesn't exist, probably because there is not much need for it.

Violate exists, but it is not a positive for *inviolate*; it is a verb with a different meaning. *Inviolate* is not quite the same as *not violated*. *Inestimable* suggests great value or high quality and has become more than just a negative of *estimable*. *Appointment* is not the positive of *disappointment*. Something *infamous* is certainly more reprehensible than something merely *not famous*.

In a few cases the positive existed before the negative and then dropped out of the language. *Kempt* was a word for combed in early English, but it is now archaic, and *unkempt* has broadened in its meaning to mean any kind of untidiness. *Inane* from Latin *inanis*, meaning empty, looks like a negative with the *in-* prefix, but the nature and meaning of the base are unknown, and it would be hard to create a positive.

To complicate this nonsense, the prefix *in-* behaves erratically, with various meanings, including both not and in. *Intelligent* and *inebriated* are not negatives; a stupid person is not *telligent*, nor is a sober person *ebriated*. The case of *inflammable* is special and confusing. The verb *inflame* developed from Latin *flagare*, to burn, with *in-* meaning in and the verb meaning to set on fire. *Inflammable* developed in the sixteenth century to mean burnable. But people misunderstood the prefix, took the adjective to mean not burnable, and in the nineteenth century produced a positive form, *flammable*, to mean burnable. So we now have two words to indicate that something is capable of going up in flames, and either one is likely to appear on a truck carrying combustible material. To indicate that something is fireproof, we have to say that it is not inflammable or not flammable.

• Semantic Change and Reading Shakespeare

Looking at changes like this from another direction, we can see why lines of Shakespeare and other early writers are sometimes misunderstood. Familiar words seem to fit into the plays with a modern meaning but actually meant something different when Shakespeare used them.

One of the best examples is Juliet's "Wherefore art thou Romeo?" which is often mistakenly understood, with the modern meaning of *wherefore*, as a plea for information about the location of the young lover. Actually, *wherefore* meant *why* in Shakespeare's day, and Juliet is lamenting the fact that Romeo is named Romeo, that he belongs to an enemy family, that it "is thy name that is mine enemy."

Or another often quoted line is "This was the most unkindest cut of all," with both *kind* and *cut* thought of in current senses. Marc Antony speaks the line referring to Brutus's stabbing of Caesar. *Unkindest* in Elizabethan English meant unnatural, and Antony is saying that Brutus's action against his friend and benefactor—a cut quite literally—was unnatural. Shakespeare did not have modern textbooks on usage and did not hesitate to double the signs for the superlative, *most* and *-est*.

When Polonius diagnoses Hamlet, saying, "This is the very ecstasy of love," *ecstasy* means *madness* or *insanity*. It has nothing to do with romantic passion and is quite different from the old Hedy Lamarr film. When Hamlet threatens to "kill the man that lets him," he is not offering to take advantage of a willing victim. *Let* meant to prevent or stop. The old meaning survives in tennis in which a let is a ball partially stopped by the net.

To call a lady "passing fair" does not mean, as it would today, that the lady is fair in a momentary or fleeting or merely adequate sense. The word was short for *surpassingly* and appeared often to emphasize a quality. Similarly, a *fond* lover was not especially affectionate or devoted. *Fond* meant *foolish* and has been elevated to its present meaning.

In *Romeo and Juliet*, after a pair of killings, Benvolio tells the Prince:

I can discover all
The unlucky manage of this fatal brawl.

He does not mean that he is about to play detective. He already knows what happened and is going to reveal or uncover it. *Discover* was like *uncover,* meaning to disclose or expose.

The verb *doubt* derived from Latin *dubitare,* meaning to waver in opinion, which is fairly close to the word's current meaning, to question or distrust or tend to disbelieve. In the Renaissance it had come to mean primarily *suspect.* When Hamlet sees his father's ghost and says, "I doubt some foul play," he is expressing his suspicions, not his incredulity.

A word that is easily misinterpreted by a modern reader is *still.* When Polonius comments about Hamlet, "What still harping on my daughter," and when the King tells Polonius, "Thou still hast been the father of good news," they are using *still* to mean always or invariably, the common Elizabethan meaning, which has disappeared.

Presently seems to be coming full circle in meaning. In Shakespeare's time it meant at once, instantly. It then came to mean in a little while or soon, the meaning that prevailed until recently. Currently there is a tendency to revert to something nearer the earlier sense, with *presently* meaning at present or at this time.

• Draining Meaning: Making Words Empty

One of our tendencies, exaggerated by the needs of mass media and especially advertising, is to generalize words out of existence. By overuse and by inappropriate applications, some words lose their significance, become vague and empty. *Nice* is perhaps approaching that state. Obvious examples are what admen have done to *breathtaking, fabulous, stupendous, outstanding, colossal,* or *super,* or what teenagers have done to *awesome.* Recently *legendary* seems to be moving in the same direction, as a movie is praised for being "very legendary." A new car model is called "extremely aerodynamic," which is a little like calling a locomotive "very steam" or "very diesel." Sizes of olives are pertinent; it's hard to find one smaller than colossal.

A more recent example appears in this sentence: "This year has just been astronomical. It just seems that more and more people are coming here." *Astronomical,* because of the large numbers associated with astronomical calculations, has come to mean very large in connection with numbers or even quantities. We call the national debt astronomical. The expression has become common enough that the writer uses it as a general term of approval, good. *Wonderful* or *fabulous* might have worked as well.

Fabulous, as it is being used these days, has nothing to do with fables, as *fantastic* has no connection with fantasy. The words signal only some vague exaggerated praise. Dictionaries list *fictitious* as a synonym of *fabulous* and *imaginary* as a meaning of *fantastic,* neither of which would suit the advertiser describing a sale of used cars or a new deodorant.

Only recently moving toward empty generalization is the word *custom,* as used in a realtor's ad for "a very custom house." The reference is not to a government building used to collect customs. This use of *custom* develops from other coinages, found only in recent dictionaries, *custom-built* and *customize,* which involve building or altering something to the tastes of a buyer. The sign shows the word becoming only a term signifying some kind of general approval. Olive oil importers do the same sort of thing. *Virgin* has a specific meaning when applied to the oil. But when the label promises *extra virgin* or *very virgin* oil, the term *virgin* becomes only a kind of general approval word.

The word *byzantine* has become recently popular in a generalized sense to refer to anything exotic or even anything unusual or strange or overly complex. The word, of course, primarily describes something belonging to or like the culture or architecture of Byzantium. But presumably because of the remoteness of the Byzantine Empire it is applied to an unusual costume or a decision that seems strange.

The word *quality* is a noun and doesn't appear in current dictionaries as an adjective, but it is widely used these days, especially as an academic buzz word in expressions like "quality education." The expression may be a welcome change from "excellence in education," although it may be even vaguer in its meaning. But the easy conversion of nouns to adjectival use is characteristic of English and seems to me usually to work, even with *quality.*

Revolutionary is drifting more and more into generalized vagueness as advertisers use it to describe eye shadow or toothpaste or a way of cutting hair. It is recognized as an exaggeration; no one really believes that the product is the result of a complete and drastic change, an overthrow of dominance of the old eye shadow. Purists, incidentally, can make a distinction among *revolution,* which designates a completed or successful change; *rebellion,* which usually fails; and *revolt,* which may or may not be successful.

• Words That Don't Change

Of a somewhat different sort are words that get associated with a particular time in history or a particular sort of writing and are hard to move into another context. *Damsel* is a perfectly good word, defined in dictionaries as a girl or maiden, but it belongs to another age. Lydia Languish was the heroine of Sheridan's play, *The Rivals,* and damsels could languish for love in Victorian novels, but *languish* has a lavender scent today. *Beauteous* and *curvaceous* sound fancy in modern prose.

Words also get associated with situations in which they appear. *Pep,* a shortening of *pepper,* was overused enough that it sounds old-fashioned when used alone to mean vigor or enthusiasm. On the other hand, the word has become standard in *pep rally* or *pep talk.* A vitamin store is currently peddling *brainpep.*

Expressions like *sticktoitiveness* and *intestinal fortitude* tend to be mildly nauseating from overcuteness and from association with people who talk about "the man upstairs" instead of God. These are like euphemisms, perhaps in reverse, trying to provide a light touch for the serious, as if the writer finds straight talk embarrassing. *Grit* and *pluck* have similar associations and are also dated. Frank Merriwell and the heroes of Horatio Alger were full of grit and pluck. *Grit* in its day designated a kind of wholesome courage and perseverance somewhat different from the virtues publicized for today's athletes, who are mainly "physical," which seems to mean strong and rough enough to injure the opposition.

• *Put Up, Put Out, Put In, Put Off, Put Over*

One of the most significant changes in English in modern times is the multiplication of verbs by the formation of new verbs with separable suffixes or verb-adverb combinations. These verbs, like *turn up* or *turn in*, have a meaning independent of the meaning of either word by itself. They are easily created, and hundreds of them are in constant use, in many instances replacing other verbs.

Often these creations seem unnecessary, with a single verb available to convey much the same meaning. We can usually substitute *discover* for *find out* or *explode* for *blow up* or *surrender* or *retire* for *turn in*, depending on which meaning for *turn in* we want. But *examine* or *peruse* is not quite the same as *look over*, nor is *appear* the same as *turn up*.

Sometimes the addition of the separable suffix makes only a slight difference or is redundant. *Fill up* means no more than *fill*. If you tell the filling station attendant to "fill 'er up," you get no more gas than from just filling it. It's hard to stand without standing up, although standing up for a cause differs from standing for one. We might say, "Please stand for the benediction," but "Stand up and take your medicine."

Up is a major offender in adding a useless separable suffix. The word is rapidly losing its meaning of specifying direction and becoming a kind of function word, an all-purpose verb creator. *Free up* is a current example of the useless *up*. We free up funds for the project, free up our schedule for the party, free up the guest room for the weekend. I find no reason for the *up* in any of these.

Sometimes *up* retains enough of its earlier meaning to provide a sense of direction in *get up* or *sit up*. *Sneak up* is different from *sneak*, and *blow up* may suggest the direction of an explosion. *Grow up* includes the notion of increased stature, involving more than just growing. But the sense of direction can be pretty vague. We can slow up or slow down without much difference in meaning. We can ask someone to sober up or sober down. We burn up or down a house, although we only burn up the road or gasoline.

Sometimes *up* adds a sense of completion to an existing verb: *buy up, grind up, clean up, tie up, wrap up, mop up*. *Shut up* is different from *shut* whether it means to be quiet or to close, or close up, the office. But often with such coinages the *up* is redundant. *Hush up, hurry up,* or *listen up* says little more than the verb without the suffix. I'm not sure how to distinguish between reading up on a subject and just reading on or about it, but the *up* may give a sense of completion or greater thoroughness. Thoroughness may be involved in the *up* in working up a proposal.

Sometimes the *up* seems to be required in order to make a metaphor work. You can whip up a salad but not whip one, charge up a crowd but not charge it, kick up a fuss but not kick it, wind up a job but not wind it, beef up a budget but not beef it. Most of the time it is hard to attach any precise meaning to *up,* although it produces a new meaning for the compound verb. Speaking up may require an act of some courage or more volume. In *step up* the suffix may indicate direction, to a platform perhaps, but often the combination means increase—to step up production, for example.

In any event, the combinations continue to multiply, with *up* and *in* and *out* and others creating new shades of meaning—and sometimes producing double meanings. One side benefit of the process is the opportunity for playing games with ambiguities like "Daphne turned into a tree," which can either record an automobile accident or recount the myth of Daphne and Apollo. Or try "Willy ran across his mother in the parking lot," which can describe either a chance meeting or a serious accident. In "The cook called up the dumb waiter," the cook either looked into the dumb waiter and shouted or telephoned a colleague with limited intelligence or perhaps an inability to speak. With the first meaning, *called* is the verb and *up the dumb waiter* is a modifier telling where the cook called. With the second, *called up* is the verb.

Here are some others that can be interpreted as either a verb with a modifier or a verb-suffix combination:

> The small boys tore up the street. (Were they running fast, with *tore* as the verb, or being destructive, with *tore up* as the verb?)
> Mary went for a tramp in the woods.
> Louise did not want to turn in her new girdle.
> Mrs. Grimes blew up the chimney.
> The inspector looked over the wall.

The next step in the process, which was to be expected, is the creation of other parts of speech from the new verb combinations. The most obvious creations are those that simply repeat the verb-adverb combination with a shift in accent. Thus, if a rocket blasts off (with the accent on *off*) there's a blastoff (with the accent on *blast*). If something spins off, it's a *spin-off* (only recently listed in dictionaries). If a person blacks out, he suffers a blackout, but that verb doesn't directly produce *blackout,* referring to the absence of light at the end of a scene in a play or during a bombing raid. All of these multiply the problems of spelling compounds—one word, two words, or two words hyphenated (see chapter 8).

There are many more. A pitcher pitches out and the pitch is a pitchout. A robber holds up a bank and accomplishes a holdup. An entertainer is held over for another engagement and becomes a holdover. An athlete holds out for more salary and is a holdout, but a prisoner of war who holds out even when tortured is not a holdout. If one picks something up, what one picks up can be a pickup, whether it is a girl on the street or by extension a small truck used to pick up things. When a marriage breaks up, there is a breakup, and perhaps a blowup with a blowout to celebrate later.

There is no consistency in the way these words develop. The noun may specialize the meaning. You can pin up all sorts of things, but only a particular kind of picture is a pinup. You can hand out not only things but also opinions, but a handout is a gift, usually to a beggar. You can break in new shoes or a new employee, or break in on someone's privacy, but a break-in is only forcible entry. You can work over the data from an experiment, or a gang of thugs can work over an uncooperative victim, but overwork is different from either of these. *Run* with suffixes has produced *rundown, runaway, run-on, run-off,* and *run-in,* but *run out* (to exhaust a supply or to abandon), *run into* (to meet), and *run up* (a bill, for example) seem not to have produced nouns, at least not yet.

Like all new trends in language, however, these creations move into standard English only slowly, and only after resistance from those who find some of the new words unnecessary or unclear or who just don't like change. A question can come up, and a birthday may be coming up without meeting much resistance, but *upcoming* to describe events in the future is regarded as bad usage by many users of the language. A publisher is alleged to have put the following on a bulletin board: "If I read 'upcoming' in *The Wall Street Journal* again, I will be downcoming and somebody will be outgoing." Similarly *input* has had a technical use for some time to refer to the electrical current put into a machine. It has been adopted in computer language and has become a kind of fad word: "We need your input in this discussion." By analogy *output* has become popular, and more recently *throughput* or *throput* or *thruput*. I tend to resist *input* just because it is overused these days; I object to *throughput* because I don't know what it means.

As recently as 1991 *Time* was bewailing "further tattering of the language" threatened by a new edition of the *Random House Webster's College Dictionary*. The main objection of the reviewer is that the dictionary editors have chosen to be "descriptive, not prescriptive." The result is that many changes in the language over recent decades are recorded. Dictionaries, of course, for many years have been descriptive, not presuming to dictate what is acceptable usage. They therefore record many changes and many usages that differ from what we may have been taught in school.

Language changes are inevitable, but so are disagreements among users of the language about the value of the changes. Speakers of English have always resisted the establishment of any authority, like the French Academy, to dictate good usage. As a result, differences in opinion multiply, experiment and linguistic humor flourish, and I am grateful for the fruitful chaos.

4

The Ordinary Sentence: Grammar and Meaning

A sentence should read as if its author, had he held a plough instead of a pen, could have drawn a furrow deep and straight to the end.
* **Henry David Thoreau**, *A Week on the Concord and Merrimack Rivers*

Let schoolmasters puzzle their brain,
With grammar and nonsense and learning,
Good liquor, I stoutly maintain,
Gives genius a better discerning.
* **Oliver Goldsmith**, *She Stoops to Conquer*

Language conveys meaning in two ways, semantically and grammatically. Semantically we get meaning because a word is a symbol for an idea, for a thought. We get meaning from *dog* because we relate it to our experience with a certain variety of four-legged animal. We get meaning from *bone* because it stands for our impressions of an object or a substance. We know what kind of action *bury* symbolizes. But just speaking those words—in alphabetical order, for instance—wouldn't say much: "bone bury dog." To make sense we have to show how the ideas represented by the words are related. We do this by creating a grammar, using grammatical devices. We can say "The dog buries the bone," and listeners know what we mean.

Grammar is a versatile and sometimes confusing word. It can refer loosely and broadly to all aspects of language usage—"His grammar is good" or "That's an error in grammar." More accurately it refers to the relationships among words in a sentence or to any system of describing those relationships. Modern linguists generally use *grammar* in the latter senses. They attempt a descriptive grammar to show how the language works and thereby how we can best use it.

Not all grammars are descriptive. In the eighteenth century, when grammarians began writing extensively about English, they were often at least partly prescriptive. They assumed that Latin had achieved linguistic perfection and that English should strive to follow Latin as a model. They often proposed rules for English based on rules for Latin, or on alleged logic, or just on intuition (see chapter 6).

Early grammatical statements had much to recommend them, but linguists in this century found them inadequate in many ways. For example, they observed that the traditional definitions of parts of speech, based on meaning, were not always adequate. Defining a noun as a word that names does not satisfactorily explain *running* or *disaster*. Calling a verb an action word does not explain *exist*, and calling it a word that asserts does not really define. Descriptive grammarians tried classifications based on function—for example, saying that a noun is a word that will work as a subject—but these were not always clear. Actually, precise descriptions of parts of speech may not matter very much; most people have a general idea of the meaning of words like *noun* and *adjective* based on traditional teaching.

In the 1950s linguists were working on a variety of new systems for descriptive grammars. Among them was what came to be called, a little pretentiously, transformational-generative syntax. The system became too complex to gain general understanding, but it changed our ways of looking at grammar. One of its basic principles is that all sentences have both a deep structure and a surface structure. The meaning of a sentence is conveyed by its deep structure; the form of a sentence is given by its surface structure. Deep structure becomes surface structure through "transformations." The same deep structure may be transformed into several surface structures. This is not the place to develop a discussion of transformational grammar, which doesn't seem to me to do much to illuminate questions about the everyday use of English. Some of the following comments about the sentence, however, are oversimplifications of views of the new grammars.

The new grammars, for instance, recognize that English employs three kinds of devices for revealing relationships in a sentence: inflection, function words, and word order. All three of these grammatical devices have been used above to make the words *bone, bury,* and *dog* into a sentence. An inflectional ending -*s* has been added to *bury.* The function word *the* has been put before the other two words, and the words have shifted from alphabetical order.

The first of these devices, inflection or form change, was important in Latin and in Old English but has been disappearing from English for centuries. Surviving examples tend to cause usage problems in a language increasingly dependent on other devices (see chapter 5). The grammar of modern English relies primarily on word order, the device that informs us that the dog in the sentence above is doing something concerning a bone.

This is the crucial grammatical relationship in the English sentence, what some grammarians call *nexus* or *predication*, the relation between a subject and a verb—something does or is something. In other words, the grammar of English can be thought of as an infinite number of possible combinations, but all of them based on a single central pattern, which grammarians sometimes call a simple sentence or a basic sentence or a core or a kernel.

This basic sentence, based on the nexus relationship, involves an actor, an action, and sometimes a goal. It has three parts: a subject, a verb or linking verb, and a complement—an object or a predicate nominative or adjective. It has three patterns:

1. Subject, verb:
   Birds sing.
   Blue fades.
2. Subject, verb, object:
   Louise sang an anthem.
   Ontogeny recapitulates phylogeny.
   The captain offered the crew hot rum.
3. Subject, linking verb, predicate nominative or adjective:
   Gordon is my brother.
   The moon was a galleon.
   George became president.
   Life is real.
   The coat felt warm.

This is gross oversimplification, of course, but theoretically, at least, all English sentences are variations on these patterns. Patterns can be combined and any of their parts can be amplified with modifiers, and the result may be long and complicated sentences. But the simple core is there and is the crucial part of sentence grammar and rhetoric. Crucial to clarity and effective style is the integrity of the sentence core.

• **Square Pegs and Round Holes: Meaning and Grammar**

Here are some groups of words that look like sentences:

Believe incongruities although.
The prejudice ambushed infelicity.
The lampshade promised Andrew.
Developments are moving rapidly.
Any person would mean the failure.

The first three are obvious nonsense. The last two seem vaguely to say something. But all five, in varying degrees, have a problem. They follow the pattern of the basic English sentence, but the words put into the slots in the pattern don't have forms or meanings that are compatible.

The first is contrived; nobody would ever utter such a combination. But it illustrates one obvious requirement of the sentence pattern, that words are not all suitable for all positions in the sentence pattern. *Banker* and *orchestra* and *apple* may be used as subjects or objects in a sentence and have privilege of occurrence in those slots in the pattern. They will not work in the verb slot; you can't *banker* or *apple* anything. *Subtracts* and *manipulates* fit in the verb slot, but not as subject or object. *Believe* would work as a verb, not as a subject; *incongruities* would work as a subject, not a verb; *although* is a function word not privileged to occur in the object slot. Some grammars classify words into parts of speech on the basis of privilege of occurrence: nouns, for example, have privilege of occurrence as subjects or objects.

The second and third sentences make no sense for a different reason. Grammatically the words have privilege of occurrence in the slots where they appear, but they have no semantic compatibility. That is, they don't make sense together. A prejudice can't ambush anything, certainly not infelicity. A lampshade doesn't make promises. Nobody would write them as sentences.

But the last two sentences did appear, in expanded form:

In the Far East this morning, developments are moving rapidly toward a possible military confrontation.

Any person ill on the day of the first performance would mean the failure of the summer program.

With the basic patterns surrounded by other words, the sentences seem to make sense, and we accept the foggy meaning, even though developments don't advance and it's the illness, not the person, that would cause the failure. The sentences aren't obviously bad, but they are less clear than good writing requires because the meanings of the words in their basic patterns don't work together.

Sentences of this sort need revision, and the best way to do it is almost always to pick a different subject and revise the basic pattern, usually trying for greater specificity. I'm not sure precisely what the first sentence intended, but this is a possibility:

In the Far East this morning, hostilities are developing rapidly toward military confrontation.

The second can be revised by shifting to *summer theater* as subject of the core sentence:

If any person were ill on the day of the first performance, the summer theater would fail.

Sentences of this sort are examples of what can be called faulty predication, a failure to use words with compatible meanings in the basic sentence. They are not always obvious blunders, but they make writing awkward or obscure. Notice another example, from a letter soliciting funds for a political campaign:

It is imperative that this necessity take place at once.

Out of context, it seems impossible to guess what this sentence is talking about. In context, I get an idea that the writer was trying to emphasize that the campaign needed money in a hurry. I didn't contribute.

Inaccurate predication occurs most frequently when a sentence is fairly long. The writer picks a bad subject for the sentence, then stays with it no matter how awkward the sentence becomes. Or as the sentence goes on the writer forgets the subject. Or the writer assumes that a modifier is the subject. Notice this more complicated sentence:

The basis for the continuing unrest, which was partly misunderstanding and partly understanding too well what our motives were, held little hope for success in negotiating new treaties.

The sentence sounds as if it ought to make sense, but it doesn't because the meanings in the basic pattern don't work together: "The basis held little hope." With a new subject and verb the sentence works:

Our representatives had little hope of negotiating new treaties because of the continuing unrest, based partly on misunderstanding our motives and partly on understanding them too well.

The original sentence got off to a bad start. The writer put down the first word that came to mind and never quite realized that the basis for unrest was not what the sentence was to be about.

Here are some other examples:

The worry it saves you will add years to your life.
Children playing with matches could be avoided if parents were cautious.

The first one comes out in praise of worrying, which is probably not what was intended. The writer of the second probably did not mean to make an argument for birth control. Again the sentences can be revised by finding new subjects:

Freedom from worry will add years to your life.
If parents were cautious, they could keep children from playing with matches.

Headline shorthand can produce inaccuracies in predication. For example, notice "Air passengers increase 16.5 percent." The story is not about air passengers going off their diets but about an increase in the number of people passing through the airport. Another, "Officer remains serious," is intended not to characterize the officer's general attitude toward life but to report on his condition after a serious accident. Shortcuts for reporting a lack of information have become journalistic formulas: "The cause of death was unavailable. The condition of the infant was not immediately available. The victim was still being evaluated." Usually these are understood, although literally they make no sense.

Other predication problems occur when the offending sentence pattern is in a subordinate part of the sentence:

> A middle ground must be found that we can all follow.

Behind the problem here is a mixed metaphor or mixed cliché. Somewhat tritely we can "find a middle ground" or "follow a path or a course." But a middle ground doesn't go anywhere. You can't "follow" it. In the pattern "We can follow a middle ground," the verb and its object are not compatible.

The chances for illogical predication are especially good when the subject governs a pair of verbs and has to fit both of them. Consider:

> The earth is covered by 71 percent water and contains two-thirds of all life on earth.

The sentence has a variety of problems, but mainly it gets into trouble because the subject isn't the right one for the second verb, *contains*. Changing the subject gives the sentence the meaning that was apparently intended:

> Water covers 71 percent of the earth's surface and contains two-thirds of all the life on earth.

The same kind of problem occurs in this sentence.

> The filling station attendant was knifed in the arm and required fifteen stitches to close the wound.

There is probably no way to make *attendant* the subject of both verbs. Making both parts of the sentence passive is the most likely revision:

> The filling station attendant was knifed in the arm, and fifteen stitches were required to close the wound.

The subject-verb-complement pattern is the core of the English sentence. When the parts aren't compatible, the sentence runs like a car with one square wheel.

- **Two Plus Two Equals Four, Not Five**

When Shakespeare used *to be* in Hamlet's soliloquy, he meant "to exist"; Hamlet was contemplating suicide. Today that is the least common meaning of what is probably the most used and most abused verb in the language, *to be,* called a copula or linking verb.

It is troublesome for several reasons. It is one of the few verbs in the language still significantly inflected; it changes form to indicate person, number, and tense: *I am, he is, he was, you are, they were,* and so on. It can be a verb meaning exist, as in *Hamlet,* or it can be merely a function word, marking the passive voice, as in "He was seen leaving the accident." *Was* has no meaning in that sentence, and has been labeled an *auxiliary,* or by teachers of the sugar-coating persuasion, a *helping word.*

As a copula or linking verb, *to be* has a variety of senses, some of them illustrated in the following:

1. A triangle is a plane figure.
2. The submarine is yellow.
3. Barkis is willing.
4. To know her is to love her.
5. She's a dream.
6. Simon is in the garden.
7. There's a unicorn in the garden.
8. That dress is 90 dollars.

The first example is probably the easiest to describe, with *is* functioning a little like an equals sign in an equation, as in "one plus one is (or *are* or *equal* or *equals*) two." The sense in the second and third is different; *is* doesn't suggest identity but says something like "has this characteristic" or "can be described as."

The fourth sentence suggests an equation, but with a difference in that the identity of the elements on each side of the equation is much less precise. And the identity of the elements linked in the equation of the fifth is still more vague, even without considering whether the dream is a nightmare. The sense in sentences six and seven is nearer Hamlet's "to exist," but the verb mainly just indicates a presence or location, with more plausibility in six than in seven. Sentence eight illustrates the flexibility of *is,* meaning something like "costs" but also something not too far from the attributive meaning of numbers two and three.

To be is obviously very versatile; but almost always when it is used as the link in a basic sentence pattern, it conveys a sense of equation—something is or equals or is like something else. Clear writing requires that the elements on each side of the equation be capable of plausible equation. Two plus two should equal four, not five or seven. Faulty equation, a kind of faulty predication, is a failure in the basic sentence pattern.

Often the problem seems to be just sloppiness, perhaps unawareness of what the subject really is. Here is a United States vice president talking about an earthquake disaster:

> The loss of life will be irreplaceable.

Perhaps the confused statement was an attempt to disguise the fact that all the sentence has to say is pretty obvious: "Lives are irreplaceable."

Frequently unequal elements get equated when a writer obscures the basic sentence with unnecessary words. Notice:

> An ego is an extremely important item for an adolescent to have.
> To realize that teachers are not able to spend a full day teaching in their field was the guiding force in preparing this paper.
> Here in America the general tendency has been the rich people looking down on the poor people.
> Mules bucking packs off and horses getting away are not unusual situations for a packer to face.

Pulling out the core pattern in each of these sentences reveals the faulty equation that makes the sentences awkward: an ego is not logically an item, tendency is not people looking down, and mules bucking off packs may create a situation but not be one. In each case the solution is to cut out the unnecessary words, although that may reveal that the sentences—these have appeared in print—don't have much to say.

> An ego is important for an adolescent.
> I prepared this paper because I realized that teachers are not able to spend a full day teaching in their field.

Here in America the rich have tended to look down on the poor.
A packer must often contend with mules bucking packs off and horses getting away.

Another common inconsistency occurs when a sentence equates one and two. Even though the meaning may be clear, there is a sense of illogicality.

One thing nice about the room is the two big closets.
The media are just one element in a vast communications network.

The reader is at least slightly put off by the notion that one thing is two closets or plural media are one element. Here's another example:

The problem for the audience was the speaker's many silly anecdotes that distracted them.

The singular *problem* is equated with plural *anecdotes*. Changing the subject helps:

The speaker's many silly anecdotes distracted the audience.

• **Equations with Modifiers**

The linking verb idiomatically can join a subject with a modifier indicating place—*in the garden* or *there*—but with other modifiers it creates an illogical equation. We think of a sentence like "The girl was in the park" as analogous to "The girl was pretty"; we think of "in the park" as if it were a modifier of *girl*. But the modifier doesn't seem to modify the subject in a sentence like

The only uniform I have been issued was in camp last summer.

The sentence suggests that the uniform was a camp resident. The problem is that the writer has picked a bad subject; general words like *way* or *problem* or *reason* or *difficulty* often lead a sentence into wordiness and a bad predication:

The way in which she wore her clothes was with an air of sophistication.
The subject of the story is about the situation in which a young girl finds herself.

Getting rid of words that muddy the subject helps:

> She wore her clothes with an air of sophistication.
> The story is about a young girl who finds herself.

The most common schoolroom error with equation also involves modifiers, particularly modifying clauses beginning with *when* or *where* or *because:*

> Impulsiveness is when you jump to conclusions.
> The study of geology is where I get my lowest grades.
> The reason Johnson wrote *Rasselas* was because he needed money for his mother's funeral.

For each sentence the solution is to make the predication more direct:

> Impulsiveness is jumping to conclusions.
> I get my lowest grades in geology.
> Johnson wrote *Rasselas* to get money for his mother's funeral.

The last two illustrate what is behind many of the sentences that seem to be illogical equations: For both sentences the solution is to get rid of the linking verb and use the verb that says directly what happened. One good practical device for improving writing is to check every use of a linking verb to see whether it can be replaced by a stronger one.

• Varying the Pattern

Frequently taught in the schoolroom, and sometimes encouraged in manuals for scientific writing or academic theses, is the notion that the use of the pronoun *I* is not desirable. It supposedly discourages objectivity and may even reveal a lack of modesty. Objectivity certainly is a worthy goal of some writing; even modesty has some value. But the effort to avoid assigning any responsibility for statements often leads to excessive use of variations on the basic predication pattern of the sentence: frame sentences, postponed subject, and passive sentences.

These variations are less direct than the basic subject-verb-complement pattern. But sometimes indirection is desirable, not just to avoid the responsibility involved in using *I*, but also to shift emphasis. Advice like "avoid the passive" or "use the passive sparingly" appears in many textbooks but is too simple. A more sensible suggestion is "vary the pattern only when there is a reason to vary it."

Frame Sentences. One reason is a need to shift emphasis from the main business of a sentence, often to clarify an introduction or transition. Here is an introductory sentence for a paragraph:

> The most important consideration is that nobody is likely to volunteer for active duty.

In order to provide a transition, the writer begins with *consideration,* making it technically the subject of the sentence, even though the sentence is not mainly about consideration but about the fact that nobody will volunteer. Similar are sentences in which a possible object gains emphasis in the subject position, creating a kind of frame:

> A good job was the only thing she wanted after graduation.

The sentence emphasizes *job;* it could have been put in the usual pattern with *she* as the subject, but with different emphasis:

> After graduation she wanted only a good job.

Postponed Subject. A similar variation uses *it* or *there* to postpone the subject. The device is useful to say simply that something exists. We could say, "A reason for the delay exists," with *reason* in the subject position. But a more idiomatic solution is to put *there* in the subject spot and say, "There is a reason for the delay." *There* doesn't have any meaning, but it serves to introduce the sentence. *Reason* is still the subject, but it comes after the verb. We can do the same kind of thing with *it:*

> It is impossible to understand the book without a dictionary.

The subject, *to understand* is postponed; *it* stands in for the subject. In the usual pattern, with the subject first, the sentence seems awkward:

> Understanding the book without a dictionary is impossible.

Passive Sentences. Sometimes the usual pattern with an actor as the subject won't work. The actor or agent may be unknown, or may be insignificant, or perhaps should remain anonymous. The solution is to reverse the usual order, making what logically is the object of the action grammatically the subject. For example, "Alice read the book first" becomes "The book was read first by Alice." Either of these would work. The first is more direct, but the second may fit better in the context.

Sometimes, however, the passive is clearly better. We might want to mention, for example, the completion of a new road. We don't know who did the completing, or if we do, the name of the construction company is not relevant to what we want to say. To put it into the actor-action pattern, we would have to say something like "Last July somebody completed the new road." Obviously, it makes more sense to use the passive: "The new road was completed in July."

Often, however, passive constructions are overused, or misused, especially in business, institutional, and scientific writing, in an effort to achieve objectivity. Notice:

> Coordination of financial planning was agreed upon by the corporation's board of directors.

There is no reason for varying here from the usual pattern. The actor is known, and the usual pattern is clearer and more direct:

> The corporation's board of directors agreed to coordinate financial planning.

• **Modifiers: Dangling**

The most obvious way to develop a sentence is to expand or qualify the basic pattern or any part of it. That dog burying the bone can become "The old tan-spotted dog that my brother had rescued from the pound ten years ago." The bone can become "the large bone from the lamb roast that we had for dinner last night."

Latin indicated what modified what primarily with endings. The little girl is *parva puella* but so is *puella parva*, with the *-a* ending showing that the two words go together. We've lost adjective endings and rely on word order to associate a modifier with what it modifies. Most of the time, and with simple modifiers, we don't have any trouble putting modifiers in the spots that convey meaning clearly. In fact, we have established fairly firm idiomatic patterns for many situations. We can say "the girl's pale blue gingham dress" but not "girl's gingham the blue pale dress." We could say "the pale blue gingham girl's dress," changing the meaning. Modifiers of nouns are almost always in fixed positions, single ones before nouns, word-group modifiers after. "The *lazy old* man *in the boat* was sleeping."

Some modifiers, however, can be put into different spots in the sentence pattern, changing meaning whenever they are moved. Compare:

> Walking in the park the old man found her purse.
> The old man walking in the park found her purse.
> The old man found her purse walking in the park.

In the first, *walking in the park* modifies the whole sentence. In the second it identifies the old man. In the third it makes the purse ambulatory.

When moveable modifiers are inadvertently placed so that meaning is unclear or distorted, the writer is guilty of one of the most celebrated of schoolroom sins—the unattached or the misplaced or, more ominously, the dangling or squinting modifier.

The title of the dangling modifier or participle is a product of the period in American education in which frustrated English teachers were turning in all directions to try to make grammar palatable to reluctant students in an expanded public school system. Parsing, analysis of the grammar of a sentence by explaining the use of every word, was translated into sentence diagramming, a more interesting game in which students could develop considerable proficiency without knowing anything about grammar. Auxiliary verbs became helpers and verbs action words as part of a campaign to make terminology simpler. Common errors were given titles to command respect: the comma fault or comma blunder, the baby sentence, and the dangling participle.

The dangling modifier or dangling participle has become one of the favorite quarries of error hunters—along with split infinitives and final prepositions—partly because of the graphic character of the term but also because of the skill of textbook writers in making up comic examples: "Having eaten our lunch, the bus went on to Chicago," or, "Having rotted in the damp cellar my brother was unable to sell the potatoes." (Actually, I didn't make up the last one; it appeared in a student paper years ago.)

Interestingly, the modifiers in those horrible examples are not unattached or dangling at all. They are very much attached, but to the wrong thing. The initial modifier attaches to the subject of the sentence, and we have a picture of the greedy bus and the putrefying brother.

Sentences of this sort, but less obviously misleading, do occur in prose more frequently than they should, usually producing a kind of awkwardness rather than serious misunderstanding. Here are some sentences that appeared in print:

> Having accepted an appointment in Illinois, all mail after August 1 should be addressed to . . .
> Convinced that reading this article will curb reckless driving, reprints in unbound form are being offered at cost.
> The next morning, while in the bathtub, the janitress came in to inspect the radiator.
> By analyzing one word, this paragraph becomes clear.
> While taking his clothes off, one of the women grabbed the gun and got into a struggle with the alleged rapist.

In each of these the subject of the sentence is not the subject of whatever happens in the opening modifier. The mail did not accept an appointment, the reprints were not convinced, the janitress was not in the bathtub, the paragraph did not analyze, and the woman was not really undressing the rapist.

It seems unlikely that anyone would misunderstand any of these. We've come to supply the missing subject for the modifier, especially when it is *I*, as in the first three sentences above. But the sentences are sloppy, and the third and last are unintentionally funny. Furthermore, revision of this kind of sentence is easy, just by supplying the subject for the modifier:

> Having accepted an appointment in Illinois, I will get my mail at . . .
> Convinced that reading this article will curb reckless driving, I am offering unbound copies at cost.

The next morning, while I was in the bathtub, the janitress came in to inspect the radiator.

The fourth is best revised by changing the construction, not using a modifier:

Analyzing one word clarifies the paragraph.

The last can be clarified by putting a subject within the modifier:

. While he was taking his clothes off, one of the women . . .

Here are some slightly different examples:

Due to their good looks and the way they are built, most sports car owners are attached to their cars.

On a pedestal in the center of the county clerk's office, protected by a glass lid, I studied with straining eyes the precious document.

The sentences seem to make sense—at first glance, at least—but they certainly suggest well-stacked sports car owners and a reporter under glass. Even when meaning seems quite clear, most sentences with opening modifiers that dangle can be improved by revision.

• Modifiers: Misplaced and Squinting

Problems are not always connected with opening modifiers, however. Notice these:

He fired three shots at the lion with a smile of triumph on his face.

No one is allowed to dump anything along the road except a city official.

To be polite he poured some of the wine first into his glass so he would get the cork and not the lady.

He finally got an answer from one small university president.

All these are potentially ambiguous because modifiers tend to attach themselves to the eligible words closest to them. Moving the modifier solves the problem:

> With a smile of triumph on his face, he fired . . .
> No one except a city official is allowed . . .
> . . . so he and not the lady would get the cork.
> . . . from one president of a small university.

Sentences are especially susceptible to ambiguity when modifiers follow a negative statement. These appeared in print:

> The horse didn't win because the track was wet.
> Nobody was ever punished because the camp was run so carelessly.

The first may be either offering an excuse for a losing horse or explaining that the horse didn't win just because he was a good mudder. The second may say that the bad management of the camp went unpunished or that the carelessness explained why everyone escaped punishment.

When two or more modifiers come ahead of a noun, they may modify the noun independently or each may modify all that follows it. In "a pretty young schoolgirl," we think of *pretty* as modifying *young schoolgirl* and *young* as modifying *schoolgirl*. In a sentence like the fourth above, however, *small* can be attached to *president* rather than *university*. Headline shorthand often slips into ambiguities of this sort.

> Aging Committee Holds Hearings
> Directions for Mailing Precinct Voters

We figure out that it is a committee considering problems of aging, not a committee with members getting old, and that directions are for voters in mailing precincts, not for mailing voters. A hyphen between *mailing* and *precinct* would have clarified the second.

Occasionally modifiers get into spots where they can be taken to apply to more than one word: "The person who lies frequently gets caught." *Frequently* can be taken to modify either *lies* or *gets caught,* with a difference in meaning. Someone thought of labeling this phenomenon, which doesn't occur often enough to be a serious problem, a "squinting" modifier, looking both backward and ahead. Another sentence has the same ambiguity: "She told me at the end of the dance she would marry me." This could mean either "At the end of the dance she told me she would marry me" or "She told me she would marry me right after the dance."

- **Writing as a Balancing Act**

Thinking is in great part a matter of seeing similarities and differences and drawing conclusions from them. We can record thinking of this sort in language; for example, we can give two ideas equal status by casting them in the same grammatical pattern, making them parallel. We can use other grammatical patterns to give one idea more or less status than another. Compare these sentences:

> He dropped to the ground, and the bomb exploded.
> After he dropped to the ground, the bomb exploded.
> After the bomb exploded, he dropped to the ground.

In the first sentence the two actions are framed in parallel patterns, and we understand that they occurred simultaneously; they have equal status. In the other two one of the events is subordinated, and different relationships are established.

Most of the time we coordinate two words or two sentences or two parts of sentences with no trouble. But with longer sentences style sometimes suffers because the elements to be coordinated are not clearly parallel in form or are not in the proper order. A reader can become confused about which things are to be coordinated. This sentence has a word order problem:

> Among the items in the collection are the only known document bearing the signatures of Queen Elizabeth and Sir Walter Ralegh and a cigar store Indian.

Technically the reporter that wrote that sentence had the coordination straight. The two items in the collection, *document* and *Indian*, are parallel, and *Elizabeth* and *Ralegh* are parallel after *signatures*. But it is also possible to read *Elizabeth, Ralegh* and *Indian* as a parallel series after *signatures*. And that gives the statue more ability than the reporter probably intended. The solution is to make the statue the first item:

> Among the items in the collection are a cigar store Indian and the only known signatures of Queen Elizabeth and Sir Walter Ralegh.

Here is another example of the same problem:

Wilson stated in his complaint that the defendant owned a large dog that walked the floor most of the night, had noisy midnight parties, and played a radio so that sleep was impossible until 1:30 in the morning.

Obviously the reporter who wrote this one wanted three items to be parallel after *defendant:* he *owned a dog, had parties,* and *played a radio.* If he had put the dog last, the dog would not have been blamed for the parties and the radio.

• Coordination and Parallel Form

The most common confusion in coordination patterns occurs when items to be coordinated are not in parallel form. Often just carelessly a writer gives one item a different form, as in this:

Anne enrolled for painting, harmony, music appreciation, and to study art history.

To study is not parallel with the other classes; here the solution is easy, just leave it out. Even inconsistency in using articles can destroy the rhythm of a sentence:

The only enemies of the sloth are the eagles, jaguars, and the large boas.

Using *the* with all items or with none would improve the sentence.

Another kind of confusion occurs when an item not intended to be coordinated inadvertently gets into a parallel pattern that is not appropriate.

I still remember the smell of burning candles, incense, and Greek chanting.

The construction makes all three items parallel so that the Greek chanting smells as much as the candles and incense. There should be an *and* between *candles* and *incense* to establish that these two items are coordinate after *smell.* Moving *Greek chanting* to come just after *remember* would clarify still more.

This longer sentence from a news report is not likely to be misunderstood, but it does get the coordination confused:

Three years of increasingly bitter fighting has scarred this small Central American nation with corpses, crumbling buildings, gutted vehicles, and left children without fathers.

The sentence reads as if there were four parallel elements after *scarred,* but the obvious intent is that *scarred* and *left* should be parallel. The solution is simple: insert *and* after *buildings* to close off the series dependent on *scarred,* and then insert *has* before *left* to create a clear parallel with *has scarred.*

• **Comparisons: Ears Like a Rabbit**

One kind of coordination occurs in comparisons, and parallel structure is needed to clarify the relationship. A common blunder fails to get one element in parallel form:

The foreman insisted that his job was harder than a laborer.

Obviously it should be *laborer's,* as "His teeth were sharper than a tiger" should read *tiger's.* This sentence has the same difficulty, less obviously:

During the war the value of the infantry was found to be on a par with the cavalry.

One revision would read:

During the war the infantry was found to be as valuable as the cavalry.

A complication is a sentence like this:

Walter believes that he is as smart if not smarter than anybody in his class.

Parallelism dictates that the first parallel unit be completed with *as,* and logic dictates that *anybody* includes Walter and that the writer has to specify *any other member* or *anybody else.* So this sentence would have to read:

Walter believes that he is as smart as if not smarter than any other member of his class.

This is more logical, but still not very graceful, and usually this kind of sentence pattern doesn't work too well. If Walter is going this far with his ego, he might just as well go all the way:

> Walter believes he is the smartest member of his class.

Winston Churchill, commenting on his school years at Harrow, said that "by being so long in the lowest form I got a tremendous advantage over the cleverer boys. I got into my bones the essential structure of the ordinary British sentence—which is a noble thing." At least part of the nobility of that structure is its susceptibility to almost infinite expansion. The most complex ideas can be accommodated in variations on the basic pattern. I suspect, however, that the nobility of the structure depends even more on its simplicity. The trick is to keep the simple core in order, logically and semantically, no matter how complex the sentence may become.

5

Embalming Problems: Preserving Vestigial Remains

"Whom are you," said he, for he had been to night school.
• George Ade, "Bang! Bang!"

For there be women fair as she,
Whose verbs and nouns do more agree.
• Bret Harte, "Mrs. Judge Jenkins"

English has, over the centuries, changed its way of conveying grammatical information (see the previous chapter). It began as primarily an inflected language, like Latin. Latin expressed its grammar by inflection, changing the form of words, usually by adding endings. For example, *agricola amat puellam* means "the farmer loves the girl." To relate the words differently, to make the sentence mean "The girl loves the farmer," Latin would simply change endings: *agricolam amat puella*. Old English was like Latin. It put endings on words to show how they were used, as the subject or object of a verb, for instance.

As English evolved, however, it became increasingly independent of inflections and became an analytic rather than an inflecting language. It came to rely on form changes instead of word order and function words to reveal basic grammatical relationships—between a subject and verb, for example. In a sentence like *The farmer stabs the girl*, because of the order in which the words appear we know who does the stabbing and who gets hurt. Reversing the order, rather than changing endings as we did with the Latin sentences, would specify a different victim.

Echoes of the older system survive, and modern users of the language are not always comfortable with them. Inflections are not compatible with the direction in which English seems to be going. They often seem unnecessary and are disappearing as the language evolves.

But they have not all disappeared. Those remaining include: the form changes of some pronouns, the use of *s* and the apostrophe to mark plurals and possessives, the *-er* and *-est* endings we put on modifiers, the *-ly* ending for adverbs, and form changes for verbs, especially the verb *to be*. Because word order handles so much of our grammar, we can usually be understood without using these devices from our older grammar. We have trouble handling distinctions required in standard written English but not always observed in speech: *who* or *whom, there is* or *there are, lie* or *lay*. In another century or two problems of this sort may disappear as we retire more of the devices of an inflecting grammar and rely more exclusively on word order and function words. In the meantime, we need to respect the remains, embalmed as requirements of standard English.

• Saving *Whom*

The pronoun *whom* is one of the words likely to be a casualty of the shift from an inflecting grammar. It is increasingly replaced by *who* in any spot usually occupied by a sentence subject, and meaning doesn't suffer. In the midst of this shift, however, writers and speakers are often confused.

The traditional grammatical distinction between *who* and *whom* is clear enough. *Who* is the subject form, to be used whenever the pronoun is subject of a sentence or a clause within a sentence. *Whom* is an object form, to be used whenever the pronoun is object of a verb or preposition. The words are to be used in this way regardless of their position in a sentence. The following sentences illustrate:

> George wondered *who* or *whom* had been put in charge of the picnic.
> They asked him *who* or *whom* he thought he was influencing by these tactics.
> He offered the job to *whoever* or *whomever* would apply for it.
> He promised a bonus to *whoever* or *whomever* the committee nominated.

The decision in each sentence depends on how the pronoun is used. In the first sentence, the pronoun is used as subject in its clause, subject of "had been put in charge," and *who* is standard. It is pretty safe to assume that whenever the pronoun immediately precedes the verb of its clause, *who* is the right choice.

In the second, the pronoun is the object of the verb *was influencing,* and *whom* is standard. With increasing frequency, *who* is likely to appear in sentences like the second because of its location before the verb in the usual subject position. With our feeling for word order we are inclined mistakenly to think of it as a subject.

The third and fourth sentences work in the same way. *Whoever* is standard in the third as subject in its clause, immediately preceding the verb. *Whomever* belongs in the fourth sentence as object of the verb *nominated.*

Difficulties in applying these principles occur when there is a conflict between the grammatical use of the pronoun and our feeling for word order. Especially when the pronoun occurs at the beginning of a question, *who,* the subject form seems natural in the subject position. So we frequently hear, "Who were you talking to?" or "Who are you voting for?" even though the pronoun is used as an object. To introduce a question, *whom* is almost gone, although formal English still requires it.

For the relative pronoun, the traditional distinctions are still standard, and failures to use *whom* as an object are usually mistakes rather than declarations of independence. In "my good friend *who* I have known for many years," the writer is misled because the pronoun appears in a subject position. But it is the object of *have known,* and should be *whom.* Or consider: "Dickens was a writer who Wilson called the 'greatest dramatist the English have produced since Shakespeare.'" Again, the pronoun is object of *called* and should be *whom.* This is similar: "The men, who police refused to identify, were arrested after a shootout." *Whom* should be the object of *refused to identify.*

In sentences like the above, the position of the pronoun makes it easy to use the wrong form, and the error is not so noticeable. But *who* sounds illiterate when used within a sentence in an object position: "The people for *whom* (not *who*) she worked recommended her."

• *Whom*-Happiness

I find the opposite error, a kind of *whom*-happiness, more bothersome because it seems pretentious, wearing a dinner jacket to a picnic. "Whom does she think she is?" may exude some ungrammatical scorn, but is not very convincing snobbery.

In the following, the use of the pronoun may be less easily determined: "Steinbrenner thirsts for power and never hesitates to let everyone know that *whomever* happens to be managing his team is merely a lieutenant." The mistake is probably an assumption that the pronoun is an object after *know*, but it is subject of its clause and should be *whoever*. Tom Brokaw reveals the same kind of reverence for *whom*, quoting "remarks addressed to whomever is elected our next president."

Or notice a couple of sentences from a popular novel by Sidney Sheldon, who seems able to turn out best-sellers without benefit of grammar. The first seems clearly to be inspired by a mistaken notion that *whom* provides some kind of instant class: "Whomever selected the hole into which the mouse would run won the prize." In the other example a character is speaking, and he may be the type of person who would try to show off with an ungrammatical *whom*, but I rather doubt that this is clever characterization: "He'll pay whomever can obtain it for him half a million dollars." I think that the character, a very sophisticated con-man, would have played it straight with *whoever*.

• *Whose* for Things

One of the difficulties in our management of inflections is that some grammarians tend to look at them logically and prescribe rules that run counter to what is actually happening. A good example is the notion that *whose* must apply only to people. The logical explanation is that *whose* is the possessive form of *who; who* refers to people, therefore *whose* refers to people. The trouble with the logic is that *whose*, even in Old English, is also the possessive form of *what*.

The practical consideration is that this is an instance in which the old form is useful for referring to both people and things; the alternative *of which* is often awkward. To avoid *whose* and write "the dog, the tongue of which was a blur as it licked its master's hand . . ." is a dubious expedient. "A country whose economy is sound" seems to me clearly preferable to "A country of which the economy is sound."

H. W. Fowler, whose *Modern English Usage* is certainly not overly permissive, is interesting on this usage: "In the starch that stiffens English style," he writes, "one of the most effective ingredients is the rule that *whose* shall refer only to persons; to ask a man to write flexible English, but forbid him *whose* 'as a relative pronoun of the inanimate,' is like sending a soldier on 'active' service and insisting that his tunic collar shall be tight and high; activity and stocks do not agree."

• An Ending That Doesn't Know Its Place

Adverbs, according to many linguists, were originally nouns and adjectives, pressed into adverbial uses until they assumed individual forms. Many were formed by adding an ending, *-ly*, to an adjective—so many that today an adverb is sometimes defined, inadequately, as a word ending in *-ly*. This is a useful ending and sometimes provides a way of making a distinction in meaning. Compare:

> The speaker fell *silent* [stopped talking].
> The speaker fell *silently* [went down with no noise].

The ending makes the difference.

But there is a complication, another example of the refusal of language to remain neat and logical. Another *-ly* ending, related to the ending *-like*, marks a number of adjectives for which we can't easily provide corresponding adverbs. Notice these sentences:

> They reacted very friendly to the proposal.
> They ate very leisurely as they waited for the bus.

The sentences are not standard English, but we can't shift to the usual adverb forms, *friendlily* and *leisurelily*. Other adjectives in *-ly* that cause the same sort of problem include: *holy, homely, weekly, deadly, sickly,* *lovely, kindly, jolly, likely, leisurely, silly, motherly, stately, timely, manly, kingly, bodily, beastly, heavenly.*

Usually, of course, we avoid the problem, framing the sentence so that we can use the adjective. We can say "They were friendly to the proposal" or "They had a leisurely meal while waiting for the bus." If we say "The natives acted friendly," we're thinking of *friendly* as an adjective, as in sentences like "The natives seemed friendly" or "The natives were friendly."

In the same way we could say "He acted silly," but we wouldn't say "He behaved silly" any more than we'd say "He behaved stupid." We would say "He behaved stupidly," and we could say "He behaved sillily"; *sillily* is standard English. I don't think most people would use it.

Holily and *jollyily*, like *sillily*, are in the dictionary, but both of them sound a little silly, not sillily, and nobody would try *lovelily* or *sicklily* or *likelily*. A few -*ly* adjectives have become established as both adjectives and adverbs: *early, daily, hourly*. But in some situations only a wordier substitution will work: a phrase like *a timely moment* or *at a leisurely pace* or *in a sprightly manner*.

• **Verb Forms: The Past Becoming Present**

Sports announcers are certainly not the best models for language usage, but they may be fairly accurate indicators of some general trends, whether for good or bad. And they seem to be leaders in at least one trend, a tendency to simplify verb forms. Indeed, they seem to be moving toward a reduction of all verbs to present forms, relying on context to make any distinctions in time.

For example, we hear, "If the catcher makes a good throw, Butler is out at second" or "If he makes a clean block, it's a touchdown." The verbs here are present forms, but they are referring to events in the past. Butler has already stolen a base, and the runner has been tackled because there was no clean block.

The sentences are probably clear in context, but standard English would require indications of time in the verbs: "If the catcher had made a good throw, Butler would have been out at second" and "If he had made a clean block, there would have been a touchdown."

It's easy to see why the announcers have hit on this simplification, and why it seems to be spreading. It's shorter, and their comments are usually not complicated. The simplification seems consistent with the drift of English grammar away from some of the form distinctions that survive in our complicated verb system.

In some ways the modern English verb is much simpler than verbs in Old English or inflected modern languages. We don't have to learn elaborate conjugations like those that used to stimulate nightmares for schoolchildren learning Latin. In other ways, because of the variety of auxiliaries we have added to take the place of endings, the English verb is very complicated: *will be about to be making, would have had to have made, might have had to make.* Native speakers learn these at an early age.

Difficulties in dealing with many of these forms—those of the sports announcers, for example—are not caused by ignorance of the forms. We learn easily to handle several ways of indicating future time: *he will speak, he speaks, he will be speaking, he is about to speak, he is going to speak,* and so on. The errors come rather from a failure to keep a point of view consistent, to stick to a logical position in time in relation to the subject matter.

We have trouble picking the right forms. For instance, here are sentences from a current best-selling novel:

> Since the first time she saw his house, Gwen remembered, she had seldom seen him happy again.
> He'd either know who they are, or he'd know they weren't real.

In each example, the choices of verbs could be used to give the reader a more accurate impression about how the events are related in time. In the first sentence, the writer is already talking about the past, "Gwen remembered," and wants to report something that happened before this time. He needs to say "the first time she had seen his house." In the second, the *are* may be just a slip, but it confuses the time. *Weren't* indicates the past time the context requires, and *were* should replace *are* in the first part of the sentence.

The verbs *may* and *might* seem especially troublesome these days. They are related in two ways. Both words can appear in the present with related but distinct meanings. *Might* in the present suggests more uncertainty than *may,* but often either word seems to make sense. If someone says "I might pay my debt Monday," you don't start thinking of ways to spend the money. But "I may pay my debt Monday" is also not very reassuring.

Confusion occurs because *might* is also the past form for *may.* This sentence should use the past form: "Steve knew he may have been exposed to the virus." *Knew* puts the sentence clearly in the past, and *might* is the form needed. This sentence has the same problem: "While the fall itself may not have been prevented, his life may have been saved had he been found immediately." *May* should have been *might,* past form, in both uses. Here is Dear Abby: "Had you let Don take his lumps from the police, it may have been a valuable learning experience." *Might* is needed.

The pattern we use to signify time relations can be put into a kind of formula: The past perfect forms (*had made*) are to other past forms (*made* or *has made*) as past forms are to present forms (*makes* or *is making*) and as present or future perfect forms (*will have made*) are to future forms. Here are examples:

> When the boss had spoken [*past perfect*], we left [*past*] the room.
> When the boss has spoken [*past*], we know [*present*] what to do.
> If the boss had left [*past perfect*] orders, we could have [*past*] acted.
> If the boss leaves [*present*] orders before noon, we'll [*future*] get our checks.

Putting everything into the simple present, the device of the sports announcers, may represent the drift of the language toward a grammar of word order. But writers can make subtle distinctions in time using form changes and auxiliaries.

- **Verbs That Can't Make Up Their Minds**

Old English, like other Germanic languages, had two ways of creating verb forms. One was to add an ending, usually *-ed*. The other was to change the main part of the verb itself, as in *swim, swam, swum*.

In the early nineteenth century, philologist Jacob Grimm, considering the Old English verb, thought those that changed their form were somehow better, more vigorous perhaps. He called them strong verbs, and the name stuck. The *-ed* ending seemed to him a kind of simple device, and he called the verbs that used it weak.

In Old English, the strong verbs were the most common, the "regular" verbs. But the system using *-ed* was easier, and gradually became more common. New verbs tended to indicate past time by adding the *-ed* ending, and many Old English strong verbs shifted to the weak pattern.

Currently it is the surviving strong verbs that are irregular. And because we are more accustomed to the pattern with an ending, we have trouble keeping the form changes of the old verbs in order. There are various kinds of difficulties.

As one complication, the regular weak verbs are often irregular because some of them have developed variations on the *-ed* ending, leaving out the *d* or changing it to *t*, even combining an ending and a form change: *tell, told, told; bring, brought, brought; build, built, built; keep, kept, kept; burst, burst, burst.*

As another complication, verbs have been changing for centuries, and not in any consistent pattern. Some strong verbs have shifted to weak, but not in all areas of the English-speaking world. Some old forms exist but have different forms in different dialects.

- **Take Your Choice**

For some verbs either a strong or a weak form is acceptable in standard English. *Wake* is a complicated example. We can say "He *woke* or he *waked* the children." In Great Britain it is also common to hear

"He had *woken* the children." There are no consistent patterns. In the United States *woke* seems more common when it is used without an object, usually with *up:* "They finally woke up." *Dove* and *dived* are also alternatives, but they didn't develop in the usual way. *Dive* was a weak verb in Old English and developed in the usual way with *dived* as the past. Later a dialect past, *dove,* was formed, apparently imitating *drove.* Today *dove* is not very common in England, but both forms exist in the United States and are standard.

Similarly, we have both strong and weak forms for *plead,* either *pleaded* or *pled,* and for *hang,* either *hung* or *hanged,* although some writers make a distinction and use only *hanged* to refer to an execution.

For some strong verbs two standard strong past forms exist. *Stink* can be either *stank* or *stunk,* although with *have* only *stunk* is standard. *Sink* can be either *sank* or *sunk* in the past, but only *sunk* with *have.* *Sunken* still appears sometimes with *have* or as an adjective, *a sunken ship.* The past of *spring* is usually *sprang* in standard English, but *sprung* sometimes appears, as does *shrunk* as an alternative for *shrank.*

• Dialect Variations

More confusing, however, are nonstandard dialect variations. Sometimes old forms are retained after standard English has adopted new ones. Sometimes nonstandard forms are created by analogy with other verbs that sound like them. The list of variants is extensive.

Drug. One common type, including *drug* for *dragged,* retains the old strong form in preference to the standard weak form with the *-ed* ending. *Drug* is common as a nonstandard variant in many American dialects.

Snuck. The origin of the verb *sneak* is a mystery. Some etymologists associate it with Old English *snican,* to creep, but others find this an unlikely relationship. The verb turned up in the seventeenth century, with its first recorded use in Shakespeare's *Measure for Measure:* "Sneak not away, sir, for the friar and you must have a word." The word became common in English with the regular past forms, *sneaked* and *has sneaked.* In the late nineteenth century an irregular past form, *snuck,* appeared, associated with dialect speech and perhaps formed with a kind of humorous intent; compare the use of *thunk. Snuck* appeared in fiction in the conversation of uneducated characters; the narrator in a Ring Lardner story says, "I snuck off down the street and got something to eat." Schools condemned *snuck* along with dialect variants like *drug* or *brung,* and usage books as recently as the 1980s consider it unsuitable for standard writing. The form has, however, become standard, as common as the earlier form *sneaked.*

Clumb. *Clumb* as a past form for *climb* was in good usage in England to the end of the seventeenth century but was gradually replaced by the now standard weak form *climbed. Clumb* is still common in the North Central states and some other areas.

Swoll, Holp. Although the standard past forms for *swell* and *help* use the *-ed* ending, the old forms *swoll* and *holp* still occur occasionally.

Blowed. Sometimes, however, the opposite happens, and the weak form is substituted for the older strong patterns in nonstandard speech. The past tense of *blow* is *blew,* but *blowed* is common in dialects throughout England and the United States.

Growed, Knowed, Throwed. *Grow, know,* and *throw* often are given weak past forms in uneducated dialects.

Brung. Some dialect forms are created by analogy; *brung* as a nonstandard past for *bring* resembles the pasts for words like *cling* or *swing.*

Come, Give. The most common deviations from standard usage are probably those in which forms of surviving strong verbs get mixed up— in which the present is used for the past or with *have.* In both England and the United States the present forms *come* and *give* are used for both present and past time in uneducated speech.

Seen, Begun, Drunk, Done. Forms reserved for use with *have* in standard usage are commonly used for the past in various nonstandard contexts: "I seen her in the store yesterday. He begun working just after lunch. He drunk the whole bottle. He done his best."

Et. The past forms of *eat* are *ate* and *eaten,* but in Great Britain *ate* is pronounced *et* and sometimes spelled *eat.* Standard American English has rejected the British pronunciation, and *et* has become a nonstandard form strongly criticized in the schools.

Go. A different sort of dialect variation is the use of the word *go* to mean *say,* a usage that became common in the 1970s, but generally confined to the speech of children and young adults. It seldom appears in print, and it is frequently lamented as undesirable slang. The use is not entirely illogical. Some idioms associate *go* with expression: "How does that song go?" or "The cannon went bang." And there may even be some reason for the use to distinguish a direct from an indirect quotation. *Go* always introduces a direct quotation: "Then he goes, 'You're cute.'" *Say* could introduce an indirect quotation: "Then he says you're cute." But the use of *go* for *say* is still clearly nonstandard.

- **Keeping *Lie* Alive**

The verb *lie,* meaning recline, developed from Old English *licgan,* related to the Greek word for bed. It has been used for a long time to say that a person or animal or thing is recumbent, in a prostrate position:

> The patient lies on his bed.
> The dog lies [or is lying] down.
> The book lies [or is lying] on the table."

The past forms of *lie* are *lay* and *lain:*

> The patient lay on his bed for a week.
> The dog lay down.
> The book lay on the table.
> The patient has lain on the bed for a week.
> The dog has lain in his bed all day.

Another common verb, *lay,* comes from Old English *lecgan* and means to put or place. It usually has an object:

> He lays his cards on the table.
> He lays linoleum on weekends.
> He lays claim to the title.

The past forms of *lay* are *laid* and *laid:*

He laid his cards on the table.
He laid the linoleum last week.
He laid claim to the title.
He has laid all his cards on the table.
He has laid linoleum in the past.
He has laid claim to the title.

The two verbs are quite separate, but for a number of reasons they have long been confused. One reason is the duplication of the past form of *lie* and the present form *lay*. Another reason is that for a long time in the past it was common to use *lay* with a personal pronoun to mean recline, as in "Now I lay me down to sleep." When the pronoun dropped out, the pattern remained, "Now I lay down to sleep."

The usage persists in much speech, and occasionally over the years even in literary writing. Grant White, writing about usage a hundred years ago, noticed Byron in *Childe Harold* writing ("incorrectly," according to White), "And dashest him again to earth—there let him lay." Laurence Sterne, in *A Sentimental Journey*, wrote: "Maria laid in my bosom." But a reviewer labeled this a vulgarism characteristic of a "city news writer" and commented, "Our readers may possibly conclude that Maria was the name of a favorite pullet."

Today the verb *lie* seems at least moribund. A few years ago I spent some time in a hospital and discovered that in those antiseptic halls, where there is almost constant involvement in lying down, the verb *lie* has virtually disappeared. I was told to lay back, to lay quiet, to lay on my back and breathe deeply, but not once in ten days did I hear the verb *lie*.

Linguistically, I suppose, the loss of *lie* would not have serious consequences for the language. But *lie* is a formidable bastion of linguistic snobbery, and I accept its passing with considerable reluctance. The distinction between the verbs has become a kind of measuring stick with which those who have mastered it, more or less, can judge the competence of others. A misuse of *lay* for *lie* brands a speaker as illiterate—in the view of those who know the distinction.

I know one zealot who taught his dog to drop to the floor on the command "Lie down," but to make no response to "Lay down."

• **Pitfalls and Complications**

Pitfalls, however, lie before even the grammatically virtuous in this matter. There is, for instance, the other verb *lie*, from a different Old English root, meaning to make a false statement, to prevaricate. If you use *lie* without some kind of modifier—*down* or *under the table*—the reader assumes you are using the verb that means tell a falsehood.

More likely to cause confusion—or at least to tempt one to bad puns—is the currently widespread slang application of *lay* to refer to sexual intercourse, and by extension, as a noun, to refer to a person especially active or qualified in this activity. An old joke illustrates: "Have you heard about the Egyptian girl who was laid in a cave and became a mummy?"

Also there are exceptions to the standard school grammar rule that *lie* is intransitive and *lay* transitive—that is, that *lie* never takes an object but *lay* always does. *Lie* does regularly appear without an object, but almost always with a modifier—*awake, in the grass, in bed,* for example. But there are a number of idioms in which *lay* is used without an object. *Lay off*, for instance, meaning to stop or desist, is an American colloquial idiom in wide use, and *lie off* would make no sense. *Lay about*, to fight vigorously or recklessly, is also American slang, but it seems similar to Macbeth's "Lay on, Macduff." There is some logic for using *lie* in "He'll get off the train and lay over in Chicago for a day. But the noun for what he does is always *layover*, never *lie-over*. *Lay off* can mean to dismiss from a job or to stop something, usually criticizing or teasing. To *lay for* is to ambush or plan some kind of usually unpleasant surprise. I'm not sure whether I'd say *lie in wait* or *lay in wait;* the first sounds stuffy, but the second sounds ungrammatical to me.

There are other problems, however. The confusion between the two verbs has had enough publicity to make the linguistically timid doubly cautious. I find overcorrection less palatable than the nonstandard *lay*. "He lay the pencil down" or "Just lie it on the bed" is an obviously bad attempt at elegance. I heard someone the other day describe a friend as "lain back." I have no affection for the currently overworked *laid back*, but certainly *lain back* makes no sense. *Lain up* with a cold is equally unidiomatic.

Even the U.S. Congress a century ago indulged in overfastidiousness. The rules in both houses read: "When a question is under debate, no motion shall be received but to adjourn, to lie on the table, or to postpone. One grammarian observes that if the rule had read "to lie *under* the table" the usage would have been standard. I don't know whether the manuals still read this way.

• *Sitting Bull, Setting Sun, Rising Star, Raising Cain*

Two other pairs of verbs, *sit* and *set* and *rise* and *raise,* are similar to *lie* and *lay* in confusing modern speakers with old form changes that tend to get mixed up.

Sit, one dictionary says, means "to rest the weight of the body on the buttocks and the backs of the thighs, as on a chair." *Set* is to cause to sit, and by extension to place. *Rise* is to get up, to assume a more nearly vertical position. *Raise* is to cause to rise, hence to lift or elevate. *Sit* and *rise* are intransitive, do not take objects; *set* and *raise* do.

The alleged errors in their use are less celebrated than *lie-lay* mix-ups. Fowler, in *Modern English Usage,* doesn't find enough misuse in England to warrant a comment, and several American manuals are similarly silent. But in some dialects, at least, it is pretty common to "just set on the porch and rock of a Sunday" or to "set right up and eat" or to "raise up and look out the window" or to "watch the bread dough raise." One source of confusion is a schoolroom tendency to formulate "rules." I have, for example, heard that *sit* and *lie* can be used only with animate subjects—or, even more restrictive, that only human beings can sit.

These rules are, of course, nonsense; the meaning of *sit* has extended beyond a reference to a person bending his knees and lowering his bottom, or making a lap, and like *lie* the verb can refer to objects as well as people. A picture can sit on the dresser or assurance can sit on the brow of a tyrant. Some dogs will obey a command to sit. Furthermore, in some circumstances *sit* can take an object: "The rider sits his horse gracefully" or "He always sits out the council meetings."

Set is equally versatile. Like *lay,* it usually takes an object: "She sets the table" or "He set the lamp on the table." It has a number of uses, however, without an object. The sun sets, not sits, in the west; one may set out to change the world; and jello and plaster set, in an extended meaning of the word. The past forms of *set* are *set* and *have set*. "I set the table this morning and I have set it often in the past."

The case of hens is interesting. In spite of some generations of school-room protest, setting hens set on eggs to hatch them, although birds usually sit on their eggs. And a hen may sit on a roost or sit to lay an egg. A farmer is supposed to have remarked, "I don't care whether she's sitting or setting; I want to know when she cackles whether she's laying or lying."

"The jar sets on the shelf" is considered a violation of standard English, even though it has a long tradition of usage. "The pancakes didn't set well on my stomach" is also nonstandard, although *sits* doesn't seem appropriate in that use either. The same is true of a variation like "The argument didn't set well with the audience."

The past forms of *sit, set,* and *rise* are survivors of old forms from Old English; *raise* takes the *-ed* ending. The past forms of *sit* are *sat* and *have sat*. There is some tendency to shy away from *have sat* in sentences like "The jar had sat on that shelf for years." *Set* often appears there, but people not wanting to risk the nonstandard *set* and uncomfortable with *had sat* are likely to avoid the whole problem and use *had been*.

Rise has a number of meanings, describing an action by the subject, not something done to something else. The subject can become vertical, get up after sleeping, return to life after dying, rebel or revolt, improve in social status. A person can rise up in anger; a building can rise above the trees; my voice can rise in pitch or in anger; a trout or a naïve person can rise to the bait; a river can rise to flood stage. *Rise* doesn't have meanings with an object.

Raise usually has an object. You can raise a fuss or Cain or the roof. You can raise a building—different from razing it—or corn or a revolt or your status or your salary or a question or your voice. But "to raise up in anger" is nonstandard, and bread dough rises rather than raises. The past forms, *rose* and *have risen* for *rise*, and *raised* and *have raised* for *raise*, seem to cause no problems for native speakers.

One instance of divided usage involves the nouns *rise* and *raise* especially as they refer to salaries. Theoretically, there is a difference in meaning, depending on whether the increase occurs by itself—a pay rise like a rise in temperature—or whether somebody else causes it, a pay raise. Practically, one increase is as good as another, and *raise* seems to be more common in America and *rise* in England.

Rear-raise. Some schools are still trying, with little success, to preserve an old distinction—that hogs or soy beans are raised, but children are reared. *Rear* started out meaning to make to stand up or to set on end. It developed new meaning in the fifteenth and sixteenth centuries: to bring up persons or animals, to nurture plants, or to rise up, as in "The horse reared." *Raise* has taken over for most of these uses; rear is no longer used in the United States to designate the nurturing of plants and animals, and usually not of children. It is now standard American usage to raise children.

• Ghosts That Walk; Making Verbs Agree

"He jump" is probably just as clear as "he jumps," and no one is likely to misunderstand "we is ready" rather than "we are ready." English grammar no longer has much need for changes in the form of verbs to indicate who is doing whatever the verb says. However, two kinds of form changes in verbs are still part of the grammar of standard English: the *s* that marks the third-person singular (*walk* becomes *walks* after *he* or *the man*) or the changes in the verb *be* (*am, was, is* after a first- or third-person singular subject and *are* and *were* after a second-person singular or a plural). Especially when they seem incompatible with our more recent grammatical devices, word order and function words, these ghosts from an inflecting grammar have trouble surviving.

One of the most obvious problems occurs in sentences beginning with *there* or *here,* in which the subject of the verb occurs after it: "There are dozens of children who use the park." *Children* is obviously the subject, and the verb should have the plural form, *are,* to agree with it. But we are so used to having a subject at the beginning of the sentence that we often have trouble realizing that in sentences like this one it has been postponed. More and more frequently we hear sentences beginning with a singular verb regardless of the number of the subject. The contractions *there's* and *here's* seem to be developing into sentence openers that don't specify what kind of subject should follow.

Standard writing, nevertheless, still requires that subject and verb indicate the same number, regardless of the position of the verb. Notice:

> Here are [not *here's*] some categories to get you going.
> There are [not *there's*] a lot of people waiting at the gate.
> There are [not *there's*] a boy and his dog at the door.

One solution for this kind of problem is to use the construction with the postponed subject only when it is needed. In the first sentence above, for instance, which just points out that something, categories, exist, the construction is really useful. But the second and third sentences would work better in the more usual pattern for English grammar: "A lot of people are waiting at the gate," "A boy and his dog are at the door."

Some other problems with the old verb forms probably occur just from our tendency to simplify, to let the form distinctions disappear. The nonstandard "he don't know" rather than "he doesn't know" is increasingly common in speech. "That boy look silly" rather than "that boy looks silly" is common in some dialects.

There are also frequent uses of the wrong verb which are just mistakes; the writer forgets what word is the subject. Notice this from a newspaper story: "The date for the oral arguments have not been set." The writer apparently was just confused by the plural *arguments* and mistakenly used *have* rather than *has*.

• How Many Is or Are a Committee?

The most common confusions with agreement of subject and verb, however, result from uncertainties about the number of the subject; is *committee* singular or plural? What about *headquarters* or *trio* or *none*? One way to describe the attitude of the English language on this subject is to say it is inconsistent. A more constructive view is that we can often sharpen the meaning of a noun subject by our choice of a singular or a plural verb form.

Headquarters is an example of a mass noun, a noun that is not clearly singular or plural in meaning, that does not refer to countable things: *butter, sunlight, cheese, mist, happiness*. Most mass nouns, like those just listed, take singular verbs: "Happiness or sunshine is . . ."

A few nouns look like plurals, even though they do not refer to countable things and have no corresponding singulars: *munitions, mathematics, news, savings, measles, riches, morals, hydraulics, economics, athletics*. These sound as if they ought to be followed by plural verbs, and many of them are. We would say, "Those savings are my only asset" or "His riches are a comfort to him" or "The statistics are misleading" or "The groceries were expensive" or "The tropics are exciting." But *news* or *hydraulics* or *mathematics* is singular, and *athletics* is singular when it refers to a system of exercise or training. *Politics* is singular or plural, depending on the meaning intended. We say "Politics is an interesting subject" or "His politics are conservative."

A similar class of words is made up of names for single articles, but the words look and act like plurals: *scissors, breeches, glasses, overalls, jeans, scales, pliers, pants, pajamas, trousers, tweezers*, and so on. We treat these as plurals even though they refer to single items: "His suspenders were broken," "Her shorts were too long."

In spite of these more or less arbitrary patterns—not always observed in dialects in which one could hear "Her shorts was too long"—English has developed some sensible flexibility in dealing with agreement. In general we use the verb form to reflect the meaning we intend for the subject. This is especially true with group words like *family, committee, trio, jury, flock, nation, orchestra, team*. Unlike mass nouns, these words can also have plural forms, but in their singular form they can take either singular or plural verbs, depending on the meaning to be stressed. Compare:

> The staff is too large. The staff are willing to work at night.
> The family is united. The family are vegetarians.
> The jury was out eight hours. The jury were unable to agree.
> The orchestra plays at eight. The orchestra keep their instruments in
> the hall.

Words designating number or quantity behave similarly, with the verb varied to indicate the user's intended meaning. Compare:

Half the cake was eaten. Half the students were failing.

An average of twenty points was considered good. An average of twenty students were absent.

Often the choice between *a* or *the* to precede the noun distinguishes singular or plural. Compare:

A number of possibilities were considered. The number of possibilities has changed.

A couple of people were dancing. The couple was dancing on the lawn.

Two hours of the required three were already gone. Two hours was a long time to wait.

In a dependent clause the form of the verb can be varied to show the meaning of a pronoun subject. Compare:

The court is concerned with the children responsible for the vandalism. John is one of those children who comes from a wealthy family.

The court is concerned with many types of troubled children. John is one of those children who come from wealthy families.

In the first, the singular *comes* signals that *who* refers to *John,* the only one from a wealthy family. In the second, the plural *come* makes *who* refer to *children,* all of whom are from wealthy families.

• More Than One Subject

The same principle, that the verb form is used to clarify the meaning intended for the subject, applies in some special cases. Compounds, for example, are usually plural, but they can be made singular with a singular verb: "Beans and corn is succotash." "Beans and corn are combined in succotash." Nouns joined by *or* or used with *neither* or *either* are thought of as alternatives, taking singular verbs if both are singular: "Either luck or wisdom was needed." "Neither of the candidates was chosen."

When *or* joins subjects of different number, the result is often awkward and usage varies. Usually the verb takes the number of the part of the subject nearest it: "Either the boys or their father was available." "Either the dog or the chickens were doomed."

• Data, Media, None

A few borrowed plurals (see chapter 8) seem to cause special agreement problems. For example, in the seventeenth century the Latin word *datum* came into the English language to refer to a bit of information, a fact. Its plural form, *data*, was also adopted. But soon people found more use for the plural than the singular; we seemed to refer to more than one fact at a time. *Data* came to be thought of as a collection of facts, of what would have been called *datums* if we had anglicized the word. That is essentially a singular idea, and today both "the data is" and "the data are" appear regularly and are considered standard. Theoretically a speaker can make a distinction in meaning by choosing one, *is* emphasizing the unity of the body of evidence, *are* the individual items. Many writers still prefer the plural, especially in the sciences, where perhaps some kinship with Latin lingers. But Bergen Evans suggests that we are not obliged to treat *data* as plural "just because Julius Caesar did." I still say "data are."

Media is a Latin plural, but it causes different problems. *Medium* and its plural form *media* came into English in the sixteenth century to refer to a middle quality or degree or a middle course. In the next century *medium* acquired a further meaning, to refer to an intermediary of any sort, an agency for getting something done. Much more recently it has come to be associated especially with methods of communication; radio is a medium or means of communication. *Medium* was anglicized fairly early, and the usual English form *mediums* developed. The persons who preside over the table-tapping in a seance, for instance, are mediums, not media.

But the older plural persisted in connection with communication, especially in *media of mass communication*. This was shortened to *mass media* and soon thought of as singular, not so much as a way of referring to newspapers and television as a term for an abstract idea, the notion in general of communication with a wide audience, especially to influence it with advertising. The Latin plural form has become so thoroughly thought of as singular that it has acquired an English plural, *medias*. In advertising, *media* is useful as a singular, and "media are" seldom occurs. In referring to materials for use in the visual arts or to cultures used in biology, *media* is still considered plural.

The confusion with *none* as a subject probably echoes the origin of the word, a combination of Anglo-Saxon words for *not one*. *One* is about as singular as you can get, but in the minds of users of the language that origin has been submerged under practicality for centuries. Like other words involving number, *none* is singular or plural depending on the sense or emphasis the speaker wants to achieve. The *Oxford English Dictionary* cites the plural meaning as "no persons" and comments "this is now the commoner usage." Notice "None are so deaf as those that will not hear." The singular, however, is often desired, and Dryden wrote, "None but the brave deserves the fair"—which was parodied with *none* in the plural, "None but the brave desert the fair."

Grammarian Thomas Lounsbury, eighty years ago, commented: "There is no harm in a man's limiting his employment of *none* to the singular verb in his own usage, if he derives any pleasure from that form of linguistic martyrdom. But why should he go about seeking to inflict upon others the misery which owes its origin to his own ignorance?"

6

Bishop Lowth to Miss Groby: Dealing with Rules

At this moment the King, who had been for some time busily writing in his note-book, called out "Silence!" and read out from his book "Rule Forty-two. *All persons more than a mile high to leave the court.*"

Everybody looked at Alice.

"*I'm* not a mile high," said Alice.

"You are," said the King.

"Nearly two miles high," added the Queen.

"Well, I sha'n't go, at any rate," said Alice: "besides, that's not a regular rule: you invented it just now."

"It's the oldest rule in the book," said the King.

- Lewis Carroll, *Alice's Adventures in Wonderland*

Our modern grammars have done much more hurt than good. The authors have labored to . . . persuade the English to speak by Latin rules or by arbitrary rules of their own.

- Noah Webster,
  Dissertations on the English Language

When I read some of the rules for speaking and writing the English language correctly, I think—

Any fool can make a rule

And every fool will mind it.

- Henry David Thoreau, *Journal*

People didn't get much exercised about how English ought to be written and spoken until fairly late in the seventeenth century. Shakespeare's printers, for example, were capable of spelling a word two or three different ways on the same page. They did not hesitate to add an *e* in order to space out a line. Schools were more concerned with Latin grammar than with the difference between *shall* and *will*.

But toward the end of that century, and then in the eighteenth century with a vengeance, grammarians began producing rules for the proper use of English. James Harris's *Hermes* appeared in 1751. Its subtitle emphasizes one of the topics that dominated writing about language during the period: *A Philosophical Inquiry Concerning Language and Universal Grammar*. As a "philosophical inquiry" the book offered the notion of "universal reason." "It may afford perhaps no unpleasing speculation," Harris says, "to see how the SAME REASON has at all times prevailed; how there is ONE TRUTH, like one Sun, that has enlightened human Intelligence through every age, and saved it from the darkness both of Sophistry and Error." This comfortable certainty about universal reason supports the notion of "GRAMMAR UNIVERSAL, that grammar, which without regarding the several Idioms of particular Languages, only respects those principles, that are essential to them all."

These concepts were shared by many of the scholars of the period. Grammarians, when they began outlining specific rules for a universal grammar, found the ideal grammar in the Greek language—"of all," in Harris's view, "the most elegant and complete"—or in Latin. Bishop Robert Lowth, whose *Short Introduction to English Grammar* appeared in 1762, praised Harris's *Hermes* as "the most beautiful and perfect example of Analysis, that has been exhibited since the days of Aristotle." Lowth's book, attempting to express notions of universal grammar as practical rules, was widely used in both England and America. It was standard at Harvard until 1841. Almost equally popular was Lindley Murray's *English Grammar*, 1795, which went through 120 editions before 1850.

The assumption of these early grammarians that English, in Lowth's words, "is easily reducible, to a System of rules," was pedagogically attractive. Their approach, to "teach correct English"—with their certainty about what constitutes correct English—still dominates many of the textbooks and much of the teaching in British and American schoolrooms. James Thurber's Miss Groby ("the shape of a sentence crucified on a blackboard brought a light to her eyes") is a fictional descendant of Bishop Lowth and Lindley Murray.

The difference between these and many school grammars and the statements of modern linguists is the difference between prescription and description. A prescriptive grammar outlines what the language ought to be. It assumes that there is, or was in the past, a correct language, and it lists rules to make writers and speakers conform. Correctness was established by Latin, or sometimes by a kind of logic, or sometimes by personal whim. Rules of prescriptive grammar often deal with relatively insignificant matters of usage. The descriptive grammars of today attempt to look at the language, describe how it works, and then devise different sorts of rules to describe how sentences are generated. These rules are not prescriptive or proscriptive. They are generalizations about how language works.

Actually the two approaches are not as different as they may appear to be. In fact, some modern grammarians are reviving interest in the idea of a universal grammar and are looking more tolerantly at scholars like James Harris or George Campbell. Many of the prescriptive rules offer sound advice about writing. But English does not always behave logically or consistently, and arbitrary prescriptions often do more to confuse than to help. Some rules, in fact, survive only in a few textbooks or in school tradition and have never had much influence on the way English is used. A few have successfully modified usage. Following are accounts of some of the conflicts between prescriptive rules and the language.

• **The Victory Over *Ain't***

One of the clear triumphs of rules over the language is the widespread condemnation of *ain't*. When I was in school any use of the word was regarded as blatant evidence of gross ignorance, and maybe of a tendency toward immorality or impiety. It was almost as bad as using *belly* or *butt* in public to refer to parts of the anatomy more delicately, if less accurately, referred to as *stomach* and *behind*. In the fifth grade it was fairly flashy humor to say "There ain't no such word as ain't."

For reasons not totally clear to me, using *ain't* is still the most popular example of improper usage or "incorrectness." When the third edition of *Webster's New International Dictionary* appeared in 1961, it met a deluge of journalistic criticism for its failure to condemn expressions reviewers disapproved. And it was most roundly castigated for reporting that *ain't* is "used orally in most parts of the U.S. by cultivated speakers." Both the *Chicago Tribune* and the *Chicago Sun-Times* echoed my fifth-grade comedians by opening their reviews: "The word *ain't* ain't a grammatical mistake any more."

The notion that *ain't* is not a word is of course nonsense; it has been around and in use for at least two centuries. The *Oxford English Dictionary* records a 1706 use of *an't* as a contraction for *are not*. Samuel Johnson's famous dictionary of 1755 includes an entry for *an't* as a contraction for *and if it,* as in "an't please you." *An't* was socially acceptable in speech, like other contractions with *not: haven't, won't, can't,* and so on.

Ain't as a variant of *an't* appeared toward the end of the century, about the time of the American Revolution. During the nineteenth century it tended to replace *an't* and also to start on its slide from favor. Partly, perhaps, because it was associated in England with Cockney speech, it began to attract labels like *vulgar* or *illiterate,* and in this century it skidded to its position as a symbol of uneducated usage.

The word of course is useful. *Am not* is not easy to say, especially in a question, "Am I not?" It also sounds stuffy. Apparently *amn't I?* has some use in Ireland, but it does not seem a likely solution. *Aren't I?* spoken in England doesn't jar, because the *r* is silent and the word sounds like *an't.* But in America *aren't I?* sounds precious or kittenish, suggesting the positive form, "Yes I are."

But, useful or not, *ain't* seems doomed for at least the present, partly because it has been extended so far beyond its logical use as a contraction for *am not.* There is not much justification for using *ain't* to mean *is not:* "He ain't playing." And there is even less reason for using it, or the variation *hain't,* for *have not* or *has not:* "He ain't got a dime."

I doubt even the claim of the *Third New International* that *ain't* is used very widely by "cultivated speakers," except for mild comic effects or as a kind of reverse snobbery. I therefore find myself reconciled to *am I not?* or to avoiding the whole business. I can't bring myself to utter *aren't I?*

But I must confess considerable affection for *ain't,* partly, I suppose, in sympathy for an unjustly maligned underdog, but also because the word is so essential to a great deal of picturesque American speech. It's not the same to identify a stack of hundred-dollar bills by "That isn't hay" or to advise, "If it isn't broken, don't fix it."

• **Latin Grammar in the Van: Final Prepositions**

The poet John Dryden, as a way of improving his writing, sometimes composed a passage in Latin and then translated it into English. He discovered that Latin prepositions do not occur at the ends of sentences. Since Latin was the ideal grammar, he concluded that a final preposition in English was an error, and he even revised some earlier writing to get rid of terminal prepositions.

The case against final prepositions was reinforced by the irrelevant literal interpretation of the meaning of the word *preposition: pre* means before; therefore, a preposition must be positioned before not after its object. This is an obvious form of circular logic, giving something a name and then defining from that name. It is like saying that a buttercup is something you might drink from—or from which you might drink.

It is hard to know why the schoolroom proscription of the terminal preposition survives. Although grammarians recognize that prepositions most often appear before their objects, even the eighteenth-century Latinists were sensible about their placement. Goold Brown, whose grammars were popular in nineteenth-century schoolrooms, notices that "Whom did he speak to?" is common, although he contends that "To whom did he speak? is "more dignified and in general more graceful." I don't find that "rule" today in even the stuffiest school texts. But the notion that final prepositions are bad is one of the most frequently remembered school admonitions.

On the placement of prepositions, as on many questions of style and usage, no rule, especially no prohibition, provides an answer. The position of the preposition is determined by the effect a writer wants. Usually this involves emphasis or perhaps the existence of a standard idiom.

Frequently the preposition falls naturally after its object—almost always when the object is *that* or *what* or *that* understood.

> To weep at what I am glad of.
> The rascal I spoke of.
> Such stuff as dreams are made on.
> The book that I read about.

The first three were written by Shakespeare, who hadn't heard about the rule. None of these could be reversed, except by changing them or inserting a pronoun: "The rascal of whom I spoke. The book about which I read."

On the other hand, there are many instances in which only the position before the object would work: "He walked *across* the street," "The girl with red hair," "The man in the moon." No one would ever say "The man the moon in." We would say "The fire occurred during the lecture," not ". . . the lecture during."

My favorite illustration of the possible dangers of final prepositions is a verse composed many years ago by Morris Bishop:

> I lately lost a preposition;
> It hid, I thought, beneath my chair,
> And angrily, I cried "Perdition!
> Up from out of in under there."
> Correctness is my vade mecum,
> And straggling phrases I abhor.
> And yet I wondered, "What should he come
> Up from out of in under for."

Obviously, final prepositions can be awkward. But probably the most serious danger to writing is not in putting a preposition at the end of a sentence but in distorting a sentence to put it elsewhere. "About what could she have been thinking?" seems to me not good English. An often-quoted comment, attributed to Winston Churchill, answers an editor who had objected to a final preposition: "This is an abomination up with which I will not put."

The main complication in this business is that those who remember the rule aren't always accurate in identifying prepositions. Many words that can serve as prepositions also work as parts of verbs, as in *blow up, look out, turn off, think over* (see chapter 3). Often it is idiomatic to use these as separable suffixes, located after their objects:

You can count me out.
Please don't turn him away.

Sometimes they can appear either before or after an object:

Turn the light off. *or* Turn off the light.
Look these plans over. *or* Look over these plans.

Using the taboo on final prepositions to object to final verb suffixes is a gratuitous absurdity.

• **Grandpa's Beard and Split Infinitives**

Late in the nineteenth century, in another futile attempt to apply logic to language, grammarians began popularizing a rule that nothing should be allowed to separate *to* and the other part of an infinitive. As a result, the split infinitive has come to be regarded as a serious grammatical sin, especially because, like the dangling modifier, it basks in an aura of mystery. It also serves as a handy weapon for would-be authorities on language, who are able to detect the phenomenon in others and massage their egos by condemning it.

An infinitive is a verb form used as a noun, usually introduced by the word *to*. If we say "To err is human," the infinitive *to err* is used as a noun, subject of the sentence. If we say "He told me to stop," the infinitive *to stop* is direct object of the verb *told*. If we say "He told me to immediately stop," separating *to* and *stop,* we have committed what has come to be called a split infinitive. Professor John F. Genung, whose 1886 rhetoric was widely used, explains, not very convincingly: "The adverb belongs to the whole expression, and should therefore stand either before or after, not in the midst of it."

There was never much reason for the rule, and it has by now disappeared from most textbooks. But the term *split infinitive* had an ominous ring, and it sticks in a lot of memories, even when its meaning has disappeared.

Like so many of these traditional rules, this one has some justification. It is not a rule of grammar, and never was. The split pattern is clearly grammatical in English, although it is relatively recent. But stylistically it is usually more logical to keep all parts of a verb form together—not only of an infinitive but also of any verb formed with a number of words.

Thus we'd usually say, "He told me to stop immediately" rather than "He told me to immediately stop." And we'd also probably say, "He noticed that I had stopped immediately" rather than "He noticed that I had immediately stopped." We'd probably not separate *had* from *stopped* any more often than *to* from *stop*.

But the location of a modifier in a complex verb is not a usage to be governed by a rule. It is a matter of stylistic choice. And frequently the split infinitive seems the better choice. Examples are common, from the sixteenth century on. Consider:

> I've heard enough to just about convince me.
> I want them to first consider the consequences.
> She was able to more than better her old position.

These are not especially graceful sentences, but revising them to avoid the split infinitive does not improve them. In the first example, *just about* could be placed before *to,* but it seems more awkward there. In the second, *first* could be placed either before or after the infinitive, but the emphasis would be different. Moving *more than* in the third seems impossible without a change in meaning. "To slowly walk down the aisle" makes a different impression than "slowly to walk down the aisle" or "to walk down the aisle slowly." The script writer who asserts that the mission of the Star Trek crew is "to boldly go where no person has gone before" seems justified in seeking special prominence for *boldly.*

H. W. Fowler classifies the English-speaking world into "(1) those who neither know nor care what a split infinitive is; (2) those who do not know, but care very much; (3) those who know and condemn; (4) those who know and approve; and (5) those who know and distinguish." The first group he finds happiest. "To really understand" comes readier to their lips and pens than "really to understand."

Grandpa, who had a long white beard, was asked one day by a grandson, "Grandpa, do you sleep with your beard under or on top of the covers?" Grandpa did not know the answer; he had never thought about it. But from then on he lay awake at night wondering where the beard should be.

• **Bad Algebra and the Double Negative**

In 1762, Bishop Lowth formulated a rule that still appears in many books: "Two negatives in English destroy one another; or are equivalent to an Affirmative." In one of the few triumphs of teachers and authorities over common usage, the rule persists. The double negative is condemned as illiterate in expressions like "The children didn't get nothing from Santa" or "Nobody told me nothing."

In Old English, or in the time of Shakespeare, it was apparently felt that using two negatives, like *not* or *no* or *never,* just made the negation stronger. When Hero in *Much Ado about Nothing* says of Beatrice:

> . . . she cannot love,
> Nor take no shape nor project of affection,

the piling up of *not, nor, no,* and *nor* just emphasizes the lady's inadequacy. In modern languages like French or Spanish it is standard to use more than one word to express negation.

But in eighteenth-century England, Bishop Lowth and other authorities, looking for ways to regularize the language, decided that multiple negatives were illogical. Apparently as an analogy with algebra, they asserted that two negatives make a positive and outlawed locutions like "He don't know nothing" or "She don't never look at me." The argument was neither good logic nor good algebra; in algebra, $-x$ plus $-x$ equals $-2x$, not $2x$. The two negatives equal two negatives.

Logical or not, the rule has been a success, and double negatives like "I don't know nothing about it" tend to label a speaker as uneducated. People with a little knowledge pounce on a double negative as self-righteously as they expose a split infinitive. Expressions like the above, involving *not* and clear negatives like *nothing* or *nobody,* seldom appear in writing.

The case is not so clear with less obviously recognized negatives. *Neither-nor,* for example, defies the so-called logic that two negatives cancel each other. We don't say "Neither snow or sleet can stop them," avoiding a double negative. In standard English we use two negatives, with no notion that they cancel each other: "Neither snow *nor* sleet can stop them."

We are also less consistent with negatives like *hardly* or *scarcely*. Although they are regarded as nonstandard, we often hear

I can't hardly hear you.
I don't hardly think I should.

Standard usage requires cutting one of the negatives:

I can hardly hear you.
I hardly think I should *or* I don't think I should.

When *but* has a negative meaning, there is still more confusion, even though standard usage dictates a single negative:

I can't help imagining [*not* but imagine] the worst.
I don't doubt that [*not* but that] she means well.

Perhaps because of the success of Bishop Lowth's rule, an intentional double negative is increasingly popular. In this use, actually a kind of understatement, a negative word qualifies a negative or derogatory word, producing a mealy-mouthed positive. If we say that "Senator Abscam is not entirely stupid," we leave very little for the positive, only whatever small amount of nonstupidity exists between entirely and not entirely. If we say that the senator's speech is "not half bad," we may be allowing at least 50 percent on the positive side. If I say that Mr. Falwell's statements on equal rights are "hardly without prejudice," I am certainly accusing him of some prejudice, but the negative approach seems to make me feel safer from libel suits.

It is not inconceivable that in a not unanticipated move in the not too distant future, no small number of bureaucrats will be turning their not inconspicuous talents to the not inconsiderable and not unchallenging task of translating all documents into not totally uncommunicative nonpositive understatements.

• Rules and Possessives

One of the most frequent schoolroom errors is failure to signal possession with an apostrophe. Omission of the apostrophe from *a day's work*
or *my father's mustache* is considered a blunder in usage, although it
is an increasingly common blunder. It is easy to see why such errors
occur, since the whole business resulted from a fairly intricate scholarly
error, an example of authorities outsmarting themselves.

In Old English, as in Latin, endings were used to designate the uses of
nouns. The possessive or genitive forms were marked with the ending
-es, which was pronounced as a syllable. In Middle English, in some
dialects, the ending was written *-is,* as in *the kingis sword.*

Scholars during the Renaissance, concerned with the nature and history of the English language, concluded that the *-is* ending was a shortening of *his,* that *Haroldis horse* was really a corruption of *Harold
his horse.*

The apostrophe, or apostrophus, had become popular in the sixteenth
century as a mark designating the omission of letters. Shakespeare, or
his printers, used it consistently in this way, and Ben Jonson, in his
grammar of 1640, described this use. Therefore, since scholars were
assuming that *Harolds horse,* which had become the standard possessive, was really a shortening of *Harold his horse,* they started using the
apostrophe to show the assumed omission of at least part of *his.*

This was nonsense, of course, but the usage prevailed, was extended
to mark the plural possessive also, and was formulated into a set of
rules required in standard edited English.

The possessive singular is the noun plus *-'s: the cat's meow, the
teacher's advice, the year's end.* When a plural does not end in *s,* its
possessive is also formed by adding *-'s: the people's choice, the children's hour.*

If the plural ends in *-s,* only an apostrophe is added to form the
possessive: *twenty cats' meows, teachers' salaries, the visitors' needs.*

When a noun ends with an *s* or *z* sound in the singular, an added *-s*
may be hard to pronounce. As an alternative the possessive is sometimes
formed with only the apostrophe added, as for *s* plurals: *Charles's* or
Charles' book, Jesus's or *Jesus' sake.*

There are complications and exceptions. For example, the apostrophe is not used with possessive pronouns like *yours* or *ours* or *its*, but it is used to mark omissions in contractions of pronouns and the verb *to be:*

> It's [contraction] an apartment with its [possessive] own entrance.

The use of the apostrophe with possessives makes no difference in pronunciation and does little to clarify writing. In Shakespeare's time writers apparently got along very well without it. But the rule survives and standard English requires the apostrophe.

A variation on the rule has not fared so well and illustrates again the hazards of trying to impose some kind of logic on the language. The term *possessive* replaced the earlier *genitive* sometime during the eighteenth century. And grammarians, with the kind of circular logic that insisted prepositions must always be pre- something, decided that possessives with apostrophe *s* could be used only to signify ownership by a person. The *king's sword* is all right, but not the *king's English,* since he doesn't own English, although he may use it.

By the time it gets to pop grammarian Wilson Follett, the rule is as firm as it is inaccurate. Follett outlaws *Cornell's Division of Industrial Relations, Florida's governor, Berkeley's president,* and *the nation's capital.* These are "newfangled and false. . . . we must stick to the ancestral rule which, with a few exceptions, reserved possessives in -'s for ownership by a person."

Jacques Barzun, who edited Follett, uses the same examples in his book on usage and points out that the forms with -'s ending grow from a "false relation in thought" because they do not mean *the governor of Florida* and *the capital of the nation.* Of course they don't mean exactly the same, but the meanings with the -'s seem to me just as legitimate as those with *of,* and *the capital of the nation* doesn't fit my sense of idiom.

We have worked out idiomatic ways of using the two forms of the genitive or possessive, with the apostrophe and with *of.* The distinctions don't always follow any discernible pattern of logic. And we can sometimes simply use a noun as an adjective, so that we have *the car's engine, the engine of the car,* or *the car engine.*

Sometimes the different forms are not interchangeable, have different meanings. Compare *hair of the dog, the dog's hair, the dog hair.* There's a difference between a *turkey's dinner* and a *turkey dinner* or a *dinner of turkey.* Some expressions can have only the apostrophe form: *a stone's throw, hell's half acre, a day's work, my mother's love.* The differences illustrate how you can get into trouble if you make up a rule and then have to try to apply it.

• **The Ecclesiastical *Shall* and Related Rules**

I remember from a Sunday school far in my past the prayers of a zealous superintendent who obviously preserved a vague memory of a rule he had learned in school. Whenever he prayed, he abandoned his usual speech habits, presumably out of respect for his divine listener. And among the distinctions of his Sunday kind of talk was a liberal sprinkling of *shall*s. He remembered that there was something funny about *shall* and *will* and assumed—not illogically—that in order to be right he should simply do the opposite of what seemed natural to him. So *will*s disappeared, and we heard "The Lord shall forgive our sins and it shall be good." I do not recall his ever saying "Thy shall be done."

There was probably another reason for his affection for *shall;* the Bible in the King James translation is full of *shall*s. And these seem quite consistently to follow a pattern exactly opposite that of the schoolroom rule still in most textbooks. *Shall* is used when *you* or *he* or a noun is its subject, *will* with a first-person subject. My superintendent's ecclesiastical *shall* was perhaps more fitting than he realized.

Shall also at the time of the 1611 Bible projected a kind of authority, a sense of certainty or determination. An exchange in Shakespeare's *Coriolanus* is revealing. Referring to Coriolanus's mind, Sicinius says:

> It is a mind
> That shall remain a poison where it is,
> Not poison any further.

And Coriolanus answers:

Shall remain!
Hear you this Triton of the minnows? mark you
His absolute "shall"?

Not long after Shakespeare's time, however, in 1653, grammarian John Wallis formulated a rule to govern the use of *shall* and *will*, which practically reversed the usage of the Bible. As part of the general effort of the time to regularize English, to make it more like Latin, Wallis specified: "With a subject in the first person, either singular or plural, *shall* is used to indicate future time and *will* to express determination. With a subject in the second or third person, the opposite applies; *will* indicates the future and *shall* expresses determination."

Perhaps because of its neatness, the rule got into textbooks. It still appears in most school grammars, and British usage more or less follows it. H. W. Fowler in *Modern English Usage* states categorically that *shall* should be used in the first person to indicate future time. He then cites two pages of examples from British periodicals using *will*—which he labels "wrong" but which illustrate a growing tendency to deviate from what he labels "right."

In America the rule has had much less acceptance. As early as 1784 an American grammarian presented a dissenting view: "*Will* as an auxiliary term is a mere sign of futurity. . . . *shall* even as an auxiliary sign always denotes something more than mere futurity, and constantly implies either obligation, possibility, contingency, or something conditional, and very often several of these together." This is still an accurate description of American usage.

A few people follow the rule and the British usage, at least in formal situations. In general, however, *will* is the sign of the future in all persons, especially since it is usually contracted to *I'll* or *we'll*. *Shall* appears more often in questions, but usually it does more than simply signal futurity. If I say, "Shall I put a log on the fire?" I'm asking for advice or permission. If I were asking simply for a prediction about my future action—which is unlikely—I'd probably say, "Will I put a log on the fire?" asking my listener to guess about what I planned.

One reason for our difficulties with *shall* and *will* is that they are less and less often used to signal future time. We are likely to say "I'm going tomorrow" or "I go tomorrow" rather than to use the auxiliary, although we'd probably say "I'll do it tomorrow." There are differences in meaning among the various ways of dealing with the future which users of the language seem to handle without much trouble and which defy formulation into rules.

• How Not to Start a Sentence

A newspaper column by Mike Royko tests a computer program designed to correct "stylistic errors" against Lincoln's Gettysburg address. Among other criticisms, the computer objects to Lincoln's sentence: "But we cannot dedicate . . ." The computer comments: "Use *but* sparingly to start a sentence."

This fairly sensible advice got translated into a rule prohibiting initial *and* or *but* that has been around for a long time; I remember it from school, and I've often heard teachers cite it. But I have no notion where it came from; I don't find it recorded in grammars or handbooks even a hundred years ago. Thos. W. Harvey's 1878 grammar says, "Conjunctions are sometimes used as introductory words, either to awaken expectation, or to make the introduction of a sentence less abrupt."

The rule probably does go back to school, originating in the kind of circular logic that creates a definition and then uses the definition to create a rule. That is, you define a coordinating conjunction—*and, or, nor, but, for*—as a word that links parallel elements in a sentence. Then from the definition you conclude that such a word can be used only within a sentence.

Actually, coordinating conjunctions work just as well to relate a sentence to preceding sentences as to link elements within a sentence. Like any device, the initial conjunction can be misused or overused, but prohibition is not the way to prevent that.

• Leaky Rules and Useful Distinctions

In a language as blessed with words as English—some half million in an unabridged dictionary—it's inevitable that meanings should get mixed up. Some common words look alike or have closely related meanings and are hard to distinguish—*accept* and *except, affect* and *effect*. Some relatively uncommon words suggest other words and mislead a speaker into malapropism.

The word *malapropism* came into the language through an eighteenth-century play, *The Rivals,* by Richard Brinsley Sheridan. In the play, Mrs. Malaprop, whose name, from the French, means something like "not appropriate," became a classic comic character by consistently mixing up words. She uses *reprehend* for *apprehend* and *derangement* for *arrangement* and accuses her niece of being "headstrong as an allegory on the banks of the Nile."

Mrs. Malaprop was not the first dramatic character to confuse words as a device for comedy. Dogberry, the constable in Shakespeare's *Much Ado About Nothing* orders the watchmen to "comprehend all vagrom men" and promises that the villain he arrests will be condemned into "everlasting redemption."

Usages not unlike these turn up in the press and on television and radio every day, and for generations rules and rules makers have been waging a battle against them. Some of the rules have made no sense, merely attempting an arbitrary attitude inconsistent with standard usage. Some have been sensible but futile. Some have tried to preserve distinctions that are useful. Following are some of the confusions that persist in spite of—or sometimes because of—rules.

Like, As. In the 1950s when a cigarette company announced that its product tasted good "like a cigarette should" there was a louder outcry about the alleged misuse of *like* than about any harm that might be done to the lungs of anyone believing the slogan. The outraged objections made the slogan a success, and usage of *like* and *as* became more confused. The rules restrict *like* to use as a preposition, with *as* or *as if* as conjunctions.

The distinction can be made, and often is in formal writing:

He grew like a weed. He grew as a weed grows.
He looks like me. He is old as the hills.
He walks like an ostrich. He walks as if he were an ostrich.
This tastes like a cigarette. This tastes as a cigarette should [taste].

But the distinction has never been observed very consistently, and examples of *like* as a conjunction can be found in the writing of respected authors from Shakespeare to the present. Here, for instance, is a sentence from *Language Arts,* a professional journal for teachers of English:

Whether we are young people or tired old college professors like I too often am . . .

Or notice the use of *like* in a number of faddish speech lines:

Tell it like it is. Do it like they do in the army. Like I said, you gotta have faith. You know, like we saw in the movies.

Like flourishes also in places where the formal tradition requires *as if:*

She talked like butter wouldn't melt in her mouth.
Marie's face looked like she'd been run over by a truck.

Uses like these are generally considered nonstandard, but they grate less than the false elegance achieved when speakers become afraid of using *like* and overcorrect. This appeared in print:

The closeness of American portrait painters, as West, Copley, and Stuart, to contemporary British artists . . .

This appeared in an Associated Press story:

Gripping the podium comfortably, as if a steering wheel, the speaker . . .

The problem is complicated because *as* and *like* are both sometimes used as prepositions; the choice between them can affect meaning. Compare:

He cried as a baby. He cried like a baby.
He worked as a stevedore. He worked like a stevedore.

In the first pair, one sentence tells what he did as an infant; the other describes the way he cried. In the second, the difference is whether he held a dockside job or whether he worked hard. A person who is "crazy like a fox" is not really crazy; one who is "crazy as a fox" may be.

To complicate matters further, it is often possible to express a difference in meaning by using *like* as a conjunction. "I can't sing like I used to" is different from "I can't sing as I used to." The first indicates that I can't sing in the same way or with the same skill. The second says that I used to sing, but now can't.

Although the *Oxford English Dictionary* points out that *like* has been used as a conjunction for centuries, the usage is still one of those about which many people are very stuffy.

Affect, Effect. These are quite different words, but they look and sound alike, and people have trouble with them. *Affect* comes from Latin *afficere*, to influence or attack. It is always used as a verb, usually meaning to influence, to produce a change, or to stir the emotions:

> The weather doesn't affect her disposition.
> He was not affected by the criticism.

Effect is from Latin *efficere*, meaning to accomplish or bring to pass. It is usually a noun. It names a result or an impression:

> The effect of his decision was chaos.
> His words had no effect on the children.
> She wore the hat just for the effect.

One complication that causes trouble is that *effect* is also a verb, meaning to cause or bring about or accomplish. It has generally the same meaning as the Latin verb from which it is derived. "To effect a decision" is to make one; "to affect a decision" is to influence it. *Effect* often makes a sentence wordy or indirect. "To effect a decision" doesn't seem to me any better than "to decide."

Fewer, Less. The schoolroom distinction, that you use *few* to modify countable things and *less* to modify quantities, is still enunciated. Wilson Follett, indeed, says in his usage book that "fewer is by nature a word applicable to number." I have no notion what "by nature" means to him.

Actually, the rule never has reflected usage. The *Oxford English Dictionary* points out that the use of *less* to mean *fewer* is "now regarded as incorrect" but goes on to cite uses of *less* with countables from the ninth century on. I can't really account for my affection for the distinction, which seldom does much to clarify meaning. But I try to observe it, at least in writing, perhaps as minor snobbery.

And in some contexts I suspect that even I would use *less* with countables. For example, I would not say "Lunch will cost $10 fewer" or "The baby was fewer than three months old" or "Do twenty-five push-ups, not one fewer." I might write "The telegram may have twenty-five words or fewer," but I probably wouldn't say it.

Can, May. A distinction drummed into all schoolchildren is that *can* is used to express ability, *may* to express permission. The distinction is observed by careful writers but is frequently forgotten in speech—often with reason, since the school rule is not so easy to apply as it may seem.

One difficulty is that *may* and sometimes *can* also express possibility. "Walter may come to dinner" is ambiguous. Does it mean he has permission to come or that it is possible he will come? "Walter can come to dinner" probably means that he doesn't have another engagement. In "Can such things be true?" can is expressing possibility.

I'm not sure how much difference there is between "It can happen here" and "It may happen here." Perhaps the second suggests greater likelihood. In the negative we'd always use *can:* "It can't happen here."

In a question, *may* is usually used to ask permission: "May I come in?" But it is less common for a negative answer, probably because "No, you may not" seems more stuffy than "No, you can't." The negative form *mayn't* is increasingly rare. "Why can't I?" would almost always be preferred to "Why mayn't I?"

The distinction seems to me worth preserving, but literal application of the rule won't work. The person who asks "Can I leave my coat here?" sometimes gets a smart answer, "I suppose you're able to, but I don't know whether it's allowed." That kind of correction is not likely to make friends. People resent having their speech corrected, especially when they're wrong.

The past form of *may, might,* has come to signify a difference in probability more than in time (see also chapter 5). That is, *may* represents a situation or event as possible; *might* represents it as possible but not likely. Between "He may come" and "He might come," the first suggests the greater chance of his appearing.

That, Which. President Franklin D. Roosevelt's statement fifty years ago that December 7 is "a date which will live in infamy" is frequently misquoted. Journalists, vaguely recalling an old rule, make it "a date *that* will live in infamy." The overcorrection is based on a rule that *that* must always be used to introduce a clause that is restrictive or defining—that identifies or limits what it refers to. According to the rule, it should be "the money that I spent" not "the money which I spent; "the youngest man that ever qualified," not "the youngest man who ever qualified."

No one is quite sure when or why the rule was promulgated. For a long time *that* and *which* seem to have been used interchangeably. Notice the following from the King James (1611) Version of the Bible: "Render therefore unto Caesar the things which are Caesar's; and unto God the things that are God's." I'm sure there is no intent here to define a difference in authority between Caesar and God.

Early in this century, however, various writers on usage were advocating that only *that* should be used with a defining clause, although Fowler in the popular *Modern English Usage,* after enunciating the principle, observed that "it would be idle to pretend that it is the practice either of the most or of the best writers."

Jacques Barzun much later, in a 1975 book on usage, says, "I recommend using *that* with defining clauses, except when stylistic reasons interpose." But on the next page he starts a paragraph: "Next is a typical situation which a practiced writer corrects 'for style' virtually by reflex action."

Barzun's practice, rather than his rule, seems to fit current standard usage. Either *that* or *which* and *who* may be used with defining clauses, but *which* and *who* are standard with nonrestrictive clauses. Either "the book that I bought" or "the book which I bought" is standard; "the other book, which had been lying in the attic" is also standard, with a comma designating the nonrestrictive effect of the clause. The Lord's Prayer in the King James Bible addresses "Our Father which art in heaven." Modern translations sometimes change *which* to *who;* but there is no tendency to change it to *that.*

If, Whether. Rules about *if* and *whether* tend to be leaky. For instance, there is the attempt to exclude *if* from use to introduce a noun clause and to prefer *whether.* Sometimes *whether* is better, but it seems to me that this sentence of Thoreau is clearer as it stands: "One may almost doubt if the wisest man has learned anything of absolute value by living." *Whether* is possible, but *if* seems to me more accurate.

Another rule, that *whether* should always be used before alternatives, frequently makes sense. "I didn't know whether I should laugh or cry" leaves no doubt that either laughing or crying is involved, not both. In a different context either word might be used, with a possible distinction in meaning: "I didn't know whether I should order cake or pie" suggests that I am choosing one dessert. "I didn't know if I should order cake or pie" suggests that I am not sure that I want any dessert at all. Or I might write, "I don't know whether he is better or worse," emphasizing that I don't know which of two possibilities is right. I could write, "I don't know if he is better or worse," emphasizing that I have no information at all about his condition.

Still another attempt at a rule affects *whether* before alternatives. Some grammarians observed that "I wondered whether I should have dessert" implied but did not express alternatives. The alternative "or not have dessert" is not there. The solution was to express the alternative along with *whether:* "I wondered whether or not I should have dessert." The insistence on *whether or not* or *whether or no* never prevailed, but about half the Harper usage panel still feel the negative should be there.

Imply, Infer. The *Oxford English Dictionary* lists *imply* as a synonym for *infer,* and the two words have been used interchangeably for a long time. Many writers and grammarians, however, make a distinction, based partly on the ancestry of the words. *Imply* is from Latin *implicare,* to fold in, the same root that produced *implicate* and *implicit. Infer* is from Latin *inferre,* to carry in. Originally, *infer* meant to bring about, to cause.

Reflecting these origins, *imply* means primarily to have as a necessary part or condition: a deed implies a doer. From this developed a secondary meaning, to hint, to indicate without saying directly: "His statement implied that he would vote no." *Infer* is to conclude from evidence, by reasoning or guessing to make an inference: "From his statement I infer that he will vote no." The speaker implies; the listener infers. Implying is a sort of saying, inferring a sort of thinking.

The distinction is one of those with a good deal of snob value, but it is also useful and seems to me worth preserving.

Different From, Than, To. One of many schoolroom oversimplifications is the rule that *from* and not *than* should always follow *different*. Like most such rules it is partly right, but also misleading.

It is idiomatic, in the United States at least, to use *from* after *different* when it simply connects a noun with the rest of the sentence: "Blood is different from water" or "His view is different from mine." But in sentences in which the word after *different* introduces a clause or an understood clause, *than* is common: "Theater is different in America than in London" or "My brother is different than I am."

Furthermore, grammarian Otto Jesperson observes that *different* is often felt to be a kind of comparative; and since *than* is the usual word in comparisons ("Bill is older than his brother"), *than* is sometimes used as the preposition after *different*. Some writers might say not only "His need is greater than mine" but also "His need is different than mine."

Just to indicate that there is no divinely sanctioned rule on this, it should be noted that British usage is commonly *different to*.

Confusing Distinctions. Many other differences in meaning are being eroded by usage in spite of efforts to keep them clear. To *flaunt* is to display or show off something, sometimes defiantly or brazenly; to *flout* is to show contempt, to jeer, or mock. The words have been confused enough that current dictionaries recognize the use of *flout* to mean *flaunt*. A *principle* is a tenet, creed, rule of conduct. A *principal* is a name for somebody in authority, a school principal, or it can be the main amount of an investment or debt. To *jive* developed from jazz slang and can refer to playing some kinds of music or to chatting aimlessly. The word meaning to be in harmony with or to agree is *jibe*.

Wrangle goes back to German *rangen*, to struggle or make an uproar, and it means to dispute or quarrel. It also specialized in the American West to refer to management of horses. The word for getting something by scheming or manipulation is *wangle,* to wangle a job or a promotion. *Liable* can be restricted to mean subject to some change or action, usually undesirable: "You are liable to be arrested," that is "liable to arrest." *Likely* and *apt* are used to suggest probability: "You are likely to succeed if you try." *Ingenious* now means clever or resourceful; *ingenuous* is open or frank, sometimes naïve. *Disinterested* and *uninterested* were once synonyms, but now *disinterested* suggests impartiality, a lack of self-interest; *uninterested* is unconcerned, showing no interest.

Over, the *Oxford English Dictionary* records, has long been standard English meaning both in a physical position above and in greater quantity. There is, however, a persistent attempt by some users of the language to condemn "We drove over a thousand miles" and substitute *more than.* It is possible to make a distinction between *farther* and *further,* using *farther* when physical distance is involved and confining *further* to figurative uses. In practice, *further* seems to be taking over in both senses. *Complected,* as in "light-complected," is a frequently heard dialect confusion for *complexioned.*

Bishop Lowth in the preface to his grammar (I'm quoting from the 1786 edition) describes a prescriptive grammar: "The principal design of a Grammar of any Language is to teach us to express ourselves with propriety in that Language; and to enable us to judge of every phrase and form of construction, whether it be right or not. The plain way of doing this, is to lay down rules, and to illustrate them by examples." His proposal is attractive, practical for teaching and satisfying for those who want to know what's "correct." It is built on an unrealistic premise—that there is a correct grammar separate from the language itself—but probably nobody's use of language is greatly handicapped even by zealous avoidance of final prepositions.

The prescriptive approach, however, is too easy. It lulls users of the language into a false security and discourages thinking about how language actually works. I doubt that good writing is much encouraged just by attention to prescriptive rules—even those that do accurately describe how English works.

7

Nothing produces such an effect as a good platitude.
- Oscar Wilde, *An Ideal Husband*

The posteriors of this day; which the rude multitude call the afternoon.
- William Shakespeare, *Love's Labour's Lost*

Elegant English for You and I: Overcorrection

An honest tale speeds best being plainly told.
- William Shakespeare, *Richard III*

Fine words butter no parsnips.
- English Proverb

I observed the attractions of extra elegance in language at a fairly tender age. When the ladies of my mother's bridge club assembled, I was usually able to eavesdrop on the opening gambits. I was impressed especially by what I've since thought of as a bridge-club *did*. One would ask as a polite opening, "What have you been doing with yourself?" The answer would be perhaps "Oh, I haven't really did anything much." On other days of the week, an ordinary *haven't done* would have served, but for special occasions the usual speech habits were suspect.

I later discovered the origin of this particular bit of self-consciousness. My sixth-grade teacher, Miss Toole, had performed in this small town for years, teaching my mother's friends as well as me. She was a demon on verb forms. *Brought* not *brung, dragged* not *drug, knew* not *knowed*," she would intone. I still remember when a young man insisted in class that he didn't know "who done it." He got his hand walloped with a ruler—not because he really knew but because he had used *done* for *did*. He stayed after school to write fifty times on the board, "*did*, not *done*." Over the years Miss Toole managed to inspire through the entire town a firm mistrust of *done* in any circumstances.

I remember other early encounters with unfortunate attempts at elegance. On special occasions, cautious speakers felt well or badly, not good or bad. People worried about *ain't* used a rather self-satisfied *aren't I,* though it was never followed by *I are.* I remember some virtuoso effects in pronunciation inspired by the same teacher who had expunged *done* from two generations. *Tiusday* was more elegant than *Tuesday, niuw* than *new*. My favorite of these childhood experiences in the niceties of usage also reflects this teacher's concern for pronunciation—the importance of the careful enunciation of the suffix *-ing*. *Goin* was bad; *going* was good. It was *getting*, not *gittin; doing*, not *doin*. This instruction worked. At my uncle's dinner table on Sunday, especially if the minister was there, we ate not chicken, but chicking. We were not, however, called childring.

I'm sure that Miss Toole's shadow no longer hovers over that dinner table, but people still pursue elegance, and sometimes catch something else. For example, classroom comments on the virtues of *whom* echo dimly and prompt some speakers to overcorrect with *whom*s where they don't belong (see chapter 4). James Thurber, in *Ladies' and Gentlemen's Guide to Modern English Usage,* a spoof on Fowler's *A Dictionary of Modern English Usage,* observes facetiously that "*Whom* should be used in the nominative case only when a note of dignity or austerity is desired. For example, if a writer is dealing with a meeting of, say, the British cabinet, it would be better to have the Premier greet a new arrival, such as an under-secretary, with a 'Whom are you, anyways?' rather than a 'Who are you, anyways?' " Thurber's joke is not as absurd as it seems. Here's a travel brochure describing a London hotel and praising the concierge, "whom in my particular case knew all the answers." The hotel also has "a darling wine bar." Or, in the general confusion about *lie* and *lay* these days, with *lie* tending to disappear (see chapter 4), an attempt at elegance produces a friend who is "lain back" or a congressman who "lies a bill on the table." And there is a kind of politically elegant revival of the subjunctive for campaign speeches: "If this be the task before me, I gladly face it."

• **U and Non-U**

Questions of usage get all mixed up with questions of image and of people's attempts to create some kind of impression through their use of language. Vance Packard pointed out in the 1960s in *The Image*

Makers that choices of usage can be considered "class-designators," social labels. Efforts for a particular effect are not always successful. Attempts to sound like one of the boys may ring false; attempts to sound educated may sound stuffy or pedantic; attempts to sound sophisticated may turn out to sound pretentious or affected. Because choices are so difficult, people interested in language are always trying to work out systems or ways of predicting what kind of effect some expressions will have, what social level they designate.

One of these systems that caused some stir nearly forty years ago is still interesting, partly because it is specific enough that anyone can have opinions about its accuracy or value and partly because its conclusions seem outdated. A. S. C. Ross wrote an article in 1954 called "Linguistic Class Indicators in Present-Day English." Jessica Mitford reprinted it in *Noblesse Oblige*, where it got a lot of attention, much of it protest.

Ross asserts that three social classes exist in England: upper, middle, and lower. "It is solely by its language that the upper class is clearly marked off from the others," Ross contends. He creates the terms *U* and *non-U* to distinguish characteristically upper-class language (*U*) from the language of those who are not upper-class (*non-U*). Since we don't recognize classes in the United States, we perhaps have to substitute some kind of translation for U—*old-fashioned educated*, perhaps, or *old-fashioned elite*. Ross, of course, insists that neither of these is "superior," only that the differences exist.

I suppose it is true that distinctions like these still exist in America as well as England, and a look back at Ross's distinctions is interesting, mainly because it illustrates how difficult it is—and was in 1954—to be sure about specific expressions. If the U–non-U distinctions are right, many great writers from Chaucer to the present were non-U. For example, Ross classified *mirror* as non-U and *looking glass* as U. Mitford quotes Shakespeare's *Richard II*:

> An if my word be sterling yet in England,
> Let it command a mirror hither straight.

Bolingbroke replies:

> Go some of you and fetch a looking-glass.

Mitford comments: "It is probable that Richard II, like many monarchs, was non-U."

Here are other examples of distinctions Ross found in 1954: *Rich* is U; *wealthy* is non-U. *Writing paper* is U; *note paper* is non-U. *Lavatory paper* is U; *toilet paper* is non-U—which, somebody commented, makes all Americans non-U. *Wireless* is U; *radio* is non-U. *Jam* is U; *preserve* is non-U. *Table-napkin* is U; *serviette* is non-U. In a card game it is non-U to speak of the jack; *knave* is the U term. It is non-U *to take a bath,* U *to have one's bath.* It is clearly non-U to say "Cheers" before a drink. Many of these are exclusively British distinctions, and I suspect that most of them have disappeared—if they ever existed. But more recently some American equivalents have been suggested. Emily Post, for instance, includes some discussions of language fashions in her books on manners. On the word *drapes,* for example, she comments that "the word is an inexcusable vulgarism." She explains: "Curtains are hung at windows; hangings as decorations for walls." *Corsage,* she says, is "a word cherished by many, but distasteful to the fastidious, who prefer the phrase *flowers to wear.* I doubt that many people share these opinions, but some expressions used only in special circumstances do seem to me clearly attempts at some kind of elegance or propriety. An example is the word *wish* as it is often used by a waiter or a clerk in a store: "Do you wish cream with your coffee?" or "Do you wish to see some other samples?" Another is the sign in public restrooms: "Please cleanse your hands." *Cleanse* for handwashing seems to occur only in this situation, although I think I have heard dentists urging cleansing of teeth, also a little pretentious. *Beverage* seems natural enough as a heading on a printed menu, but it seems affected when a waiter asks what you prefer for a beverage. I remember from long ago a less common example of beverage gentility. I ordered whiskey in a small country bar in the Midwest, and the waitress asked me with special politeness what I'd "like for a rinse"—pronounced *rench.*

Here are suggestions put together by linguists Thomas Pyles and John Algeo a few years ago as American examples of U and non-U. The non-U speaker says *dentures;* the U speaker *false teeth.* The non-U speaker takes *medication* but may have to resort to *surgery;* the U speaker takes *medicine* and if it doesn't work has an *operation.* The U speaker shuns a non-U euphemism like *halitosis* and simply uses *bad breath*. Non-U are *perspire* for *sweat, pass away* for *die, powder room* for *toilet, mentally ill* for *insane, senior citizen* for *elderly person,* and *finalize* for *complete*. Pyles and Algeo suggest that these are or were at one time "characterized by pretension, subterfuge, vanity, or some other quality generally regarded among U speakers as mildly amusing or even somewhat reprehensible." These seem to me to provide material for endless arguments—in which I have no desire to participate.

They also provide hints about the kinds of blunders that can result from well-intentioned efforts to speak well. Attempts to sound sophisticated or proper may become only overcorrection or misguided snobbery. Even quite precise learned language may sometimes seem inappropriate. There's an old story about an Oxford don who greeted T. E. Lawrence on his return from London.

> "Was it very caliginous in the Metropolis?"
> "Somewhat caliginous," Lawrence replied, "but not altogether inspissated.

London had been only moderately foggy.

• How Do You Say It?

We tend to get stuffy about pronunciation, and there is no doubt that certain pronunciations are associated with prestige dialects and others with uneducated speech. In Shaw's "Pygmalion," later "My Fair Lady," Eliza Doolittle becomes a lady, not laidy, mainly by changing her pronunciation to that of a prestige dialect. *Hoof, roof, root,* and *soot* to rhyme with *goof* are probably regarded as classier than the common pronunciation with the vowel of *put. Either* that sounds like *eether* is the pronunciation in most of the United States west of the Hudson, but *eyether,* common in England, has been adopted in stage and much television English.

Two misconceptions are behind a good deal of our concern about pronunciation. One is the notion that there are "preferred" pronunciations dictated by dictionaries. Dictionaries are said to distinguish these by putting them first in the listing. This is pure myth. The dictionaries I happen to have in front of me put *eether* ahead of *eyether*, but this order makes no statement about preference. Dictionaries record; they do not dictate.

Another misconception is that the pronunciation should attempt to sound every letter in a written word. I remember in school being drilled to spit out the *ru* in *February* and to make distinct the *dnes* in *Wednesday*, not as a tribute to the Germanic god Woden, for whom the day was named, but in deference to the infallibility of the writing system. It's not easy to do, but I tried, and I still find myself making some effort toward the *ru* in *February*. We were taught to put a *you* sound in the middle of *news* and to be sure that *literature* had four syllables, the last pronounced *tyour*, not a sloppy *cher*. A similar affectation is the pronunciation of the final four letters of *permission* or *controversial* as two syllables—*seeun* or *seeal* rather than *shun* or *shul*. I still try for the first *r* in *surprise* and imagine that I'm sounding the *d* in *handkerchief*. People taking this view forget that sound precedes; written words are attempts to record sound, not guides for speech. And as spelling problems demonstrate, pronunciation often changes while the written record remains stable.

A number of individual quirks account for other variations in pronunciation. I knew one man, for instance, with a gift for metathesis who pronounced *debris* as *derbis* and called a tree shaped like a pyramid *primedal*. And I have known two people who reached adulthood, after long addiction to reading, pronouncing *misled* with the accent on the first syllable as *mizled*, the past form of a verb *to mizle*. Compromises between English and foreign patterns produce *chick* for *chic*, *pot poury* for *potpourri*, *gormay* for *gourmet*, and all sorts of things for *hors d'oeuvre* and *croissant*. *Amateur* has been pretty well assimilated, but dictionaries record several variations for the final syllable: *choor*, *tuhr*, *toor*, or *tyoor*.

Or pronunciation may reflect a kind of folk etymology, which may ultimately produce a new spelling; *duct* tape becomes *duck* tape. A similar example is the pronunciation *script* for *scrip*, based on confusion between the similar words. The confusion goes back a long way. *Scrip* was current in the seventeenth century, maybe altered from *script* or from *scrap,* to refer to a small piece of paper, a scrap. This became a word for small-value paper currency and then acquired its modern meaning as a certificate of a right to receive something—for example, a stock certificate. *Script* can refer to a style of writing or printing or to a written document.

I have preferences, based, I am sure, on some kind of snobbery. I prefer accenting the first syllables of *formidable* and *impotence,* even though other pronunciations are equally acceptable. I pronounce *finance* and *research* with the accent on the last syllable, probably because they sound more educated or sophisticated to me, but I'm not sure they sound so to other people. I say *joogular* vein, but I think the short *u* is more common. I was taught somewhere to say *cyoulinary,* but most members of the union call it *cullinary,* and I pronounce *err* as *ur,* but I'm sure *air* is commonly accepted. I can't, however, adopt *sheik* to rhyme with *lake,* although the British do, and Rudolph Valentino remains in my book the *sheik,* to rhyme with *seek,* of Araby.

Most of our pronunciations, including what we call our accent, come from our childhood, and early habits almost never totally disappear. My wife, who grew up in Connecticut, pronounced the word *tomahto;* I grew up in Indiana and said *tomayto.* Both our children say *tomayto,* not because of any male dominance in the family but because they grew up in the Middle West. We tend to develop loyalty to the pronunciations of our geographical area; speakers from other areas have accents. At one time there was some agreement that some ways of speaking were better than others. Teachers tended to push accents from around Boston, perhaps as being closer to British sounds. This notion has pretty much disappeared, but we still nurture our ethnocentrism. I remember from a few years ago a neighbor in the Middle West who criticized newcomers to the neighborhood: "Why, you know they say *you-all* and *we-all* instead of *you-uns* and *we-uns.*"

I have additional prejudices that I got from my journalist father, who had unqualified respect for the dictionary. He found *poinsettEEa* so pronounced in a dictionary, and I still pronounce two final syllables. I am similarly faithful on another flower, the clematis vine, which I stubbornly pronounce in the dictionary way with the accent on the first syllable, even though nursery workers correct me to *clemAtis.* I have more or less given up my father's *gladEYEola* in favor of the more common *gladiOla*. And I have given up pronouncing *cantaloupe* with the last syllable rhyming with *group*. I find the pronunciation in my 1910 dictionary but not in more recent ones.

There are, however, still deviations that seem to me genuine mispronunciations, likely to label a speaker as uneducated rather than just an old fogey or a speaker of another dialect. Here is a list of some favorites:

> *nucular* for *nuclear*—even though at least two presidents have said *nucular*
>> *realator* for *realtor*
>> *calvary* for *cavalry*
>> *irrevelant* for *irrelevant*
>> *larnyx* for *larynx*
>> *mischeevious* for *mischievous*
>> *enviorment* for *environment*
>> *deef* for *deaf*
>> *colyum* for *column*
>> *assessories* for *accessories*
>> *pronounciation* for *pronunciation*
>> *ekcetera* for *etcetera*

• Being Careful with *Me* and *Him*

When I answer a telephone inquiry and don't recognize the voice, I say, "This is he." But most of the time I do what most people do and say "It's me" or "That's her." The long schoolroom campaign invoking the authority of logic and Latin grammar to preserve the use of the subject form after a linking verb has pretty much lost to the pressures of word order. When the personal pronoun appears after the verb, even a linking verb like *is,* it appears in the spot usually occupied by an object. And the object form increasingly appears. On the rare occasions when I say "It is I," I sound like a schoolteacher.

We have not, however, given up logical patterns entirely, and we still tend to use the subject form when the pronoun after a linking verb is modified: "It was he who told me." I might also say "It was she standing on the corner," but *her* often would appear. Usage is equally varied in sentences involving a comparison: "My brother is older than I [or *me*]." The subject form has been prescribed here on the ground that it is subject of an understood clause, "I am." But again, the pressures of word order have been working, and "My brother is older than me" is common.

But the schoolroom efforts to preserve the old forms seem to have had an effect. They are apparently behind a currently widespread suspicion of *me* and *him* and *her*. Teachers warn about "It is me" and also about using *me* or *her* as a subject, "Him and her went deer hunting." And, at least partly as a result, *I, he,* and *she* turn up in all sorts of places where they have no reason to be.

The awkward sentences that try too hard almost always involve a pronoun in a pair, coordinated with a noun or another pronoun. Here are samples:

> Blank claims the alleged extortion was merely an attempt by he and John Doe to determine if Jane Doe was behind the conspiracy.
> It should be an interesting match, since this is the worst surface for both he and I.
> Just between you and I, she isn't telling all she knows.
> The hostess invited Alice and I to leave.

In all these sentences the object form of the pronoun would be standard. In the first three the pronoun is object of a preposition: *him* and *John Doe* after *by, him* and *me* after *for,* and *you* and *me* after *between.* In the fourth, *Alice* and *me* are objects of the verb *invited.*

An old rule of thumb works if you want to determine consciously which pronoun to use in sentences like those above. Leave out one of the pair, and the choice is clear. We would never say "an attempt by he to determine" or "worst surface for I" or "just between I" or "invited I to leave."

Overelegant *he* also occurs when it is not part of a pair in a sentence like this from a recent editorial: "Let he who has clean hands cast the first stone." The New Testament translators did not make the mistake: "He that is without sin among you, let him first cast a stone at her."

An obvious example of overcorrection is this from a recent newspaper column: "true love until death do we part." I cannot, however, quarrel with a usage I was reminded of by a revival of the movie version of *Gentlemen Prefer Blondes*. One blonde, played by Marilyn Monroe, reveals her desire to appear cultured with frequent references to things not suitable "for a girl like I."

For those who are faint-hearted about *me* or who have been told that it's immodest to use *I* too often, *myself* has become a popular cure-all:

> Joe and myself were the first to arrive.
> He promised to save tickets for Jenny and myself.

The standard use for *myself*, however, is as a so-called reflexive pronoun, one that turns back to repeat the subject: "I'd rather do it myself" or "I hurt myself." Used to avoid making a choice between *I* and *me, myself* is the coward's way out and usually sounds affected. The sentences above should use *I* and *me*.

The Harper dictionary usage panel is stuffy, but it seems justified in condemning, by 88 percent, this use of *myself*. The adjectives used by panel members to describe the usage are interesting: *fluffy, illiterate, delicate, ignorant, grotesquely formal*.

• How Does the Dog Smell?

Good is one frequently misused word that attracts attention. Teachers and editors are quick to jump on "He played good" or "You did good on the test" or "Walter done real good." They are right, of course. Sentences like the examples are using *good* as if it were an adverb, which it is not. The adverb corresponding to *good* is *well*.

It is possible to do good, in the sense in which a do-gooder accomplishes something. It is also possible to do well, meaning to profit in some way. Tom Lehrer's Old Dope Peddler is "doing well by doing good." But when simply a modifier of the verb is required, *well,* not *good,* is the word. "He worked well in the new environment," or "She played well through the first set."

As a result of all the fuss about misusing *good* instead of the adverb form, the word *good,* like the pronoun *me,* has become an object for suspicion. People recall that something about *good* causes trouble and find it safer to avoid the word. "I feel well" is considered more elegant, or perhaps safer, than "I feel good." And by analogy "I feel badly" is the form that accompanies the crooked little finger on the teacup.

The confusion with such sentences involves only a few words in one of the basic patterns of the sentence, a subject linked to an adjective that modifies it: "The rose is red." The verb *is* carries little meaning here, not even much of the verb's usual meaning to exist, but serves only to link *rose* and *red*. The sentence is not much different from "the red rose."

The verb *be* is the most common in these patterns, but a number of other verbs have come to act like the verb *be,* to function as linking words. We can say "The rose looks red" or "The rose seems red" or "The rose became red" or "The rose turned red." The usage problem is to determine whether the verb is being used as a linking word or as a regular action verb.

It's easy to tell with *be,* which is almost always linking, and with *become* and *seem,* which usually are. But *feel, smell, turn, look, stay, remain, taste, walk,* and others can be either linking words or action verbs. When it merely links or joins, we use an adjective after the verb: "The weather turned cooler" or "The soldier walked tall." When the word is used as an action verb, an adverb modifies it: "He turned the corner skillfully."

The verb *wax* I've noticed recently tempting some good writers to overelegance. Here's a syndicated columnist: "Nor does anyone wax lyrically today about the little people of America." *Wax* can describe an action and be modified by an adverb; the moon can seem to wax or wane slowly. But when *wax* is used to mean become or grow, it links a subject to an adjective. A speaker may wax eloquent, not eloquently.

The verbs conveying impressions of the senses seem behind most of the confusion: *see, hear, smell, taste, feel.* And these behave differently. *See* and *hear* do not work as linking verbs; *smell, taste,* and *feel* do. We can smell a rose or a rat or smell like a rose, and a rose can smell sweet. We can feel the heat or feel hot. We can taste an apple which tastes good.

Smell and *taste* can be used as nouns, but for *see* and *hear* we have *seeing* or *sight* and *hearing*. And we have words to express the absence of sight and hearing, *blindness* and *deafness*, but no words for a loss of smell or taste or feeling. *Look* and *sound* are linking verbs to parallel *see* and *hear*, when a characteristic of a subject is to be defined.

> The music sounds good when we hear well.
> The picture looks good when we see it clearly.

With these words the choice between adjective and adverb makes a difference in meaning. A dog that smells bad needs a bath; one that smells badly will never succeed as a bloodhound. A person who looks sharp dresses well; one who looks sharply is discerning. A person who tastes good would please a cannibal; a person who tastes well might have a future in judging wines. To act wise is to show off perhaps, to act smart; to act wisely is to make a good decision and proceed. To act stupid is to assume the manner of a simpleton; to act stupidly is the opposite of acting wisely.

Most of the usage questions with these equating sentences involve the verb *feel,* the adjectives *good, bad,* and *well,* and the adverbs *well* and *badly.* You can use *feel* as an active verb when you feel pressure or feel the softness of a loaf of bread. If you do a good job on the bread you can use an adverb to specify how you did the feeling, *skillfully* or *carefully* or *well.*

That's an unlikely meaning. Usually you use *feel* as a linking verb, to reveal awareness of your own sensations. You feel happy, not happily, sad not sadly, vigorous not vigorously, good or bad, not well or badly. Water can feel warm or cold, not warmly or coldly.

Although you usually feel good, when you are describing your general well-being you can also feel well if you mean that you are not ill or are cured. That is, *well* is not only an adverb, paralleling the adjective *good,* but it is also an adjective meaning in good health. "She is quite well" means that she is in good health or perhaps recovered from illness.

Usually, however, such sentences are not intended as reports on health but indications of a general attitude: "I feel good about her progress." "I feel bad about what's happened." "I feel good when I hear her play." There would be no question if we used other adjectives in those sentences: "I feel discouraged about what's happened." "I feel proud when I hear her play." We would never say *proudly*.

• **Fancy and Phony**

The sportswriter who produced the following was trying, perhaps too hard:

> He looked forward to spring training with eager anticipation, always expecting a plethora of promising material and a new atmosphere of optimism.

The sentence is clear, but it sounds phony, as if it were transmitting a formula rather than communicating. It relies on trite expressions and seems pretentious rather than clever. "With eager anticipation" is a set phrase that could be omitted without much loss of meaning. "Plethora of promising material" is a dated sports bromide.

Freshness and originality are worthy goals for a writer. New metaphors and unusual diction can be clever. But variations just to be different often do more to obscure than to brighten prose. One can, for example, understand the efforts of the sportswriter to vary day after day reports that one team has beaten another. Teams conquer, overwhelm, devastate, trounce, pulverize, flail, maul, batter, overcome, triumph, clobber, wallop, prevail, blow out, squeak past, edge, or eke out a victory. These may accurately define the nature of the win, but often they just exaggerate. Or notice entertainment writers hitting on an unusual word and overusing it until it becomes trite or pretentious: *segue* generalized from its use in music to mean follow in a sentence like "He segued across town"; or *venue* generalized from law to refer to the site of any event.

Trying to dress up writing with fancy diction almost always backfires—is counterproductive, to use a current fad word. Notice the following two sentences, which I constructed from a list of words that were being used over and over at the time I was writing:

The incremental parameters of marginal management with a responsive functional contingency program will facilitate the time-phase capability of reciprocally compatible conceptualizations.

Any scenario for a state-of-the-art commitment impacts on the bottom-line formulation of all viable throughput.

Unless I have slipped up, neither of these means anything at all, but at first glance they look like English and have some similarity to a good deal of the high-sounding writing that turns up these days.

Fashions in words, as in hemlines, are constantly changing, and some of the words in the nonsense above are already outworn. Writing that relies on repeating stock phrases is likely to sound stuffy or pretentious—often because it is repeating stock ideas. But it is not easy to generalize about the use of set expressions, to distinguish between success and failure in efforts to make writing clever and graceful. What is a cliché?

In the first place, we have hundreds of set expressions in the language—like "in the first place"—that we use over and over without thinking of them as trite. In fact, deviations from some formulas would sound strange—"butter and bread" instead of "bread and butter" or "eggs and ham." Conventions like "good morning" or even "have a nice day" are useful.

Furthermore, recognition of a cliché, like perception of irony, depends on the experience of the audience. Frank Sullivan, in the 1940s, did a series of *New Yorker* pieces in which he created a "cliché expert." One of these multiplies sportswriting clichés: the expert points out that when there is a tang of autumn in the air the pigskin sport will hold undisputed sway with throngs of rabid fans. Long ago, in an effort to explain clichés, I read the following conclusion of the piece to a writing class:

> Life is a game of football, Mr. Sullivan, and we the players. Some of us are elusive quarterbacks, some of us are only cheer leaders. Some of us are coaches and some of us are old grads, slightly the worse for wear, up in the stands. Some of us thump the people in front of us on the head in our excitement, some of us are the people who always get thumped. But the important thing to remember is—Play the Game!

The exercise didn't work. About 90 percent of the class made comments like "I certainly agree with Mr. Sullivan" or "What the author says teaches an important lesson." Partly, I suppose, the students had been conditioned to think that teachers would never make fun of a subject like football or life. Even if they were suspicious, they didn't want to rock the boat. But mainly they just hadn't read enough to recognize the staleness of both the language and the ideas. Triteness to one person may be cleverness to another.

Is "to rock the boat" in the paragraph above a cliché? It is not a fresh metaphor, but it seemed to me better than anything else at the time, and many such phrases are certainly not fresh or original but seem to work naturally in many contexts: "to put the cart before the horse," "the tail is wagging the dog," "out of the frying pan into the fire."

These were clever when they were first used and useful enough to become part of the standard language. Somehow they seem less trite than "busy as a bee" or "white as a sheet" or "clear as crystal" or "too cute for words," but I'm not sure why. The key is probably in the tone of the passage, whether it seems to be slipping into set expressions as a way of showing off or of avoiding direct statements.

An example that leaves no doubt is the following from Sinclair Lewis's *Arrowsmith*, in which Mr. Pickerbaugh talks about his jingles to sell health:

> You'll see how one of these efforts of mine just by having a good laugh and a punch and some melody in it, does gild the pill and make careless folks stop spitting on the sidewalk, and get out into God's great outdoors and get their lungs packed full of ozone and lead a real hairy-chested life.

The parody makes fun of Pickerbaugh's attempts to be clever or original—*ozone* for air—and to rely on automatic combinations of words like "God's great outdoors." Or he slips into "gild the pill," mixing two clichés, "gild the lily" and "sugar-coated pill."

The attempts at cleverness that fail most obviously are those like Pickerbaugh's that manage not only to rely on clichés but also to distort them somehow. In the following examples, from various sources, bromides get ludicrously tangled and dead metaphors unexpectedly revive:

I racked my brain back and forth over the problem.

She finally weathered the problem.

The girl had apparently taken part in the limelight of life when she was younger.

I don't want to jump the gun and be left out on a limb.

The sonnet says that since the man is about to die, the girl should love him up to the hilt.

Gonzales has had a lot of experience under his belt.

• Fancy Fillers and Pretentious Padding: Cereal in the Hamburger

Sometimes, I suppose, writers have reason to aim for obscurity. An official hoping to conceal embarrassing information or a politician trying to keep from taking a stand may want to sound informative without saying anything. A handy resource is the ready-made phrase that can be dropped in without much thought. George Orwell called these fillers jargon. They give prose more pomposity than clarity.

A current favorite, *in terms of,* will illustrate. Here are some samples from the press:

> . . . in France, where prices in terms of francs have risen.
>
> The Republican party in terms of numbers has fewer members than . . .
>
> Divorce wasn't something Kennedys were supposed to do, so in family terms she'd felt humiliated by that already.
>
> . . . the operation on Lin and Win was the most complicated ever performed, in terms of number of organs separated.

Term has extended from its earlier meaning, a limit or boundary, to designate a word or phrase with special significance to a science or discipline, as in "*cosine* is a term in trigonometry." So *in terms of* supposedly means something like "in the special language of the subject being discussed." The phrase, however, has become mainly a kind of filler. Usually it can just be omitted, as in the first and second sentences above. The third is a little different, but the phrase "in family terms" repeats the first part of the sentence and can be omitted. In the last example, *terms* is just the wrong word; there are no terms of numbers of organs. The sentence could be direct: ". . . the most complicated ever performed because so many organs were separated."

Fashions in jargon change, of course, but there are a few words that have long been favorites of jargon fanciers; it's a good idea to think before using one of them: *case, factor, character, condition, circumstances, situation, picture, line, persuasion, level, position, nature, variety, degree, type, outstanding, worthwhile.* Here are examples of ways to use them to make short stories long:

> He had been working in the real estate line for several years. [Why not just "in real estate"?]
>
> He came home in an intoxicated condition. [That is, he was drunk.]
>
> In the case of Jim, the field of mathematics was very difficult in nature. [Mathematics was hard for Jim.]
>
> The dangerous nature of the assignment made him lapse into a frightened condition. [The danger of the assignment frightened him.]
>
> After considering the inadequate housing picture, they took an opposing position on the legislation. [After considering the inadequate housing, they opposed the legislation.]
>
> She was a young type girl who liked clothes of a modern character. [She was a young girl who liked modern clothes.]

The following student sentence defies translation into English:

> There were several instances where Hamlet could have put the quietus on the king, but he failed to come through because the situations were not applicable to the circumstances in his case.

• Bondoony

Interest in being clever with language develops at an early age, and these observations on combining euphemism and cuteness began when I was informed by a four-year-old lady—with some scorn for my ignorance—that in her nursery school what you sit on is your bondoony.

I have not heard the word in other contexts; in fact I'm only guessing at a spelling, and this may be the first time the word has been written. It may have no currency beyond the young lady's nursery school, and I doubt that it will become part of the language. But it makes me think of various aspects of our interesting tendencies to create euphemisms and at the same time gently violate taboos for a kind of decorous humor.

Bondoony is part of an extensive vocabulary of names—with varying degrees of social acceptability—for parts of the human anatomy. And that part of the human anatomy designated by *bondoony*—the gluteal portion—seems especially susceptible to interesting labeling.

One reason, I suppose, is that this portion of the body houses functions that are usually considered private, and society resists open discussion of them. Another reason undoubtedly is that the bondoony has more potential for low comedy than any other body area. Human beings are easily afflicted with steatopygia, which readily inspires obvious jokes. The pratfall is basic to slapstick comedy. *Prat*, or *pratt*, of obscure origin, has been in the language since the sixteenth century.

There aren't many straightforward and also polite forms that will work, and one can see the need for *bondoony*. *Buttocks* and *rump* are perhaps the most likely, although I think that for some people they have at least an inelegant sound. *Gluteus maximus* provides a scientific name for the muscular content of the buttocks, but kicking someone in the gluteus maximus is not the same as attacking the rump or tail.

Several terms, depending on location or direction, are popular but not entirely satisfactory: *behind* and *bottom*, for example, or *rear end*. *Posterior* is clearly an attempt to cover some sort of embarrassment by using a learned-sounding word, but both it and *derriere* sound a little cute. *Fundament* is certainly not widely used or understood.

Bondoony, my four-year-old explained, is a substitute for *butt*, which was regarded as improper in her social circle. And I remember *butt* from my childhood as a taboo word. A line I recall as a triumph of third-grade cleverness, certain to make the girls giggle and blush, was "She's got freckles on her but she's pretty." Even worse than *butt* was *ass*, the American version of the old English word *arse*, created perhaps from the English tendency to print *arse* with a blank as *a-se*. One of the highlights of Sunday school was the story of Balaam, accompanied by much snickering and poking as we found the name of his animal actually printed in the lesson. The teacher's embarrassed substitution of *donkey* whenever possible didn't help matters.

Both the American *ass* and the British *arse* are still considered vulgar, at least, although they appear in print without restriction. In conversation they are only mildly naughty, especially when connected with horses or amalgamated in allegedly clever coinages like *bassackwards*. Politicians are considered macho rather than vulgar when they promise to "kick ass."

British *bum* existed in Middle English as a name for the buttocks. It is sometimes explained as a shortening of *botem,* meaning bottom; but the *Oxford English Dictionary* says firmly "not a contraction of *bottom.*" It may be an echoic word related to *bump* or *boom*. Shakespeare uses it as a neutral term, but about the end of the eighteenth century it began losing caste and is still considered mildly improper. It never has caught on in America, although a different word *bum*—apparently from German *bumler,* a loafer—has developed dozens of slang uses.

These words move in and out of respectability, sometimes fairly rapidly. As an example, I remember the saga of *boress*. When I was an undergraduate in one university some decades ago, a widely used but clearly taboo word was *boreass*. It could refer to a dull lecture, an uninteresting date, or what I think is now called goofing off. It's origin was obvious. When I returned there a few years later, the word had moved into total respectability. The broad utilitarian meaning had not changed, but the spelling had become *boress* to disguise its origin, and the student newspaper even produced an etymology tracing the word to a German root. So far as I know, the word never caught on outside that campus and is now happily extinct.

Both *bun* or *buns* and *fanny* remain gently humorous anatomical labels in America, although in England their earlier, more vulgar, associations persist. *Keister* or *keester* and *tush* or *tushie,* apparently adapted from Yiddish *tokhes,* have limited use. They don't solve the problems much better than the others. Perhaps there is a future for *bondoony.*

• *Jammies* and Other *Cozzies*

What really made me recall *bondoony* was a headline a few years ago proclaiming that "Jammies add luxury, touch of yuppiedom" to the

Reagan family "romantic evenings." I think it's fine for a president to wear lounging garb, but the head writer's use of *jammies* suggests the whole interesting business of euphemisms and diminutives like *bondoony*. When are they appropriate? Should an adult answer to "Poopsie"?

I react to some of them irrationally. For example, I tend to lose my appetite—even though I'm fond of raw vegetables—when I'm offered a plate of carrot sticks and celery with "Won't you try the veggies?" It seems worse when they are "these lovely veggies," which seems somehow to imply that I am incapable of appreciating them on their own merits. My mail as I write this offers me a magazine called *Veggie Life* for $14.97 a year. I am not subscribing.

My real question is one of appropriateness, whether it's in character for one grown person to address another in cutesy terms—whether doing it suggests something about the adult. I have no objection to telling a child to put on his jammies or woolies or nightie and go potty and then beddy-bye. I'm spelling it *bye* on the assumption that it has something to do with *bye-bye* and *bye-baby*.

Tummy, like *potty,* started as a euphemism, when all direct references to one's anatomy were suspect—*belly* was worse than *stomach*—but *tummy* survives mainly as baby talk, used by adults partly humorously. *Tum tum,* used with whimsical affection in the song "Button Up Your Overcoat"—"or you'll get a pain and ruin your tum tum"—is actually a Chinook word referring to the beating of the heart. It came into the language in the eighteenth century to mean heart or mind. I'm not sure of the implications of *bod* for *body*. I suppose it's mildly humorous praise in "What a bod!" But there may be a tinge of euphemism even here, from delicacy about any anatomical reference.

Terms like these, basically affectional diminutives, are relatively uncommon in English. Compare, for instance, Italian, with its *-ino* and *-etto* and *-ello* suffixes. The most common English suffix is *-y*, used with names like *Billy* or *Dickie* but also with words intended for talk with children, *birdie* or *auntie*. Suffixes *-let* and *-ling* have only limited use, *leaflet* or *gosling*.

We do a lot of abbreviating, however, which is partly a matter of efficiency but which may also suggest affection, or at least familiarity, as with car owners who may have a *Jag* or a *Caddy* or a just a *Chevy*. On the other hand, *vac* for a vacuum cleaner may reveal latent contempt or resentment. *Sax* for saxophone is almost standard. *Mag* is a little less respectful than *magazine*. *Cig* for *cigarette* seems to have gone out of fashion.

Some abbreviations go back a long way and have shifted meaning over the years. *Hussy* appeared in the early sixteenth century as an innocent slurred pronunciation of *housewife*. By the seventeenth century it had started to take on its modern meaning as an uncomplimentary way of addressing a woman. *Middy*, a shortening of *midshipman*, has become almost entirely restricted to a blouse modeled on naval garb. *Bunk*, a shortening of *buncombe*, seems just a more direct expression of the longer word. *Buncombe* originated in the speaking habits of congressional representatives from Buncombe County, North Carolina.

Curiously, the English, whom we usually think of as conservative, even stuffy, about their language, seem more devoted to cute abbreviations and diminutives than Americans. Many of their words never catch on in the United States, but American news magazines have at least for a while taken over *twee*, which developed as British slang early in this century to mean dainty or elegant or affectedly chic. Apparently it originated as a baby-talk version of *sweet*.

Lolly, abbreviated in the middle of the nineteenth century from *lollipop*, is the common English word for candy. It is not much used in the United States, nor is *pram*, from *perambulator*. *Telly* for *television* is used in America, but it always sounds a little self-conscious, as does *din-din* for dinner or *mummy* or *mum* or *muzzy* for *mother*. Americans of course have *tube*, which may reflect some kind of awareness of technology, and *boob tube*, and *mom* or *mommy*. As terms of endearment, *ducky* or *ducks* goes back to Shakespeare's time and *pigsney* to Chaucer's.

Australian creations often out-English the English. *To perve*, meaning to look at someone libidinously, perhaps comes from *pervert*. A shortening of *cockatoo* to *cockie* has become a name for a farmer. Other Australian diminutives are *footy* for *football*, *mozzy* implying unintended affection for a mosquito, or *cozzy*, a bathing suit, abbreviated from *swimming costume*.

8

The Writing System: Conventions

What custom wills, in all things should we do't.
- **William Shakespeare, *Coriolanus***

Custom reconciles us to everything.
- **Edmund Burke, *A Philosophical Enquiry into the Sublime and Beautiful***

They spell it Vinci and pronounce it Vinchy. Foreigners always spell better than they pronounce.
- **Mark Twain, *The Innocents Abroad***

Language works by agreement. People agree that they will designate a four-legged animal with a corkscrew tail with the word *pig* rather than *ostrich*. There's usually no clearly discernible reason why we should agree on one word instead of another. Most of these choices were made long ago, and sometimes we can guess at a reason. *Whisper* may have prevailed because it sounds like what it denotes, but it goes back to an Indo-European root, **kwei,* which isn't clearly onomatopoeic. And we can see various ways in which new words are created, often out of old ones. But the association of any given word with its meaning, as well as the way it is pronounced, is arbitrary. It communicates only because users of the language agree on what a dictionary records.

For languages that have a writing system—and most live languages do—some additional arbitrary agreements are necessary. A language must agree on what written symbols will be used to convey the sounds of the language. Modern languages have developed alphabets, more sophisticated than, say, signs for words. There is nothing certain or consistent, however, about how the alphabet is related to the sounds of English, and the spellings that have been adopted are often illogical. The writing system also includes conventions in punctuation and typography that are inconsistent and arbitrary.

Not all people, of course, agree on the same words or same conventions. French and Germans don't agree to call that animal a pig, but use *cochon* and *schwein*. The same English word may have quite different pronunciations in Texas and Yorkshire and Oxford and Australia and Chicago. The English spell *labour* and *harbour* with a *u;* Americans don't. We start to write at the upper left corner of a page and proceed from left to right horizontally. But in some languages writing starts at the lower right corner. Punctuation conventions differ. English publishers mark a quotation with a single inverted comma; Americans use two inverted commas. Book publishers and newspapers differ in punctuation styles.

These agreements, especially the arbitrary conventions, may be complex, and users of the language sometimes are unsure about what they are. Dialect differences in pronunciation can evoke arguments as people defend their habits. Arbitrary spelling and punctuation conventions have to be learned, and not everybody learns them. The following comments do not attempt any comprehensive description of conventions—this is not a style book—but rather they discuss a few of the problems of dealing with conventions.

• **How Do You Spell *Fish?***

There's an old schoolroom joke that goes, "Do you know how to spell fish?" The answer is, "Sure, g-h-o-t-i—*gh* as in *rough, o* as in *women,* and *ti* as in *nation*. English spelling is not consistent. Most of the inconsistencies, however, can be explained, although that doesn't make them any easier to deal with.

Language develops as speech; a writing system follows. Spelling or orthography is just a way of recording sounds with agreed-upon symbols. The shorthand we use to teach a child to read—what does *b* or *s* say?—is useful for teaching, but theoretically it has the cart and horse reversed. More accurately, one would ask how to record the first sound in the word *bad,* and the answer is the letter *b.*

English has been written for a long time, but not until the introduction of printing into England did the need for standardized spelling become apparent. Writers and printers did not all follow the same system or any system. Spelling varied among writers, and often what appeared in print depended mainly on the whims of printers, who did a good deal to regularize spelling but also a good deal to confuse it.

One striking example of the inconsistency is a pamphlet by dramatist Robert Greene, *A Notable Discovery of Cozenage,* published in 1591. The pamphlet, like a modern sensational tabloid, was an alleged exposé of cony-catching, swindling or cheating. *Cony*—in modern slang it would be *pigeon*—is spelled *cony, coney, conny, conye, conie, connie, coni, cuny, cunny,* and *cunnie.* The pamphlet also contains five variants of the word *fellow: fellow, felow, felowe, fallow,* and *fallowe.*

By the middle of the seventeenth century, English spelling had become relatively stable, but it was no more consistent then than it is now. Confusions had various origins. For example, Old French provided ways of recording some sounds, but they were used only part of the time. The letters *gu* were used in French to denote the so-called hard sound of *g* before *e* and *i.* The English retained it in French words they adopted, but they also applied the spelling to words already in the language: *guide, guise, guess, guilt, tongue* and even *guard,* although the French spell it *gard.*

Scholars also complicated matters in an effort to preserve the authority of Latin and put a useless *b* in *debt* and *doubt* in deference to Latin *debita* and *dubito,* even though the words had been written earlier in English as they had been taken from the French, *dette* and *doute.*

Other variations survive from different ways of indicating whether vowel sounds are long or short. Sir John Cheke had a consistent system of doubling long vowels—*taak, haat, maad, miin, thiin* for *take, hate, made, mine,* and *thine.* His system never caught on, but the use of a final *e* to indicate a long vowel, or the doubling of the consonant to indicate a short vowel, did survive—sometimes. And then some of the short vowels changed to long in their pronunciation, and we have spellings like *roll* and *toll* as well as *staff* and *glass.*

Toll and *roll* survived because spelling, once it is set, is much less flexible than pronunciation. The written word is preserved in print in spite of changes in sound. When *colonel,* to take a common example, was adopted by the English from the French at the end of the sixteenth century, it was pronounced as three syllables. The spelling accurately recorded the sound. But as the word was used by the English, who are fond of dropping an occasional syllable, it shifted to sound like *kernel,* so that now the spelling seems—and probably is—illogical. The British have done the same thing with some proper names; *Worcester* is pronounced "Wooster" and *Cholomondeley,* "Chumly." The pronunciations that were represented by *gh* in *slough, rough,* and *ought,* have disappeared, but the spellings remain.

Actually, our system is not as bad as it seems. In 1966 a government publication reported—in 1,716 pages—the results of a Stanford University project to study the correspondence in English between sounds and letters. An oversimplification of what the study and its computers revealed is that English spelling is much less inconsistent than we usually assume and that we can learn to spell a great proportion of the words in the language by learning which symbols are customarily used to designate which sounds. About 90 percent of the words in the language are spelled consistently. The other 10 percent, however, are inconsistent enough to cause a good deal of trouble, and there have been protests and attempts at reform since the sixteenth century.

• Spelling Reform

Explaining the origin of spellings like *knife* or *thought* or *psyche* does not make spelling easier for fourth-graders or depress the market for computer software spelling correctors. Everyone seems to agree that reform would be good, but for four centuries proposals have played to unresponsive audiences.

One of the earliest and most comprehensive efforts was Richard Mulcaster's 1582 treatise. It included a list of seven thousand common words with the spellings he recommended, some reformed. He recommended, for example, omitting the *u* in words like *guise, guide,* or *guest.* The proposal—and most of his other reforms—never caught on. Nor did the recommendations of Richard Hodges, who proposed, sixty years later, that we drop an unnecessary consonant and write *al, bal, hal, wal, cal, chaf, bras,* and so on.

Early in the eighteenth century Jonathan Swift proposed, on the model of the French Academy, a group of persons "best qualified for such a work" to deal with all sorts of problems in the language. They were to correct the defective grammar, eliminate "gross improprieties," throw out useless words, and then insure that the "correct language should last, although it might be enlarged." Although it created a stir at the time, Swift's proposal was never adopted, and there has never since been a serious attempt to establish an English Academy.

Proposals for reform have continued, by formal societies and individual writers, often attempting the same changes as those proposed centuries before. Benjamin Franklin proposed adding letters to the alphabet to allow more consistent spelling, and he even had a special font of type cut to implement his system. It never worked. George Bernard Shaw left a bequest in his will to support research into reforming spelling, but no reform has occurred. In 1898, the National Education Association adopted a dozen simplified spellings, a couple of which, *catalog* and *program*, are accepted today, at least as alternatives. Most of them have not been accepted: *altho, prolog, demagog, thoro.*

In 1935 the *Chicago Tribune* adopted a number of reformed spellings—*hocky, staf, skilful, crum, missil, yern,* and so on. Some readers applauded and some objected; the reforms were dropped. As recently as 1988, the *Washington Post* gave up on a logical simplification that had been for ten years in its style book, *employe,* with a single final *e.* The paper announced its decision because "loss of that *e* still enrages a substantial part of our population."

Noah Webster's widely popular dictionaries and spelling books did establish a few simplifications in American English, although earlier forms persisted across the Atlantic—*color* and *honor* rather than British *colour* and *honour,* and *ax, plow, tire,* and *jail* rather than *axe, plough, tyre,* and *gaol.*

And there have been carefully developed systems to make English more suitable as an international language. Here is the beginning of Lincoln's Gettysburg Address in Anglic, proposed about 1930:

> Forskor and sevn yeerz agoe our fadherz braut forth on this kontinent a nue naeshon, konseevd in liberti, and dedikaeted to the propozishon that aul men are kreaeted eequel.

This is easily read and more consistent than conventional spelling, but it has not been adopted. And there are potent reasons suggesting that significant change is not likely to occur: the difficulties of coping with change and keeping any system up to date, the fact that a new system would make thousands of printed volumes obsolete, the fact than no clearly perfect system has been devised, and possibly the fact that those who have learned conventional spelling are reluctant to spare a new generation from the discipline.

• Silent Letter *E*

I don't know how people learn to spell. Some people seem to get the hang of it very early, and I'm always impressed when moppets in a spelling bee confidently toss out *phylaxis* or *syzygy* or some other favorite they probably will never use. For a lot of adults and near adults spelling seems difficult. And the difficulties are compounded in a variety of ways, among them the behavior of words with silent letters, especially *es*.

The letter *e* is frequently used in English spelling not to represent a sound but to indicate something about other sounds in the word. For example, a final *e* often signals that the vowel preceding it should have a long sound: *mate, rote, rite, cute, cede.* This isn't always true, however, and words with short vowels sometimes end with a silent *e*, but it works often enough to be important. The main spelling problems with silent *e* occur when a suffix is added to a word. Does the *e* stay or go?

Judgment or *judgement* is a good example. There is a rule that applies here, one of the few spelling rules not made useless by exceptions. A silent *e* is usually dropped before an ending beginning with a vowel and retained before an ending beginning with a consonant: *love, lovely; care, careful; nine, ninety;* but *love, loving; care, caring; dine, dining.* There are exceptions, but they usually follow patterns. If the *e* is preceded by a vowel, it is usually dropped before any ending: *true, truly; argue, argument.* If the silent *e* appears after a soft *g* or *c* sound, it is usually retained even before a vowel: *notice, noticeable; courage, courageous.*

Judgement, with the silent *e* retained before the consonant that begins the ending, fits the rule. This is the older spelling of the word. But current dictionaries list both spellings, with usage seeming to prefer the older spelling with the *e* in England and *judgment* without the *e* in America. *Likeable* and *likable* are also alternatives.

• **The Sounds of *K* and *S***

There are thirteen different ways in English to record the sound most obviously signaled by the letter *k: c* in *cab, cc* in *accuse, k* in *keep, lk* in *talk, ch* in *chorus, ck* in *crack, kh* in *khaki, cq* in *acquiesce, q* in *liquid, qu* in *bouquet, sc* in *viscount,* and *x* in *exit.* Some of these spellings reflect the foreign origin of a word.

The sound of *s,* however, can be written in only nine ways, and *cc* is not one of those, although *c* is. The letter *s,* according to the elaborate Stanford study mentioned above, is used 72.09 percent of the time for this sound, and the single *c* 16.85 percent of the time. For the *k* sound, the single letter *c* is used in 73.25 percent of the words, and the double *cc* in only 1.61 percent, although that percentage is 76 words of those examined.

I'm not sure that all this provides much comfort for spellers. It does suggest that if one has trouble with these spellings, the thing to work on is the relatively small list of *cc* words, most of which use the spelling for historical reasons. *Occur,* for example, comes from Latin *currere,* to run, plus the prefix *ob-,* which changed to *oc-* before *c. Accuse, accommodate, accord,* and *accomplish* all contain the Latin prefix *ad-* changed to *ac-.*

• **Compounds**

When should two related words be combined as one, when written separately, and when joined with a hyphen? As a general pattern, when related words are used together, they start as separate words; then as they appear more frequently together they are hyphenated; and eventually many combinations become a single word. The language, however, is far from consistent in following this pattern. It's hard to see the logic of some dictionary entries. Why, for example, should it be *post office* and *post road* and *post horse* but *courthouse* and *postmaster* and *postmark?* Why *high school* but *highroad, pitch pipe* but *pitchfork?*

It's probably too late to do anything about the inconsistencies that seem established, like *nightcap, nighthawk,* and *nightspot* but *night robe, night owl,* and *night club.* But it is worth while considering some of the ways in which spelling signals meaning in compounds, especially ways in which the hyphen can be useful. Two general patterns are worth observing.

First, compound adjectives and verbs are regularly hyphenated, and it makes sense to follow that procedure. A *high school building* is a school building with many stories. Usually when we use the phrase we mean a *high-school building*—that is, a building that houses a high school. An *old car salesman* differs from an *old-car salesman,* the first commenting on the salesman's age. An *Oriental rug dealer* is different from an *oriental-rug dealer.* A *green vegetable grower* is inexperienced; a *green-vegetable grower* produces lettuce. Even when there is no possibility of ambiguity, compound adjectives are hyphenated in standard writing: *seventeenth-century history, seven-foot fall, do-it-yourself kit, pay-as-you-go taxes.*

The other general pattern is that when the second part is stressed, a compound is written as two words. If the first part is stressed, the compound is hyphenated or written as one word. An antique lover, with *lover* stressed, is getting on in years; an antique-lover likes old furniture. A model-agency finds jobs for models; a model agency is an agency to be admired. A French-teacher teaches French; a French teacher was born in France.

Two compounds are interesting enough for special attention, *alright* and *worthwhile. Alright* has been in use for a long time, but it is still labeled "unacceptable" in many handbooks, although the *Oxford English Dictionary* puts no restriction on its use. It does allow a useful distinction in meaning. In speech if we say "his answers are all right," we indicate by stress whether we mean that they were all correct or mean that they were generally acceptable. In writing, the same statement is ambiguous, unless we use *alright* for the second meaning. British slang writes two words in "She's a bit of all right." American English uses a hyphen for a similar meaning in "He's an all-right guy."

Worthwhile and *worth while* also are frequently distinguished in usage. *While* developed as a noun referring to a period of time, "I'll be here only a short while," or "It's hardly worth my while." Phrases like this were shortened to *worth while*, and then an adjective *worthwhile*. *Worthwhile* is generally used before a noun and *worth while* after: "A worthwhile job is worth while."

• Homonyms

English has a considerable number of homonyms, sets of words that sound alike but have different meanings and often are spelled differently. It's easy to confuse the ones with different spellings.

The set most frequently confused is illustrated in the old gag: How do you write this sentence: "There are three *to*s [or *two*s or *too*s] in the English language? The same problem, of course, would exist for any group of homonyms.

To, two, and *too* are quite different words, although *to* and *too* have the same origin in Old English. *To,* however, is the preposition, with a considerable variety of uses, from indicating direction, "going to Boston," to preceding a verb to form an infinitive, "wanting to scream." *To* is occasionally used as an adverb, as in "He rocked to and fro." *Too,* however, is the standard adverbial form of the word, used to indicate an addition, like *plus,* "The students spoke too," and to indicate an excess, "too much, too many, too late." *Two,* the number, comes from a different Anglo Saxon word, *twa,* which produced other modern words with a numerical sense: *twain,* and *twin,* for example. *Twig* also comes from *twa,* presumably referring to the forking of a twig; *twine* names the cord produced when two strands are twisted together.

There are many other groups of homonyms in English, some of them confusing. I think of only one quartet: *right, rite, write,* and *wright.* These are all different words, with different origins: *right* from Old English *riht,* direct; *rite* from Latin *ritus,* a ceremony; *wright* from Old English *wyrcan,* to work; and *write* from Old English *writan,* to scratch. There are many trios: *sent, scent, cent; flew, flu, flue; meat, meet, mete; sight, site, cite; so, sew, sow;* and more. And there are many pairs, some of them frequently confused: *pour, pore; peal, peel; style, stile; pain, pane; fair, fare; fete, fate.*

The homonyms that are different words but are both pronounced and spelled the same way don't cause trouble, but they are interesting. *Pole* as in a tent pole comes from Old English *pol,* meaning stake; *pole,* as in the north pole, comes from Greek *polus,* axis of the sphere. *Bark,* what a dog does, comes from Old English *beorcan,* probably an imitation of the sound. *Bark,* the skin of a tree, goes back to Old Norse *borkr,* meaning to take the bark off a tree. There is also a differently spelled homonym, *barque,* from Latin *barca,* a small boat.

• Demons

There is one perfectly logical theory about improving spelling. That is, surveys all seem to point out that a very few words account for most of the spelling errors that people make. Therefore, it is logical that memorizing a hundred or so irregular spellings will eliminate most errors. The plan doesn't seem to work very often. Even people who memorize the list perfectly don't always remember when they need the word. But here is a shortened list of words frequently misspelled: *their, there, they're, its, it's, two, to, too, receive, existence, occurred, definite, believe, lose, benefit, experience, seize, embarrass,* and *liquefy.*

Sometimes it helps with frequently misspelled words to know how they got the way they are. *Separate* owes that *a* to its root, the Latin *parare,* to arrange. *Innuendo* and *innocuous* have a double *n* in the first syllable, reflecting the merging of the prefix *in-* with roots beginning with *n.* But *inoculate* puts the prefix *in-* before *oculus,* Latin for eye. *Straightjacket* for *straitjacket* reflects a misconception about meaning; the word *strait* means narrow or strict or rigid, as to be "in desperate straits." *Strait-laced* once referred literally to the state of a woman's corset. *Sacrilegious* gets misspelled from the mistaken notion that it is formed from *religious* instead of *sacrilege.*

• Borrowed Plurals

The English language has been the most active borrower in history, but we aren't consistent in handling what we acquire. Plurals from other languages cause confusion. Among those especially difficult are plurals of words like *medium* and *datum* and *agendum* (see chapter 4). The plurals of these Latin words are formed with the ending *-a*, and we have retained the Latin spellings: *media, data, agenda*. The difficulty is that these forms have become so common that their singular forms have almost disappeared. Although formal style requires that *data* take a plural verb, it is more and more thought of as singular. *Agenda* is no longer thought of as plural things to be done but as a singular list of things. And we have developed an anglicized plural, *agendas*. *Candelabra*, the plural for *candelabrum*, is similar. It was used for ornate branched candlesticks; the singular disappeared and we use the singular with an anglicized plural *candelabras*.

For a few of the *-um* Latin words, however, we retain the Latin plural: *curricula* for *curriculum, errata* for *erratum, bacteria* for *bacterium, addenda* for *addendum, strata* for *stratum*. A number of others seem to be in transition, and we have both the Latin plural in *-a* and the English in *-s: stadia* or *stadiums, memoranda* or *memorandums, referenda* or *referendums*. And many have become completely anglicized, with only *-s* plurals: *asylums, museums, linoleums, pendulums, premiums, geraniums*.

A small group of words ending in *-s* keep Greek plural forms: *axis-axes, crisis-crises, analysis-analyses, basis-bases, thesis-theses, hypothesis-hypotheses*. For these, English plurals would create an unpleasant string of *s* sounds. Two Greek plurals of another sort have resisted anglicizing: *criterion-criteria, phenomenon-phenomena*. And *stigma* from the Greek has both the English *stigmas* and Greek *stigmata*. Words from Greek ending in *-x* usually have both plurals: *appendix–appendices* or *appendixes, index–indices* or *indexes*. *Seraph* and *cherub* are of Hebrew origin, and the biblical plurals, *seraphim* and *cherubim*, survive, even though *-s* plurals have developed.

Latin words ending in *-us* and *-a* have developed inconsistently, although some words with scholarly associations have kept Latin plurals: *nebulae* and *larvae*, and *formulae* in scientific settings. We have both *radii* and *radiuses*, *syllabi* and *syllabuses*. For words to designate graduates of an academic institution, we get thoroughly confused. We keep two Latin words with a gender distinction—*alumnus*, masculine, and *alumna*, feminine—with their Latin plurals, *alumni* and *alumnae*. But we usually pronounce the two plural forms alike, with the final sound as in *eye*, and the gender distinction disappears.

• **Articles:** *A, An, The*

There's a difference among *truth, a truth,* and *the truth*. Articles, words that introduce nouns, can be used to produce shades of meaning in different contexts. The differences are not always obvious, and there are problems.

One of these is the distinction between *a* and *an*, which is a simple matter of pronunciation. *An*, a form of *one*, existed before *a*. It was shortened to *a* because it was hard to pronounce *an* before a consonant, and the *n* dropped off. So we now use *a* before a consonant sound and *an* before a vowel sound.

The use of *an* before the *h* in words like *historical* or *humble* is a relic of a time when the *h* was considered silent. An before *h* sounds affected today, especially when the *an* is used before *h* sounds that were never silent.

A or *an* is called the indefinite article, but it is not really indefinite; it often distinguishes a definite but unspecified individual: *a book I read* or *a piece of candy*. To be clearly indefinite, we would use *any: any book I read* or *any piece of candy*.

The, called the definite article, defines, tends to make a noun more specific. There is a difference between "She married the nephew of the king" and "She married a nephew of the king." The first implies that the king has only one nephew. The distinction between *the man in the street* and *a man in the street* is less obvious, but the indefinite article, *a*, seems to make the more nearly definite designation. The first version, with *the*, is much like *any man on the street*. It is like *the average car buyer* or *the person who likes quiche*.

A noun with *the* is identified in a previous sentence or by an immediately following modifier. We can say *the man next door* because *next door* identifies. If we start a passage with "The man came up to me and spoke," we are idiomatic only if the man has been introduced in a previous passage. Without such identification we would use *a*.

When no article at all is used, the noun tends to refer to an entire class or an abstraction. "Money is tainted" condemns all money. "The money is tainted" refers to a particular quantity of cash that has been identified in previous sentences.

• Punctuating for Confusion:
Errant Commas, Including Inverted Ones

Punctuation has developed as a convention to help in understanding the written version of the language, which lacks devices of speech like stress and pauses. It has existed in one form or another for centuries, used in manuscripts before the invention of printing, but current conventions are relatively modern.

William Caxton, England's first printer, who set up his press in England in 1476, relied almost exclusively on a single mark, a slash (/) that marked pauses, without much consistency. During the sixteenth century, punctuation began to look much as it does today; most of the modern marks appeared. Most of the punctuation, however, was rhetorical. That is, marks or "points" were thought of as stage directions for speaking, locating pauses. Punctuation, therefore, was likely to be unpredictable, depending in great measure on the whims of the writer, or often of the printer.

Even during the sixteenth and seventeenth centuries, however, Ben Jonson and others were advocating standardized patterns of punctuation, designed to clarify the grammatical structure of the sentence. And today, although punctuation marks and pauses often coincide, the marks theoretically clarify sentence structure according to general rules.

Modern punctuation is either arbitrary and conventional—like commas in addresses—or it is supposed to keep the main sentence pattern flowing and to set off anything that might interrupt that flow. Writers and publishers exhibit a good deal of individuality in the way they use punctuation for those purposes, differing even in their attitudes toward standard conventions, or sometimes using punctuation to try for special effects. The following are only a few of the kinds of questions that keep coming up as people worry about punctuation.

• Restrictive and Nonrestrictive

One of the so-called rules of punctuation makes some sense. It proposes that any expression that is not essential to the meaning of the central sentence pattern, that merely provides incidental information, should be set off by commas. The idea is that this clarifies the main message of the sentence.

It's not always easy to decide whether an expression is essential or not, and another way to look at the rule is to observe that it is a way in which a writer can clarify intent, can show whether an insertion is intended to be limiting. Consider this sentence:

> The newspapers which had been competing for morning circulation were closed by the strike.

The question is whether to put commas before and after the clause *which . . . circulation*. The answer depends on what you mean. As it stands, with no commas, the clause identifies the newspapers and distinguishes them from other newspapers. (With this meaning some writers would prefer *that* rather than *which*. See chapter 6.) The modifier is restrictive. Only those newspapers competing were closed. With commas after *newspapers* and *circulation*, the meaning changes. We assume that the papers have already been identified, and the clause supplies additional information about them.

Here's another sentence involving a choice:

> All the officers who had gone to the briefing were killed in the explosion.

Commas determine how many officers were killed. With no commas, the sentence says that only the officers in the briefing room were killed.

With commas after *officers* and *briefing,* the sentence says that all the officers went to the briefing and all of them were killed. Usually the choice is easy, as in this sentence:

> My mother, who still had a powerful voice, went to the door and shouted.

The modifier is obviously intended to be nonrestrictive; it is unlikely that the writer had more than one mother.

Although this punctuation is devised to clarify the grammar rather than provide stage directions, it does coincide with speech devices. To speak the sentence above without commas, we'd raise pitch on *voice* and pause slightly after it, but we'd not pause earlier in the sentence. To speak it as it stands with the commas, we'd raise pitch on the first syllable of *mother,* lower it on *voice,* and pause after both *mother* and *voice.*

• Ornamental Quotation Marks

One of my favorite signs appears on a motel, WHERE YOU CAN "SLEEP" UNDISTURBED. The sign maker apparently thought that the quotation marks provided some kind of distinction. Actually, the effect is the opposite, suggesting that the word is used ironically and that what you are invited to do there is not literally sleep. I received recently an engraved announcement that friends had on June 1 been "married" in an informal ceremony. The motel would have been ideal for their honeymoon.

Quotation marks are conventions, and their purpose is to identify something as a quotation, something somebody has said. Sometimes the speaker is identified, sometimes not.

> The Declaration says that "all men are created equal."
> Bill asked, "Who is calling?"
> What is meant by "created equal"?

In addition to marking quotations, the inverted commas have two purely conventional uses. One is to designate a word mentioned as a word:

"Naïve" has two syllables.

Most styles, however, specify italics for this purpose:

The word *ain't* appears in expressions like "That ain't hay."

Commonly italics are used for book titles and quotations for smaller units. There's no particular logic for this convention, but it seems to work.

These uses are fairly straightforward, but they have led to a myth that accounts for a considerable spattering of quotation marks where they don't do what they were intended to do. The myth is that quotation marks provide a kind of all-purpose apology. For example, students are sometimes told that it's all right to use slang if you put quotation marks around it, "to show that you really know better," according to one popular textbook. This, of course, makes no sense. If the slang is appropriate, it needs no apology. If it's not, it's better left out.

The myth has its origin in a legitimate variation on the use of quotation marks, to indicate that a word or phrase is actually a quotation even though no speaker is mentioned—a record of the way somebody said something or habitually says it.

He reported that a "lady" had greeted him at the door.

The inverted commas around *lady* indicate that he, whoever he is, characterized her as a lady. The implication, however, because the writer has gone to the trouble of the quotation marks, is that she may not be a lady, only that he had called her one. The marks indicate that the word is used ironically. In this the punctuation has the same effect:

In my night class it "ain't easy" to understand.

The quotation marks are not apologies for the nonstandard expression; they show that "ain't easy" is the way it's said in that class.

Sign makers seem particularly partial to an extension of the myth, that inverted commas somehow lend a touch of class. Here's another sign: MIKE'S GARAGE: "BODY WORK" AND "REPAIRS." The intent is probably just to mention the garage's capabilities, but the effect is to indicate that somebody has called them body work and repairs—

and they may be something else. The marks suggest that the work may not be very good. Another sign, WE PROMISE "SERVICE" WITH A SMILE, makes you wonder what kind of service is promised.

Incidentally, quotation marks, double inverted commas, are not the only punctuation marks that seem to be acquiring popularity as ornaments. The apostrophe, a single inverted comma, appears frequently, apparently to give a passage some extra distinction—or more likely to express the confusion of someone aware only that the apostrophe is somehow related to a final -s. Here are sentences from a bulletin circulated by the U.S. Postal Service for passport applicants:

> Prices: Under 18 year's—passport cost $27 and is good for 5 year's. 18 year's and over passport cost $42 and is good for 10 year's.
> Note: Every person has individual passport's, no more family passport's.

- ### Save the Semicolon

A friend of mine once characterized a colleague as the only person he knew who could speak a semicolon. He meant his remark to be disparaging, but I considered it a compliment, because I admire the semicolon as a noble mark of punctuation, and I lament its apparent passing from much contemporary writing.

The semicolon came into use in the seventeenth century and became popular with prose writers of the period. A random look suggests that Samuel Pepys in his *Diary* used about half a dozen per page. Thomas Browne did about the same. One sentence in Sir Walter Ralegh's *History of the World* has five semicolons, along with ten commas and a colon, which allows it to wind on almost interminably, but clearly.

A quick check of some modern prose reveals nothing to match this copiousness, even in a writer like William Faulkner, who manages some pretty lengthy sentences. In general, our tendency toward shorter sentences has eliminated much of the need for the semicolon. In fact, one current usage manual suggests that "if a writer wishes to use an informal narrative style, he should avoid semicolons as much as possible."

This advice seems to me unduly hard on the semicolon, which still has valuable uses. Primarily it provides a way to separate independent ideas when a period makes a sharper break than you want and a comma isn't enough. This from T. S. Eliot, for example, could have been written as two sentences:

> Humility is the most difficult of all virtues to achieve; nothing dies harder than the desire to think well of oneself.

Using the less abrupt mark of separation makes the relation between the ideas clearer. Similarly, the following from E. B. White works better as a single sentence, with the connection between the ideas preserved:

> It is easier for a man to be loyal to his club than to his planet; the by-laws are shorter, and he is personally acquainted with the other members.

The semicolon is especially useful in sentences in which a second idea is introduced by a word like *then* or *however* or *therefore*. Macauley comments on Charles II:

> He had been, he said, a most unconscionable time dying; however, he hoped they would excuse it.

Or it can mark a main division when the sentence has other punctuation, as in the following from Mark Twain:

> When angry, count four; when very angry, swear.

I skimmed through half a dozen issues of *Newsweek* searching for semicolons. I didn't find many, but there are a few; I am not yet ready to consider the mark obsolete.

• **Conventions and Politeness**

Language and etiquette get involved together in various conventional expressions that fit social occasions. These set phrases often have lost most of their meaning and have become simply formalities. "How do you do?" is not really an inquiry anticipating an answer. In fact, the response may be another "How do you do?" *Hello,* as a greeting or a telephone convention, has little meaning.

Phrases like these are useful and cause no trouble, but some expressions are not so completely conventionalized, and their meanings sometimes intrude. For example, I am sometimes uneasy about "How are you?" How do I respond? I can, of course, take the request literally and provide a fulsome response. This is likely to discourage a friend from inquiring again. I can use "fine" or even "wonderful," whether they are accurate or not. "All right" may be no more honest and not very informative. One solution is to even the score by turning the question back: "How are you?" But you may find out, in detail.

I'm resentful when the telephone interrupts my dinner and a caller introduces himself as a member of a brokerage firm and then offers a cheery "How are you?" I understand that he is trying to be friendly, but I also know that he is setting me up for a sales pitch. I am tempted to do silly things like asking if he is really concerned about my health or launching on a detailed fictional account of medical problems.

I also have an irrational reaction to the currently popular "Have a nice day," a perfectly innocent, well-intentioned expression. Abbreviated to "Have a good one," it seems to me even less palatable. I try to rationalize my attitude by observing that the wish is not really sincere, that it's only an automatic phrase, sometimes, apparently, prescribed by an employer. But that's true of phrases like "Good morning" or innocent euphemisms like "Thank you for the beautiful dinner"—which we accept readily even though we're not thinking much about the morning and the dinner was quite ordinary.

I suppose I object partly because the expression is a newcomer to conventional talk and seems to be used more widely than it deserves. The abbreviation to "Have a good one" perhaps indicates that store clerks can get bored using one phrase all day. And I'm never quite sure how to respond. "Have a good one yourself" or "I've had a good one" seems not very gracious. "Thank you" seems hardly adequate for so specific a wish, and I tend to resort to silence, which is probably surly.

Other conventional expressions carry similar social overtones that are hard to explain and often hard to identify. For example, there are the phrases associated with an introduction: "Pleased to meet you" or "Pleased to make your acquaintance." These are what my grandmother would have called "common," but I'm not sure why. Perhaps there's a hint of insincerity, of pushing too hard, of a rehearsed response.

Somehow, saying the same thing in a different pattern seems more acceptable: "I'm happy to know you" or "It's good to meet you." The standard "How do you do" is probably safest, though it may seem stiff. It has been in the language since the sixteenth century with all sorts of variations: "How do ye?" "How d'ye do?" and finally just "Howdy?" which usually seems humorous or part of a nonstandard dialect.

• What Do You Call a Preacher?

Frequently these days one hears a reference to "Reverend Jones" or "Reverend Jim" or sometimes "Revener Jones." Conventions change, but style books still try to preserve some linguistic etiquette on this one. The question of how to address a clergyman turns on whether *reverend* should be regarded as an adjective like *honest* or *honorable* or whether it should be considered a title like *professor.*

The traditional assumption accepts the first view and requires that *reverend,* like *honorable,* be preceded by *the* and used only with a first name or a title like *Mr.* or *Miss:* "the Reverend Joseph Smith," "the Reverend Mr. Smith." *Honorable* in a title is treated the same way: "the Honorable Winston Churchill."

The question, of course, is what impression the different usages will make, and it seems likely these days that even "Good morning, Reverend" will seem natural to many speakers, especially in so-called evangelical churches. That is, we are coming to think of *reverend* as a title, not a description. Others are likely to accept the view of H. W. Fowler that the use is a "common vulgarism."

Similarly, social customs—and a certain amount of snobbery—affect the use of other titles. *Doctor,* for example, is accepted, often insisted upon, by medical doctors but is used much less frequently by people with any other sort of doctor's degree. On one university campus, in professional colleges, where relatively few professors have doctoral degrees, those who do want to be addressed as *Doctor*. In the arts and sciences college, by a kind of reverse snobbery, *Professor* is the only acceptable title, on the assumption that everyone has a doctorate. In at least some prestige universities the young Ph.D. who answers the phone, "This is Dr. Smith" or signs his name with *Ph.D.* after it is considered pretentious or showing bad taste.

One interesting development in recent years in titles in the United States is the steady disappearance of last names. Apparently on the assumption that the informality somehow enhances communication and exudes friendliness, people in all sorts of situations address strangers by their first names, a practice considered improper only a generation ago. I'm not sure that the practice has the desired effect. When a seductive voice on the phone asks for me by my first name, I'm suspicious. I assume at once that this stranger got my name from a directory or mailing list and is trying to ingratiate herself under false pretenses. I am prejudiced from the start and unsympathetic to the sales pitch—if I wait to hear it. I have much the same reaction when a bank teller or clerk or nurse in a doctor's office whom I don't know makes a point of addressing me by my first name. Furthermore, I am not especially impelled to vote for a candidate for political office who supplements his official name with a parenthetical nickname: "William (Buster) Smith" or William (Billie Boy) Smith."

In general, I like our democratic informality and have no desire to emulate the Japanese system of honorifics or the European affection for titles. But frequently, I think, the current enthusiasm for first names, especially used as a public relations gimmick, may backfire and create an impression different from the one intended.

9

Fun with Language

All work and no play makes Jack a dull boy.
  • James Howell, *Proverbs*

Then does the Jolly Maiden Aunt propound the query: What is the difference between an elephant and a silk hat?
  • Stephen Leacock, "Winter Pastimes"

A pun is a pistol let off at the ear; not a feather to tickle the intellect.
  • Charles Lamb, "Popular Fallacies"

On with the dance! Let joy be unconfined.
  • Lord Byron, *Childe Harold's Pilgrimage*

The purpose of language is communication, but language communicates in various ways—through the meanings of words, through grammatical patterns, through gestures. It also communicates in ways that capitalize on people's interest in language for itself—in its sound, in its ability to stimulate ideas by relating words in new ways, in its ability to evoke pleasure.

Children at an early age are fascinated by language games. They make up nicknames that rhyme, chant counting or jump-rope verses. They like the sound of nursery rhymes before they know what the words say. They may create separate meanings, relating the sounds to their experience. People remember childhood misconceptions. I remember creating a character named Andy who appeared at the beginning of a Sunday school hymn: "Andy walks with me, Andy talks with me." Richard Sans or Stans is a schoolroom character in the Pledge of Allegiance, "and to the republic for Richard Stans." José also appears in "José, can you see," perhaps partly because of the popularity of "No way, José." The Lord's Prayer inspires "Give us this day our jelly bread" and, in New York, "Lead us not into Penn Station."

Some years ago Sylvia Wright in a *Harper's* article even coined a name for these mishearings, *mondegreens*. As a child she sang the Scottish folk ballad "The Bonny Earl of Murray." The first stanza came out this way:

Ye Highlands and ye Lowlands
O where have ye been?
They have slain the Earl of Murray
And Lady Mondegreen.

Sylvia Wright grew up and discovered that the last line of the stanza is "And laid him on the green." Mondegreens turn up regularly. The pledge of allegiance, according to one first-grader, begins "I led the pigeons to the flag." "Gladly the cross I bear" emerges as "Gladys, the cross-eyed bear." A friend's children lost their appetites when served au gratin potatoes, which they heard as "old rotten potatoes." "One nation indivisible" is "One nation and a vegetable." I suspect that another variation on that line may be an adult creation, "One naked individual." And an alleged mondegreen on "While Shepherds Watch Their Flock by Night" seems to me too pat: "While Shepherds Washed Their Socks at Night."

Mondegreens merging with malapropisms turn up in the writings of older students. One reported that in 1957 Eugene O'Neill won a pullet surprise. Another wrote that she kept her clothes in a chester drawers.

Grown-up games may involve our love of alliteration that produces hundreds of combinations like *rough and ready, black and blue, tit for tat.* Our feel for rhyme produces *bigwig, claptrap, hotshot, wheeler-dealer.* Word play may range from silly puns to elaborate rhetorical devices, sometimes intended as ways of expressing subtleties of meaning, sometimes concocted as ornamentation. Tropes and figures of speech, for example, were cataloged by Aristotle. And then the Renaissance went mad in noticing ways in which language can be manipulated for special effects. Henry Peacham's *The Garden of Eloquence,* published in 1577, classifies 184 different figures of speech, ways of manipulating the language to produce special effects. These, of course, developed naturally and existed in writing long before they were named and classified. Most of these rhetorical names don't concern us much today— *prosopopoeia* or *hyperbole* or *synecdoche*—but we use the devices they signify all the time.

• Metaphor: Happy as a Bear

I remember that when one of our children was about three or four, an age when language-learning is going on with a vengeance, he heard somebody profess to be "hungry as a bear." To the young man the cliché was a fresh and brilliant—and useful—metaphor, and for about a year he was tired as a bear or sleepy as a bear or cold as a bear or funny as a bear. What he was doing with *bear* isn't greatly different from what all of us do with, say, the word *hell*. We can find something tired or sleepy or funny or cold as hell, as well as hot as hell. The meaning behind the comparison has pretty much disappeared, and *hell* has become just a vague word for emphasis, meaning not much more than *very* or *extremely*.

Comparisons of this sort, however, can be a much more significant part of language. Metaphor, exploiting a comparison to make a point or sharpen a meaning, is one of the most delightful devices language can use. It is the essence of poetry, a way of brightening and clarifying writing. Robert Frost comments in a poem that thinking "is just saying one thing in terms of another."

Metaphor expands the language, adds precision without adding new words. When Macbeth says,

> Life's but a walking shadow; a poor player
> That struts and frets his hour upon the stage
> And then is heard no more,

he is, in a way, expanding the supply of words. The complex of metaphors makes a comment about life that only the comparisons can produce.

Analyzing a metaphor isn't always very useful, but it is possible to see how some metaphors work by using terms proposed long ago by I. A. Richards to distinguish the elements of a metaphor—what is being compared and what it's being compared with. Richards called what is being compared the *tenor;* the *vehicle* carries the comparison. Richards attempted to clarify his terms with a bad pun, "Caruso (tenor) was a caravan of song (vehicle)." In the Shakespeare metaphor above, *life* is the tenor and *walking shadow* and *poor player* are vehicles. A great many metaphors in a book of quotations involve *life* as the tenor, with not only the Shakespeare vehicle but a lot of others as well: *beer and skittles, a bowl of cherries, a dome of many-colored glass, an incurable disease.*

It's hard to say why metaphors work, or why some work and others don't. Scholars have tried to make up rules: that the resemblance between tenor and vehicle must be close, that metaphors must be kept clearly separate, that the comparisons must be logical and pleasing. Another critic proposes that the most effective metaphor is the one that discovers some point for comparison between the most incomparable elements. None of the rules seem to work consistently.

A metaphor can be a single striking word or it can be an elaborately worked-out figure like John Donne's well-known comparison of the souls of two lovers to the legs of a compass, the kind used in drafting to draw circles:

> If they be two, they are two so
> As stiff twin compasses are two.
> Thy soul the fixt foot makes no show
> To move, but doth, if the other do.

Donne continues the image for another stanza, and it works, even though the resemblance between souls and a compass is not very close.

Another bit of poetry of the same period does not work. It is no more contrived than Donne's, but it gets betrayed by its own cleverness. Richard Crashaw describes the tear-filled eyes of Mary Magdalene as:

> Two walking baths, two weeping motions,
> Portable and compendious oceans.

The exaggeration seems silly.

A rule that metaphors must come one at a time seems theoretically plausible, but it would rule out much poetry, including Shakespeare's. Using the rule, one eighteenth-century critic faults Shakespeare for these lines:

> A stubborn and unconquerable flame
> Creeps in his veins and drinks the streams of life.

The critic worries that the flame is doing two things, both creeping and drinking. I doubt that many readers find that hard to accept.

On the other hand, mixed metaphors can get ludicrous. Here's a comment offered in the press a few years ago in defense of Admiral Hyman Rickover.

> I am not prepared to sail into the teeth of Rickover's excellent batting average compared to that of the others with braid on their sleeves. He is a different drummer.

The comment tops its confusion with ignorance by half remembering Thoreau's "he hears a different drummer."

Here's another reported in the press from Rep. Al Swift of Washington, who was commenting on cutting the number of nuclear dump sites being considered:

> If we're going to play the game and slog around with hogs, you're going to get muddy. We may have to go back to square one. . . . But if we have to play on his turf, we should go all the way and get everyone else off the hook.

Although the metaphors have been used so long that the comparisons behind them are almost gone, they regain enough life here to confuse us about how that mud became turf and where the hook fits in.

Metaphors can work in many ways, however, even exploiting clichés. A popular song asserts: "The world owes me a loving." Muriel Rukeyser strains a pun to "separate the chic from the goats," from "separate the sheep from the goats," and a dress designer "turns the other chic." A sportscaster "never pulls his hunches." Samuel Butler reverses Pope's line in "An honest God's the noblest work of man." Clare Booth Luce comments on some chauvinistic fervor: "The politicians were talking themselves red, white, and blue in the face." One of my favorite critical insights is Mrs. Henry Adams's reversal of "bites off more than he can chew" to comment on the writing of novelist Henry James: "Poor Henry, he always chews more than he bites off."

Metaphors often work by exploiting quite unexpected relationships. An example is T. S. Eliot's

. . . the evening is spread out against the sky
Like a patient etherized upon a table.

It is not the visual image so much as a complex of intellectual associations that makes the figure work.

Or a metaphor can work from sheer perverseness, as in this World War II valentine by Ogden Nash:

More than a catbird hates a cat,
Or a criminal hates a clue,
Or the Axis hates the United States,
That's how much I love you.

An excess of love is expressed amusingly as an excess of hate. Nash also comments:

One thing that literature would be greatly the better for
Would be a more restricted employment by authors of simile and
metaphor.

Regardless of what authors do, however, metaphor continues to be very much a part of our everyday use of English. It provides a major way in which the language grows, in which new meanings are created. To take an obvious example, somebody long ago noticed a resemblance between a human face and the front view of a clock. The word *face* was transferred to the clock. The comparison was apt, and the metaphor stuck. The same thing happened and is still happening, with hundreds of words: *front, leg, arm, head,* and so on.

Metaphors like these have become so much a part of the language that the original sense of comparison is nearly lost. We think of them as "dead metaphors." When we talk about the first leg of a relay race or the head of the house, we aren't conscious of any association with a body.

We also are constantly creating live metaphors in everyday speech. Slang is often metaphorical. A phonograph record is a platter or a disc and may be played by a disc jockey. Beer is suds; two single-spot dice are snake-eyes; a helicopter is an eggbeater. Often these lose their freshness and drop out of the comic strips to semioblivion. And some of those that survive become clichés, staled by overuse. It's no longer clever to call a wife a ball and chain or to call a basketball a casaba. Even those that are taken into the language, that become dead metaphors, are subject to ludicrous resurrection in some contexts. *Every walk of life* and *bad eggs* are expressions that normally are not thought of in terms of the comparisons that formed them. But in this student sentence the dead metaphors come back to life:

> In every walk of life there are bad eggs.

The eggs unexpectedly start crunching under foot.

• **Word Games**

Metaphor and other figures are serious ways of playing with language, able to add clarity and subtlety to communication. We also exploit language in various ways just for the fun of it, getting amusement and some intellectual stimulation from a variety of word games. Some, like crossword puzzles and double acrostics, are widely distributed in periodicals; games like Scrabble are commercial successes, available now as computer software; and games like Wheel of Fortune are popular as television programs.

Many games, including Wheel of Fortune, are based on anagrams in various forms. One type is the jumble, currently popular in newspapers, in which the letters of a word are mixed up and you guess the word—*giheth* is *height*, *immci* is *mimic*, *burcs* is *scrub*. Or there is the game in which you change one word into another by changing one letter—*mate* to *male*—and then, going from one player to another, keep the sequence going: *male* to *mile* to *mite* to *site* to *sire*, and so on. Players are eliminated when they can't think of a word that has not already been used.

A different kind of game that I remember from years ago is making the rounds again under the name Aunt Het. The person in the know, who is in charge, offers a series of examples of Aunt Het's preferences on any subject. The audience tries to determine the basis of her choices. "Aunt Het likes apples but not oranges." "She likes sheep but not lambs." "She likes trees but hates flowers." This goes on until somebody discovers how Aunt Het's sentiments are inspired. The game has been popular, and the discovery may not take long.

I remember another game that never got far because it was difficult to find examples. It involves taking a long word and breaking it up into parts as a kind of half pun. The example I remember is changing *ragamuffins* to *ragged little muffins*. Not exactly the same, but similar, are *bulldogmatic*, used by someone to describe Big Daddy in *Cat on a Hot Tin Roof*, *numbskullduggery*, *junior-mischievous*, and *highbrow-beaten*. An Ellen Goodman column produced *rose-colored retrospectacles*.

A more workable game that I remember with the name Whee—which may have been a purely local name—involved making puns, the more atrocious the better, on long words. To play, one person holds a dictionary and selects a word of at least three syllables, the longer the better. Then everybody tries to use the word in a sentence as a pun. The example I recall is the word *horticulture* as used in a sentence attributed to Dorothy Parker, "You can lead a horticulture, but you can't make her think." Here are a couple of the type more likely to be produced in an informal gathering:

> That manzanita dresser since his wife started buying his clothes.
> I'm going to reel in my line, but I think artificial while and hope to get a bite.

Try *barbiturate*.

I had a friend some years ago who was addicted to what we called the adverb game, which involved dramatics as well as language. In this game the party chooses sides, and one side selects an adverb: *majestically, flamboyantly, reluctantly,* or anything else that sounds interesting. Then those on the other side require the adverb proposers—who have not revealed the adverb—to perform specific acts in the manner of the adverb. So you get those on the side of the adverb buying a fur coat reluctantly or putting on eye shadow flamboyantly or playing billiards majestically, until the other team guesses the adverb.

In many ways my favorite is one called "ink-pink," or sometimes less respectfully "stink-pink" and a number of other names. It's a good game for automobile travel—good with children, though not always easy to stop. It may even be mildly educational. In the game one person provides a definition for a pair of rhyming words; the others guess what the rhyming words are. For example, the definition is "a corpulent feline," and the answer, of course, is "a fat cat." Or the definition is "an untamed juvenile" and the answer is "a wild child." Creations can get much more ambitious. "Fat cat," "spare chair," and "late mate" are ink-pinks; the words are single syllables. But there can also be inky-pinkies and even inkety-pinketies. Inky-pinkies have two-syllable words: "a humorous rabbit" is a "funny bunny"; "a minor automobile accident" is "a fender bender"; "a small bird with a closed mind" might be "a narrow sparrow." Inkety-pinketies are harder to discover. "An ominous cleric" is a "sinister minister"; or a "moral fable that you can listen to without great discomfort" is a "bearable parable." You can even find inkititity pinkititities; an "unsuccessful scholar" is an "ineffectual intellectual."

Aunt Het's interests, by the way, if you haven't spotted her secret, are purely orthographic, a passion for double letters. The game can be varied by providing different bases for Aunt Het's taste. She can like only words with a *t* in them, or only words that begin and end with the same letter, or only words that begin with a vowel, or what not.

• **Highbrow Games**

Games like Scrabble and double acrostics certainly require some intellectual agility, but word play may be at its most challenging when it merges with literary creativity. The limerick illustrates. The limerick depends in part on discovering novel or ironic or bawdy relationships. But I suspect that the creation of a limerick, which follows a rigid verse pattern, usually occurs through playing with words, especially finding ingenious rhymes. *Aberystwyth* is known to limerick fanciers less as a watering place in Wales than as a name inspiring some unusual rhymes. *Worcester* can be rhymed with *seduced her.* Contrived spellings enhance the rhyming in this well-known comment on the form:

The limerick form is complex.
Its contents run chiefly to sex.
   It burgeons with virgeons
   And masculine urgeons
And swarms with erotic effex.

The prevalence of erotic effex possibly inspired another game which appeared in 1977 in the *London Times Literary Supplement*. The trick is to translate a limerick into highly proper prose and then challenge players to reconstruct the verse. Here is a sample:

> There existed an adult male person who had lived a relatively short time, belonging or pertaining to St. Johns (a college at Cambridge), who had amorous designs on the large web-footed swimming birds with long and gracefully curved necks and a majestic motion when swimming. But the person in charge of the gate, remembering his obligations to his employers, reacted negatively. "Instead," he suggested, "possess as something at your disposal my female child. The large web-footed birds are set apart and specially retained for the Head, Fellows, and Tutors of the college.

Here is the limerick:

There was a young man of St. Johns
Who wanted to bugger the swans,
   But the loyal hall porter
   Said "No! Take my dorter!
Them swans are reserved for the dons."

Another verse game, not as well known as the limerick, is the clerihew. One Edmund Clerihew Bentley (1875–1956) gave his name to a verse form consisting of two short rhymed couplets characterizing a well-known person. He is said to have concocted the first sample while in school listening to a chemistry lecture:

Sir Humphrey Davy
Abominated gravy.
He lived in the odium
Of having invented sodium.

A more elaborate game turned up in the 1960s in a book called *Jiggery Pokery,* defining a light-verse form beginning with a nonsense line composed of two dactyls—a dactyl being an accented syllable followed by two unaccented ones. *Jiggery pokery* and *higgledy piggledy* are examples. Then there must be a proper name in the same metrical pattern—Joseph B. Kennedy or Ralph Waldo Emerson or John Greenleaf Whittier, to provide a few to work on. Then there is a four-syllable line and then the pattern is repeated. If this seems contrived and complex, it is, but here are samples:

Higgledy piggledy
Hans Christian Anderson
Sat with some tow-headed
Lads on a shelf,
Mythopoetically
Hoping that fairy tales
Added to keeping
His hands to himself.

Here's another with a historical subject:

Jiggery pokery
Benjamin Harrison
Twenty-third president
Was, and as such,
Served between Clevelands, and
Save for this trivial
Idiosyncrasy
Didn't do much.

• Playing with Sound

How much does the sound of a word reveal meaning? Can a word have significance from its sound alone? Are some languages or some words more beautiful or ugly than others?

Much of our talk about the beauty of language depends on more than just sound. An old story turns on a comparison of the words for butterfly in various languages. The notion is that Spanish *mariposa*, Italian *farfolla*, French *papillon*, and even English *butterfly* are beautiful words, whereas German *Schmetterling* is not. Many people would agree; native speakers of German might not. We often hear that *mother* is a beautiful word, never that *smother* is. The beauty is probably in the meaning of *mother* and not its sound. One often cited example of words communicating by their sound is Lewis Carroll's poem "Jabberwocky":

Twas brillig, and the slithy toves
 Did gyre and gimble in the wabe.

But even here meaning is involved. Humpty Dumpty tells Alice how the words were created: " *'Brillig'* means four o'clock in the afternoon— the time when you begin *broiling* things for dinner. . . . *'slithy'* means 'lithe and slimy.' . . . You see it's like a portmanteau—there are two meanings packed up into one word."

Some words do relate sound and sense because they originated as imitations of real phenomena; they are echoic or onomatopoeic. Words like *beep, honk, buzz, clang, whinny, ack-ack* have their origin in the sounds they represent. Tennyson's line, "And murmuring of innumerable bees," sounds like what it says.

Curiously, however, even without such specific associations, words can seem to sound like something they don't properly mean, perhaps from context, perhaps because they sound like other words, perhaps for some other reason. It's easy, for example, to contrive a paragraph like the following:

The room was gonfalon and uxorious. In front of the antiphony a red-adumbrated propitiate suggested comfort, and a gold-plated articulate on the round punctilious drew attention. A philander in full bloom grew in a terra cotta indemnity in the corner.

At first glance, this silliness seems almost to make sense, and I'm not sure why.

Neither am I sure why certain combinations of sounds seem to occur in different words with similar meanings. For example, there are all the *fl*-words suggestive of moving water or air: *fly, flow, flee, float, flight, fleet, flotsam, flotilla, flutter, flue, flood, fluvial, fling,* and many more.

These do not seem connected etymologically, although it is possible that many of them go back to the same Indo-European root.

No such explanation, even speculative, accounts for the curious association of initial *sn-* with words that refer to something unpleasant: *snot, snout, sneak, sniveling, snide, snake, snag, snail, sneeze, sniffle, snore, snatch, snitch, snarl, snippy, snub, snook, snort, snob,* and so on. Only a few refer to something pleasant: *snuggle, snow, snug, snack.* Many *sl-* and *sm-* words also refer to distasteful objects or actions: *slum, slander, slobber, slink, sludge, slime, smear, smudge, smirk, smell, smirch.*

We sometimes call these ugly sounding—like words with the sound of *g* plus a consonant: *gripe, grudge, grumble, gloom.* It is interesting to speculate about whether some words are more pleasant than others by virtue of their sound alone. Are *moon* and *mellow* and *mellifluous* beautiful, or do we just associate them with pleasantness? How about *mildew* and *millionaire,* which have the same sounds? Is *grinch* uglier than *grin?*

• Glorified Clichés and Twisted Idioms

Clichés and stock metaphors can be exploited in various ways. One obvious game is to supply part of a phrase and have others complete it: "throw down the . . ." elicits "gauntlet"; "grin and" is completed with "bear it." The game can go on almost indefinitely: "bolt from . . . ," "out of the frying pan . . . ," "kick the. . . ."

A more interesting game that has been around long enough to qualify as folklore has had recent newspaper revivals. Following are some inflated versions of set phrases. The trick is to translate them back to their familiar forms. For example, "Scintillate, scintillate, asteroid minific" converts to "Twinkle, twinkle, little star."

> Pulchritude possesses solely cutaneous profundity.
> Members of an avian species of identical plumage congregate.
> Surveillance should precede saltation.
> It is fruitless to attempt to indoctrinate a superannuated canine with innovative prestidigitations.

Eschew the implement of correction and vitiate the scion.

The ogled utensil resists achieving a temperature of 100 degrees centigrade at sea level.

Male cadavers relate no narratives.

Freedom from incrustations of grime is contiguous to divinity.

The stylus is more puissant than the claymore.

Selectivity on the part of mendicants must not be allowed.

Physical possession of a solitary member of the avian species is commensurate with the presence of twice as many in the shrubbery.

Accurate appraisal of a volume's content cannot be feasibly predicted exclusively upon external evidence.

Don't calculate too freely upon the juvenile poultry population until the process of incubation has fully materialized.

A mere scintilla of erudition is fraught with hazard.

In a situation in which a lack of erudition produces euphoria, it is injudicious to pursue sagacity.

If a machine, device, contrivance, or other object operates in an apparently satisfactory manner, evincing no evidence of malfunction, one is best advised to refrain from actions interfering with its operation with a view to improving its performance.

Related are examples of unintentional distortions that illustrate how heavily the English language relies on idiomatic patterns. Whenever nonnative speakers of any language attempt translations with only a dictionary as a guide, strange statements may occur. Samples of English created without a sense of idiom are circulated from time to time; the following are signs noticed by travelers:

Japanese hotel: "You are invited to take advantage of the chambermaid."

Bangkok dry cleaner: "Drop your trousers here for best results."

Rhodes tailor shop: "Order your summers suit. Because in big rush we will execute customers in strict rotation."

Norwegian lounge: "Ladies are requested not to have children in the bar."

Copenhagen airline: "We take your bags and send them in all directions."

• A Low Species of Wit and Shaggy Dogs

Noah Webster called punning "a low species of wit." The eighteenth-century literary critic John Dennis once characterized a colleague: "A man who could make so vile a pun would not scruple to pick a pocket." But I take comfort in the comment of Charles Lamb that a pun "is a noble thing per se. It fills the mind; it is as perfect as a sonnet, better."

Technically, a pun is any expression in which the use of words in different applications, or the use of words with similar pronunciations, produces a ludicrous idea, or at least an idea different from the usual meanings of the words. Puns can be spontaneous, or nearly so, or they can develop in the mysterious ways in which jokes become folklore, moving by word of mouth across the country and often surviving for years. For example, a 1977 book presents as a new joke a version of a song that I remember as popular in the fourth grade fifty years earlier:

What did Delaware boys; what did Delaware?
She wore a New Jersey, boys, she wore a New Jersey.
What did Tennessee, boys; what did Tennessee?
She saw what Arkansas, boys; she saw what Arkansas.

Puns can be almost unobtrusive quibbles, or they can be elaborately worked out stories. Getting just the right mixture of plausibility and outrageousness is the trick for their success. Among the most common of those in circulation—and most of them must have originated spontaneously—are quibbling definitions:

Freebooter—an amateur soccer player.
Chandelier—a French rooster.
Arcade—a beverage invented by Noah.
Allegro—a chorus line.
Aloha—a Pullman berth.
Senator—a creature half man and half horse.

There are more elaborate contrived puns, some with a literary flavor. For example, there is the Swedish chef who refused to make pastry because he didn't want to waste his Swedeness on the dessert air. Or there is this that stretches tolerance to the breaking point, combining punning with a spoonerism—the reversing of sounds in a pair of words. A student in her second year gave up love for studying because she thought she would sophomore if she put the heart before the course.

Or there is the punning game that involves taking a literary title and giving it a new use, as a name for a product or a business activity. Here are some samples:

White Fang—a toothpaste.
Middlemarch—a boot-camp exercise.
Kenilworth—a pet store or veterinary office.
Adam Bede—a maker of rosaries.
Ivanhoe—a gardener.

Shakespeare was an incorrigible punster. His puns were often bawdy, but he also used them for grim black-humor effects. Mercutio in *Romeo and Juliet* lies mortally wounded and comments: "Ask for me tomorrow and you shall find me a grave man."

Puns and spoonerisms become most pleasantly outrageous in combination with shaggy dog stories, those lengthy contrived narratives that build to an absurd surprise ending. A friend of mine is fond of one which involves a native king who collects thrones in his grass shack on a tropical island. After a royal disaster, the story ends with the observation that people who live in grass houses shouldn't stow thrones. A similarly complex story, involving a successful biologist, ends with his arrest for making an obscene clone fall. Another involves Shakespeare and Anne Hathaway planning a swimming party. Will asks Anne to check on his bathing suit, which he thinks may have been vulnerable to moths. She does so and reports, "No holes, Bard."

I like another with Shakespearean flavor, set in Australia. A pair of lost, weary, and thirsty hikers providentially come upon a desert nunnery, run by the Sisters of Mercy. They stagger to the gate, are welcomed by the Sisters of Mercy, and like good Australians ask for a cup of tea. The sisters comply, offering the rare delicacy that is their outback specialty, tea brewed from the Australian koala bear. The hikers drink eagerly, but at first sip can only sputter that the tea is full of hair. "Ah yes," replies a sister, "the koala tea of Mercy is not strained."

Perhaps my favorite of these is the story of a devoted husband intent on pleasing his wife on her birthday with her favorite flowers, anemones. But three florists disappoint him, and he settles for a bouquet of feathery ferns. His wife rises to the occasion with complete understanding: "Darling, with fronds like these, who needs anemones?"

• Language Traps for the Unwary

I remember being embarrassed at a fairly tender age when a mathematics teacher had me puzzling over this problem: One train leaves New York at 8 A.M. going to Chicago at 60 miles per hour. Another leaves Chicago for New York an hour later but at a speed of 65 miles per hour. The distance between the cities is 818 miles. Assuming that the trains maintain steady rates of speed, which is nearer Chicago when they pass?

Language traps like this are part of folklore; one of the earliest is the nursery rhyme, "As I was going to St. Ives . . ." Here are a few more, perhaps not so familiar, but all attempting some kind of misdirection:

1. Which is correct: "Nine and seven is fifteen" or "Nine and seven are fifteen"?

2. If a rooster and a half lays an egg and a half in a day and a half, how many eggs will three roosters lay in three days?

3. How do you pronounce BA CKA CHE?

4. How much dirt is in a hole three feet by three feet by three feet?

5. One child playing on a beach has 4½ sandpiles and another has 3½ sandpiles. They decide to put them all together. How many sandpiles do they now have?

6. I have two United States coins that total 30 cents in value. One of them is not a nickel. What are the two coins?

7. Pronounce boast, then coast, then roast. Now, what do you put in a toaster?

8. A farmer had 17 sheep. All but nine died. How any were left alive?

9. How many three-cent stamps are there in a dozen?

10. In America is it legal for a man to marry his widow's sister?

11. If an airplane crashes on the California-Oregon border, where are the survivors buried?

12. I have five sisters, and each of them has a brother. How many children did my parents have?

In case anyone is more than momentarily deceived by any of these, here are answers: (1) neither, the sum is 16; (2) roosters don't lay eggs; (3) backache; (4) none, the hole is empty; (5) one; (6) one coin is not a nickel, but one is, and the other is a quarter; (7) bread; (8) nine; (9) twelve; (10) a man with a widow is dead, not marrying; (11) survivors are not buried; (12) six, the five sisters and the one brother, the speaker.

• Punditry and Puntificating

This started with a question: "If lawyers can be disbarred and clergymen defrocked, doesn't it follow that electricians can be delighted, musicians denoted, models deposed, tree surgeons debarked, and dry cleaners depressed?"

The temptation to continue this sort of thing seems irresistible, and I have collected a variety of examples. If a waitress is hit by a swinging door, would she be *betrayed?* Could the queen of the May be *dismayed,* a mule-driver *discussed,* a member of Parliament *dismembered?* Would you call a successful dermatologist *irrational?*

And here are more: an electrician might also be *diffused,* a trapper who has been robbed *deferred,* a grounded cowboy *deranged,* a defrocked podiatrist *defeated,* a knife sharpener *defiled,* an outwitted fisherman *debated,* a girl with a wrinkled skirt *depleted,* Venus de Milo *disarmed.*

If a cow who loses her offspring is *decaffeinated,* then a mare with the same problem would be *defoliated.* If a colt loses his father, he is *desired.* Is a man who ran a public stable but was put out of business by the automobile a victim of *delivery?* Is spring in Georgia *unimpeachable,* unless there's a killing frost?

A variation, on about the same intellectual level, is the following menu for a meal that might feature Rockin' Rolls with Traffic Jam or Forest Preserves:

Hors d'oeuvres: Snails pace, Liver Die, Goldi Lox.
Breads: Raga Muffins, Barca Rolls with Middle Age Spread.
Fish: Immortal Sole, Pride of Plaice.
Entrees: Girded Loin, Unmitigated Tripe, Mutton Jeff.
Vegetables: Dead Beets, Chard Remnants, Capri Corn, Peas at Any Price, Gretna Greens.
Desserts: Flim Flan, Atom Bombe, Stoma Cake, or for those preferring fruit or cheese, Man or Candi Dates and De Brie.

Nonsense like this—which has been called puntificating or punditry or punishment—does not do much to further the development of good usage, but it provides a diversion during a walk.

• **Swifties and Merriwells**

I was interested to find not long ago in an issue of *English Today* an editor introducing as a new creation from Canada a "minor genre of word-play," called the Tom Swiftie. The Tom Swiftie is not a recent development, and many of us remember it as one of the better word games that flourished some thirty or forty years ago, along with knock-knocks and inky-pinkies.

Tom Swift was the hero of a series of "books for boys" in the early years of this century. He was not a favorite of mine, partly, as I remember, because his interests leaned more toward science than mine. I was, however, addicted to the adventures of Frank Merriwell, created by Burt L. Standish about the turn of the century but still going strong during my childhood. Frank had no deep interest in science, but he had remarkable athletic ability, as he played in all sports through Fairfield Academy and then Yale. He also had unlimited charm, with golden-haired Elsie Bellwood and dark-eyed Inza Burrage pursuing him from volume to volume.

Most of the books are laced with rather heavy-handed humor. Merriwell's followers include a young man afflicted with spoonerisms and an English youth who says "fawncy." The Rover Boys, the heroes of another series, include Tom, "the fun-loving Rover," who was a little tedious even for a ten-year-old.

I'm afraid the Merriwell novels as well as the Tom Swift books are not great literature, although I would defend them as infinitely superior to the comic books that apparently superseded them. They have stories and excitement and some characterization, and although the style is stiff, it seems to me more effective than the "Pow"s and "Bam"s of Batman.

The style of the Swift books often seems especially amateurish, and the Tom Swiftie is based on the writer's reluctance ever to let Tom just say something without a qualifying adverb. Tom and his friends speak *reluctantly* or *vigorously* or *hesitantly,* and the Tom Swiftie game involves devising tag lines with double meanings. For example,

> "Where are my crutches?" asked Tom lamely.
> "Doctor, your scalpel slipped," said Tom halfheartedly.
> "My EKG looks good," said Tom wholeheartedly.

English Today revived some of the old examples, and others have been turning up. I've selected only a few as samples.

> "I never did trust that buzz saw," he said offhandedly.
> "I love my new negligee," she said transparently. "And also my new bikini," she said briefly.
> "You're no longer the Pope," she said innocently.
> "No, thanks, I'm on a diet," he said stoutly.
> "You have foot trouble," said the podiatrist callously.
> "Please help me, Doctor," she said patiently.

Swifties can become more complicated with puns or literary references:

> "I'll have to glean alone," said Naomi ruthlessly.
> "That's a really big whale," said Captain Ahab superficially.

Or they can produce a pun on a proper name:

> "I hate Reading gaol," said Oscar Wildely.
> "Don't touch that violin," said Isaac Sternly.
> "That's just a fairy tale," said the brothers Grimmly.

The characters in the Frank Merriwell books never just say anything either, but I'm glad to report that they use verbs rather than adverbs to classify utterances. For example, in one chapter in which

Frank, or Merry, as his friends call him, is pitted against a group of cads and rascals, the characters *grated* several times, *grunted, admitted, cried, laughed, smiled, murmured, drawled, sneered, entreated, snarled, flung, exclaimed, softly exclaimed,* and once *mentally exclaimed.* I haven't done much toward the creation of Frank Merriwells, but there are possibilities:

> "I'm just a self-taught doctor," he quacked.
> "I think I'm dying," he croaked.
> "I just planted the vegetables," he ceded.
> "Do you like my new rouge?" she blushed.
> "I've lost the mine," he exclaimed.
> "I'm thinking about Dolly Parton," he tittered.

• **Palindromes**

Napoleon, after the Battle of Waterloo, is alleged to have said, "Able was I ere I saw Elba." It is unlikely that he said it. But the statement is possibly the best-known example of a palindrome, an expression that says the same thing when it is reversed, reads the same backward or forward. *Palindrome* comes from two Greek words combined to mean "running back." Another unlikely speculation is that the first words in the language were a palindrome, that the first man introduced himself to Eve, "Madam, I'm Adam."

The most obvious palindromes are single words: *madam, deed, noon, deified, level, radar, rotator,* and so on. But much more elaborate examples exist and can be contrived by anyone with patience and ingenuity who is not too critical about the plausibility of the result. *Stressed desserts* and *stinker reknits* make a kind of sense. Another well-known example is "A man, a plan, a canal: Panama," the story of the Panama Canal.

Palindrome enthusiasts have created fairly long palindromic sentences and even snatches of dialogue, but most of them seem obviously contrived. Here, however, are a few of the better long ones:

> Ned, I am a maiden.
> Nurse, so no noses run?

Sex at noon taxes.
Won't lovers revolt now?
Some men interpret nine memos.

• Oxymorons, Some Moronic

Oxymoron is a name for one of the more interesting of the rhetorical figures or tropes. Associating it with *moron* is almost inescapable, and the association is etymologically sound. *Oxymoron* comes from the Greek words *oxys*, meaning sharp, and *moros*, meaning foolish or dull, and *moron* derives from *moros*. An oxymoron is a figure of speech that combines two opposites, like the meanings of its two Greek roots, *sharp* and *dull*. The resulting contradiction usually has an ironic effect: *sweet sorrow, thunderous silence, cruel kindness, wise fool, abject arrogance, sweet pain, make haste slowly,* or *conspicuous by his absence.*

The device can be striking because it suggests possible similarities in what are usually considered opposites, often producing unusual insights or sometimes a kind of shock effect. Shakespeare, as a young man playing all sorts of games with language, gives Romeo a virtuoso speech loaded with oxymorons:

Here's much to do with hate, but more with love:
Why, then, O brawling love, O loving hate,
O anything of nothing first create,
O heavy lightness, serious vanity,
Misshapen chaos of well-seeming forms,
Feather of lead, bright smoke, cold fire, sick health,
Still-waking sleep, that is not what it is!

The speech is improbable, but at least it demonstrates how far you can go with this sort of thing.

The oxymoron has been enjoying a small revival of attention recently in variations from the classical figure. These are combinations of ideas that are not necessarily opposites, but become opposites when the phrase is labeled an oxymoron. The suggestion is that the phrase is self-canceling, and the figure becomes a device for criticism.

For example, labeling *postal service* an oxymoron suggests that the parts of the combination are incompatible, that the post office provides no service. *Airline food* as an oxymoron makes a satiric comment on what we eat on airplanes, as *British cuisine* comments on cooking in England. Here are others that are satiric comments or are self-canceling: *jumbo shrimp, Pacific storm, business ethics, original copy, numb feeling, nondairy creamer, plastic glasses, military intelligence.*

• Taking Words in Vain

I've never been quite sure about the meaning of the commandment about taking the name of the Lord in vain. I suppose it means something like using it out of context or using it frivolously, but real swearing is not frivolous. If it doesn't have any significance, it probably isn't worth the trouble, especially since swearing still risks some disapproval from society.

As a serious business, however, I think I share the view Robert Graves stated a long time ago and find swearing on a decline in ingenuity and picturesqueness. At least, it seems to me, there have been some distinct changes in our habits, especially in the euphemisms we use to take the curse off cursing. We still rely on three basic types of expletives: pretended appeals to a deity or references to a deity's business, such as damnation; the use of so-called four-letter words primarily referring to the body and useful only because they are forbidden; and disrespectful references to people, especially to our immediate ancestors. But fashions in the words, especially the euphemisms, have changed.

When I was a child, for instance, *darn* was a forbidden word. Therefore, although I didn't know that it was really a substitute for *damn,* it served as a satisfactorily wicked way for me to relieve my feelings on any subject. When *darn* ceased to be forbidden, I'm afraid it lost most of its usefulness. Many other euphemisms involving the functions of deity or deity itself have gone out of fashion entirely, mainly, perhaps, because *O God* and *By God* are no longer seriously shocking. We've lost many of the more colorful oaths that spiced Elizabethan speech: *egad* or *ecod; swounds* for God's wounds; and *snails* for God's nails on the cross, *adzooks* for the same nails referred to as hooks, or *Odds bodkins,* calling the nails bodkins.

Elaborations on these are sometimes picturesque but no longer in widespread use: "Christ on a crutch," "Holy jumping mother of Jesus," or "By the ripping, roaring, jumping Jerusalem." Some of the common euphemisms that now sound old-fashioned or naïve, like boys whispering in the back row at Sunday school, are words like *gee* or *gee whiz, gosh, golly, jeeze, cripes, cripey, jeepers-creepers,* or *jiminy crickets.*

British *bloody,* still frequently printed *bl——y* in England or Australia, probably is a descendant of one of these, *sblood,* for God's blood, with echoes of both the crucifixion and the sacrament as well as associations with menstruation. Although almost meaningless in America, it is still perhaps the most versatile oath in Australia, even turning up in such grammatical oddities as *absobloodylutely* or *of bloody course*— like the American use of *goddam* in *too indegoddampendent. Bloody* is still sometimes in questionable taste in mixed company in Australia, even in euphemistic variations like *bleeding* or *sanguinary* or *ruddy,* as is the still unprintable but widely used *f*-word in America.

Next to references to deity, slurs on family members and their conduct, often combined with four-letter taboo words, provide the most heavily worked epithets in English. The Elizabethan *whoreson* has been replaced, especially in America, by *son of a bitch,* the most widely used insult, along with *bastard* and in England *bugger,* which is relatively harmless in America but obscene across the Atlantic. In recent years in America, *mother,* with various uncomplimentary additions, has become probably the most serious insulting expletive.

All of these through overuse have tended to lose their sting. *Son of a bitch* and *bastard* can be terms almost of affection, and the few four-letter words not in daily print are so common in use that they have lost their shock value. The musical *Hair* spoofed the use of so-called obscenities with a song piling up scientific terms for parts of the body and their functions. It sounded naughtier than the unprintable terms.

• Giggles of Geese and a Pure of Meadowlarks

The Roman goddess of love, Venus, provides the source for the word *venereal* in its most usual current sense, to refer to something having to do with sexual activities, especially sexually transmitted disease. Another *venereal*, however, is a quite different word, coming from the Latin verb *venari*, to hunt, and is the adjective from *venery*, for what the British at least have long called the "art of hunting." If you really respect hunting as an art, you know the right words to use; you refer properly to a *skulk* of foxes or a *bouquet* of pheasants.

I remember that we were exposed to such hunting terms as part of our English course somewhere around the fifth grade, spending some time learning what were considered standard group names. I remember being especially intrigued by what I thought were the giggles of geese, which we understood as a kind of condescending pleasure the geese took in contemplating the pride of lions. I remember that we found these fascinating and for a day or two occupied ourselves in what might now be called an informal creative project, developing our own vocabulary of group terms. I recall a *nectar* of chipmunks, a *sniffle* of sparrows, a *mortal* of hens, and my favorite, a *pure* of meadowlarks.

We did not then realize that hundreds of these terms had been conceived in England during the early Renaissance as part of the rituals associated with hunting and had been preserved in books on hunting. They're not much used anymore, although "a bevy of beauties" turns up occasionally and a few are in common standard use: *a swarm of bees, a slate of candidates, a brood of hens, a litter of pups, a school of fish.* I like many of the authentic terms, although I seem not to have much use for them today. *A murder of crows* seems to me highly appropriate, as do *a kindle of kittens* and *a leap of leopards.*

Most of the terms I've mentioned are contained in *The Book of St. Albans*, 1486, which is the source for much of the information in a modern book by James Lipton, *An Exaltation of Larks*. Lipton turned up a historical novel, *Sir Nigel*, by Sir Arthur Conan Doyle, published in 1906 after Doyle had given up Sherlock Holmes. In the novel a knight instructing young Nigel advises: "But above all I pray you, Nigel, to have a care in the use of the terms of the craft, lest you should make some blunder at table so that those who are wiser may have the laugh of you, and we who love you may be ashamed." The knight proceeds to a catechism:

> "Answer me now, lad, how would you say if you saw ten badgers together in the forest?"
> "A cete of badgers, fair sir."
> "Good, Nigel—good, by my faith. And if you walk in Woolmer Forest and see a swarm of foxes, how would you call it?"
> "A skulk of foxes."

The conversation continues through *a singular of boars, a sounder of swine, a gaggle of geese, a badling of ducks,* and *a pitying of turtledoves.*

Sometimes origins of the terms are obvious, sometimes obscure or unknown. *A gaggle of geese* simply reflects a verb, *to gaggle.* The other term used with geese, when they are in the air, *a skein of geese,* is metaphoric; presumably the geese in flight look like a skein of yarn. *A pod of seals* apparently derives from a pea pod and a sailor's notion that a group of seals are like peas in a pod. *A rafter of turkeys* has nothing to do with a beam, but is related to *raft,* in the sense of many, as in *a raft of people. Cete,* for badgers, is probably derived from Latin *coetas,* meaning a company or assembly. But there is another word *cete* still in use, from Latin *cete,* meaning whale. *School,* for fish, is a totally different word from the one designating a place for learning. It comes from Old English *scolu,* meaning a troop or multitude, and is a variant of *shoal,* also used with groups of fish. *Dule,* in *a dule of doves,* is a corruption of French *deuil,* mourning. *Nye,* in *a nye of pheasants,* comes from Latin *nidus,* nest.

Lipton ends his book by recommending the creation of new terms as an amusing word game. Here are examples of Lipton's inventions: *an indifference of waiters, an odium of politicians, a piddle of puppies, a flush of plumbers, an unction of undertakers.*

I am comfortable about concluding these observations with a chapter on fun with language. In a sense, all discourse involves playing with language, at least manipulating it. Certainly much of the satisfaction of using language, in writing or conversation, comes from the pleasure of a happy choice of words or an apt comparison. Not all language is jiggery pokery, but the jiggery pokery is useful. And I am glad to have a native language so compatible with humor and nonsense. The future of English seems to me safe as long as we have fun with it.

Index

Abbreviation
  clipped words, 159–60
  and word magic, 11–12
Ade, George, 95
Adjectives
  absolute, 57
  after linking verb, 149–52
  ending in -ly, 99–100
Adverbs
  after linking verb, 149–52
  -ly ending, 99–100
Advertising, 19–23
affect-effect, 134
Afro-American, 8
agenda, 171
aggravate, 56
Agreement
  with borrowed plurals, 115–16
  to clarify subject, 112–15
  with compound subjects, 113–14
  postponed subject, 112
  pronoun, 17
  subject-verb, 111–12
ain't, 119–21
alcoholic, 61
Algeo, John, 143
Alliteration, 183
alright-all right, 168–69
Amelioration. See Elevation
American Heritage Dictionary, 57

Anagrams, 188
and, to begin a sentence, 131
Anglic, 165
Anglo-Saxon. See Old English
antimacassar, 43–44
Apostrophe
  and possessive, 127–29
  redundant, 177
apt-liable-likely, 139
aptitude, 64
aren't I, 120
argosy, 42–43
Articles: a, an, the, 114, 172–73
ass, 157–58
astronomical, 67–68
Autoantonyms, 61–63

Back-formation, 26, 56
backlog, 41
Bailey, Nathaniel, 25
barbecue, 60
Barclay, James, 7
Barzun, Jacques, 58, 128, 136
bastard, 12, 205
bat, 33
be, 81–84
belfry, 30
belly, 38–39
Bentley, Edmund Clerihew, 191
bertha, 40

between, 51–52
between you and I, 148
beverage, 143
billy, 38–39
billycock, 39
Bishop, Morris, 122
black, 7–8
bloody, 12, 205
bloomer, 36
blowed, 105
bondoony, 156–58
boondocks, 42
boor, 53
boress, 158
Borrowing, 25–26
boy, 17–18, 54
Boyd, L. M., 28
Brown, Goold, 121
brunch, 44
brung, 105
Bryant, Margaret, 24
Bryson, Bill, 2
buckle, 62
bugger, 12, 205
bull, 35
bully, 39
bunk, 160
Burke, Edmund, 161
but
    to begin a sentence, 131
    as negative, 126
buxom, 54
Byron, Lord, 182
byzantine, 68

can-may, 135–36
canary, 32
Carroll, Lewis, 117, 193
cat, 34
Caxton, William, 173
Century Dictionary, 7, 37, 42

chairman, 15
chaise longue, 29
Chase, Stuart, 3
Cheke, Sir John, 163
chicken, 32–33
Chinaman's chance, 10
chippy, 35–36
Chomsky, Noam, 2
Churchill, Winston, 94, 122
churl, 53
cleanse, 143
Clerihews, 191–92
Clichés, 153–55, 188
    inflated, 194
    mixed, 154
clumb, 105
cock, 33
cock a snook, 33
cockney, 33
cocktail, 47–48
cole slaw, 30
collaborator, 54
collectable, 27
colonel, 163–64
colored, 8
colossal, 21, 67
come, 105
Comma, 174–75
Comparison in sentence, 93–94
complected-complexioned, 139
Complement, 76
Compounds
    conflicting, 63–64
    spelling, 167–69
    as subjects, 114–15
Conjunctions
    to begin sentences, 131
    and prepositions, 132–34
contact, 58
Conventions
    and politeness, 178–80

and titles, 180–81
in writing, 161–81
Coordination in sentence, 91–94
coot, 31
cop, 48–49
Copula. *See* Linking verbs
corybantic, 55
couth, 64
crane, 32
Crashaw, Richard, 185
cricket, 49–50
critical, 62
crow, 32
custom, 68

damn sight, 47
damsel, 69
darn, 204
data, 115, 171
debut, 59
Deep structure, 75
deer, 54
Degradation, 53
demagogue, 53
Dennis, John, 196
Dialect
  American, 143–44
  British, 142–43
  class, 142
  prestige, 144
  and verb forms, 104–6
did-done, 105, 140
different from, than, to, 138
Diminutives, 159
discover, 66
disinterested-uninterested, 139
dive, 104
doctor, 180–81
dog, 33–34
donate, 56
Donne, John, 185

Double negative, 125
  as understatement, 126
Doublespeak, 3–6
  NCTE committee on, 4
doubt, 67
Douglas, Norman, 1
downhill, 62
downturn, 64
Doyle, Arthur Conan, 206
Draining meaning, 67–69
drug, 104
Dryden, John, 121
duck, 32
duct tape, 29–30, 145
dumbfound, 44
dust, 62
Dutch courage, 9
Dutch rub, 10

ecstasy, 66
either, 144
either-or, 114–15
Elegant English, 98, 140–60
Elevation, 53
Eliot, T. S., 186
Empty words, 67–69
engagement, 62
enthuse, 56
Equation, 82–84
  faulty or illogical, 81–82
  with modifiers, 83
escape, 60
et, 105
Etymology, 24–50
Euphemism, 4, 11, 20, 156–59, 204
Evans, Bergen and Cornelia, 50
exit, 59

fabulous, 20, 67, 68
Fad words, 55
Fancy diction, 152–56

fanny, 40, 158
fantastic, 68
farther-further, 139
fast, 63
Faulty equation, 82–84
February, 145
fewer-less, 134–35
fight with, 62
Fighting words, 10–13
Figures of speech, 183
finalize, 52
finance, 146
First names, 181
Fitzgerald, F. Scott, 1
fix, 62
flabbergasted, 45
Flag burning, 13
flaunt-flout, 138
flustrated, 44
Folk etymology, 27–29
  and errors, 30
  and pronunciation, 145
Follett, Wilson, 128, 134
fond, 66
formidable, 146
Fowler, H. W., 59, 99, 109, 124, 130, 136, 141, 180
fox, 35
Frame sentences, 85
Frank Merriwells, 200
Franklin, Benjamin, and spelling, 165
French disease, 9
French kiss, 9
Frost, Robert, 184
Function words, 75
Functional shift, 26, 59

gaudy, 28
gay, 54–55
Generalization, 53
Genitive. *See* Possessives

Genung, John F., 123
gerrymander, 45
Gill, Alexander, 25
girl, 17–18
give, 105
go for say, 106
Goldsmith, Oliver, 74
gong, 50
good-well, 149–52
goose, 33
gourmet, 145
Grammar, 74–94
  analytic, 95
  descriptive, 74–75, 118–19
  devices for revealing, 75–77
  inflection, 95–96
  Latin, 75–76, 86–87, 95, 117–19, 121
  and meaning, 74, 77–84
  prescriptive, 74–75, 118–19, 139
  transformational-generative, 75
  universal, 2, 118–19
Greene, Robert, 163
Grimm, Jacob, 103
gringo, 29
grit, 69
Grose, Francis, 9, 39, 46
grouse, 32
guinea, 32
gull, 32
guy, 37–38

hamburger, 61
handicap, 62
hang, 104
harlot, 54
Harper usage panel, 52, 56, 58, 149
Harris, James, 117
Harte, Bret, 95
Harvey, Thos. W., 131
hawk, 32
he and sexism, 15–17

headquarters, 112–13
hell, 184
help, 19–20
Heraclitus, 51
hi-bred corn, 29
Hobson's choice, 37
Hodges, Richard, 164
holp, 105
homely, 63
Homonyms, 169–70
honest Injun, 8
honorable, 180
hooker, 48
Hooker, Richard, 51
hoosier, 29
hopefully, 58
horse, 35
Howell, James, 182
humble pie, 30
Hunting terms, 206–7
hussy, 160
Hyphen, 167–69

I-me, 147–49
Idioms, distorted, 195
if-whether, 137
imply-infer, 137–38
improved, 20
impudent, 65
in terms of, 155–56
inane, 65
incessant, 65
incognito, 65
Indian, 8
Indo-European language, 24
infamous, 65
Infinitives, split, 123
inflammable, 65
Inflection, 75–76, 81, 95
ingenious-ingenuous, 139
input, 73

intestinal fortitude, 69
Irish legs, 9
is when, is where, is because, 84
Italics, 176

jammies, 159
Jargon, 155–56
jay, 32
jeep, 44
jerry-built, 49
Jew, 7
jibe-jive, 138
Johnson, Samuel, 2, 120
Jonson, Ben, 173
judgment-judgement, 166–67
judy, 28, 39
jury, 49

kind, 66
knave, 18, 53
knight, 53
knockout, 62

lady, 18
Laird, Charlton, 1
Lamb, Charles, 182, 196
Language
  "beautiful words," 192
  change, 51–74
  and class designation, 142
  deceptive, 19
  hypothetical, 25
  Indo-European, 24
  racism and, 5
  sexism in, 14–18
  society and, 1–23
  sound and, 192
  and thinking, 2
Language traps, 198
languish, 69
lark, 32

Latin, 95, 119
Leacock, Stephen, 182
legendary, 67
lend-loan, 57–58
Leonard, Sterling, 52
let, 52, 66
lewd, 53
Lewis, Sinclair, 154
lie-lay, 106–9
like-as, 132–33
Limericks, 190–91
Linking verbs, 76, 81–85, 149–52
Lipton, James, 206
lolly, 160
loony, 31
Lounsbury, Thomas, 116
Lowth, Bishop Robert, 118, 125, 139
-ly, 99

Malapropisms, 132, 183
man, 15–18
Marquis, Don, 54
mary, 40
maudlin, 36
may-might, 102
Meaning and sound, 192
media, 115, 171
Mencken, H. L., 61
Metaphors, 184–88
  bird, 31
  confused, 186
  dead and live, 187
middy, 160
misled, 145
Mitford, Jessica, 142
mob, 55
Modifiers
  dangling, 86–89
  misplaced, 89–90
  moveable, 87
  order of, 87

restrictive and nonrestrictive, 174–75
  sentence, 58
  squinting, 89–90
  in verbs, 124
molly, 40
Mondegreens, 182
Montezuma's revenge, 9
Moore, John, 24
mother, 12
Mulcaster, Richard, 164
Murray, Lindley, 118
myself, 149

Nash, Ogden, 187
native American, 8
Negative words with no positive, 64–65
Negro, 8
neither-nor, 125–26
new, 20
New Yorker, 64
Newman, Edwin, 51
Nexus. *See* Predication
nice, 54, 67
nigger, 7
none, 112, 116
Nosey Parker, 36–37
not hardly, 126
Nouns, 75
  collective, 112–13
  countable, 113
  mass, 112
Novelty words, 60
Number
  borrowed plurals, 115
  collective nouns, 112

Object, 76
  of preposition, 121
OK, okay, 45–46
Old English, 25
Onomatopoeia, 161, 193

Orwell, George, 57, 155
out of whole cloth, 41
outback, 63
outlay, 63
outlook, 63
output, 63, 73
outsell, 63
over-more than, 139
Overcorrection, 140–60
  with linking verbs, 149
  pronouns, 148
overlay, 63
overlook, 62
overpass, 63
oversight, 63
overtake, 63
*Oxford Dictionary of English
  Etymology*, 43
Oxford English Dictionary, 15, 28, 36,
  44, 57, 116, 120, 134, 135, 139,
  158, 168
Oxymorons, 203

Packard, Vance, 141
Palindromes, 202–3
pander, 36
Parallel structure, 91–93
parameter, 59
Partridge, Eric, 6
Parts of speech, 75
passing, 66
Passive sentences, 85–86
Paul Pry, 37
Peacham, Henry, 183
peeping Tom, 36
Pejoration. *See* Degradation
penthouse, 30
pep, 69
perve, 160
pigeon, 31
pigsney, 160

plead, 104
pluck, 69
Plurals
  borrowed, 115, 171
  with singular meaning, 113
plus, 60
Political correctness, 10–13
politics, 113
Polls, 22
pony, 35
Pop grammarians, 51
Portmanteau words, 44, 193
Positives and negatives, 64–65
Possessives, 127–29
  with *of*, 128
  of personal pronouns, 128
  restricted to ownership, 128
  rules for, 127
Post, Emily, 143
Predicate adjective, 76
Predicate nominative, 76
Predication, faulty or illogical, 78–80
premiere, 59
Prepositions, at end of sentence, 121–23
presently, 67
prevent, 52
principal-principle, 138
Privilege of occurrence, 77
Profanity, 204
Pronouns
  common-gender, 15–16
  form changes, 96
  overcorrection, 147–49
  possessive, 98, 128
  relative, 97
Pronunciation, 144–47
  errors, 147
  and folk etymology, 145
  of foreign words, 145
  "preferred," 144
  "sounding" letters, 145

punch, 28
Punctuation, 173–78
  apostrophe, 177
  development, 173
  quotation marks, 175
  of restrictive and nonrestrictive
    modifiers, 174
  semicolon, 177
Punditry, 199–200
Puns, 196–200
Pyles, Thomas, 143

quality, 68
Quin, Jim, 51
Quotation marks, 175–76

Racism and language, 5
raise-rear, 111
*Random House Webster's College
  Dictionary*, 73
rat, 35
raven, 31
rent, 62
reverend, 180
revolutionary, 68–69
Richards, I. A., 184
rise-raise, 109–11
rooster, 33
Ross, A. S. C., 142
Rosten, Leo, 56
Rotten Row, 30
Royko, Mike, 131
Rules, grammar, conflicts with
  usage, 117

sanction, 62
scrip, 145
sector, 59
seed, 62
Semantic change, 53–61
  degradation, 18, 53

  elevation, 53
  generalization, 17, 53
  and reading Shakespeare, 66–67
  specialization, 17, 53
Semantics, 11
Semicolon, 177–78
Sentences
  basic patterns, 76
  choosing subjects, 78–83
  clear modification, 86–90
  comparisons, 93–94
  coordination and parallelism, 91–93
  equation in, 81–84
  faulty predication, 77–80
  frame, 85
  passive, 85–86
  postponed subject, 85, 111
  subject-verb-complement pattern, 76
Sentence modifiers, 58
serendipity, 41
setup, 64
Sexism and language, 14–18
  animal metaphors, 34
  female names, 39
  methods for avoiding, 16
Shaggy dog stories, 197
Shakespeare and semantic change, 66–67
Shakespeare, William, 140, 161
shall-will, 129–31
shambles, 54
shamefaced, 29
Shaw, George Bernard, 165
Sheridan, Richard Brinsley, 132
shibboleth, 43
shitepoke, 42
silly, 53
Simon, John, 51
singular, 57
sink, 104
sirloin, 30
sit-set, 109–10

skunk, 36
Slang, 187
smog, 44
snipe, 32
snow, 2
snuck, 104
son of a bitch, 12, 205
spaz, 13
Specialization, 53
Spelling, 162–74
  borrowed plurals, 171–72
  common errors, 170
  compounds, 167–69
  homonyms, 169–70
  reform, 164–66
  silent letter *e*, 166–67
  sounds and letters, 164
  sounds of *k* and *s*, 167
Spoonerisms, 197
squirrel, 35
Statistics, misleading, 21–23
Sterne, Laurence, 107
sticks, 28
sticktoitiveness, 69
still, 67
stink, 104
stump, 50
Subject of sentence, 76–84
  postponed, 85, 111
Subordination in sentence, 91
Sullivan, Frank, 153
Superstition and language, 11
suspect, 67
Swearing, 204
Swift, Jonathan, 164

teetotal, 42
Tenor, in metaphors, 184
term, 155
that-which, 136–37
there, 111

Thinking and language, 2
Thoreau, Henry David, 74, 117, 186
throughput, 73
Thurber, James, 118, 141
tinker's dam(n), 46
to-too-two, 169
Tom Swifties, 200–2
tomato, 146
tomcat, 34
transpire, 56
tremendous, 20
Tropes, 183
tules, 41
turkey, 31
turndown, 64
Twain, Mark, 1, 50, 51, 161, 178
twee, 160

U and non-U, 141–44
uncouth, 53
unique, 56–57
Universal grammar, 2, 118
unkempt, 65
up, 70–73
upbeat, 64
upcoming, 72
uphold, 64
upset, 64
upstart, 64
Usage, 52–61
  descriptive and prescriptive, 73
  and semantic change, 55–61
  systems for, 142

veggies, 159
Vehicle, in metaphors, 184
Venereal game, 206–7
Verb-adverb combinations, 70–73,
  122–23
  ambiguous, 71

Verbs
  agreement, 111–12
  alternative forms, 103
  dialect variations, 104–6
  future tense, 130–31
  linking, 76, 81–85, 149–52
  principal parts, 103–6
  sequence of tenses, 102
  strong and weak, 103
  tense, 100–1
  transitive and intransitive, 108
villain, 53
virgin, 68
virtually, 19
Vogue words, 59, 152

wake, 103
Wall Street Journal, 73
Wallis, John, 130
wangle-wrangle, 138
wax, 150
weasel, 36
Webster's New International Dictionary,
  46, 119
Webster, Noah, 117, 165, 196
Wednesday, 145
Weekley, Ernest, 37
wer, 15
wherefore, 66
White, Richard Grant, 56, 107
who-whom, 96, 98, 141
Whorf, Benjamin Lee, 1, 2
whose, 98
Wilde, Oscar, 140
wish, 143
woodchuck, 30
Word formation
  acronyms, 26

affixing, 26, 60–61
back formation, 26, 56
birds and animals, 31–36
coinages, 26, 60
compounding, 26
metaphor, 26, 31
portmanteau words, 44, 193
proper names, 26, 36–40
specific sources, 40–44
speculative, 45–50
from verb-adverb combinations,
  72–73
Word games
  adverb game, 189
  anagrams, 188
  Aunt Het, 188, 190
  Clerihews, 191–92
  inflated clichés, 194–95
  ink-pink, 189–90
  jiggery pokery, 192
  limericks, 190–91
  Swifties and Merriwells, 200–2
  whee, 189
Word magic, 11
Word order and grammar, 75
Words
  derogatory, 12
  "dirty," 12
  in established contexts, 69
  new, 55–60
  as symbols, 13
  vogue, 59
worth while-worthwhile, 168–69
Wright, Sylvia, 182
Writing system, 161–81

you-uns, 146